PROMOTING HEALTH

THE PRIMARY HEALTH CARE APPROACH

Andrea Wass

Lecturer, School of Health, University of New England, Armidale

W. B. Saunders

Baillière Tindall

Harcourt Brace & Company

Sydney   Philadelphia   London   Toronto

Acquisitions Editor: Jeremy Fisher
Production Editor: Janet Healey
Cover and Page Design: Pamela Horsnell

Harcourt Brace & Company, Australia
30–52 Smidmore Street, Marrickville, NSW 2204

Harcourt Brace & Company
24–28 Oval Road, London NW1 7DX

Harcourt Brace & Company
Orlando, Florida 32887

This editon copyright © 1994, by
Harcourt Brace & Company, Australia, ACN 000 910 583

Reprinted 1995 (twice)

National Library of Australia Cataloguing-in-Publication Data

Wass, Andrea, 1960– .
Promoting health: The primary health care approach.
Includes index.
ISBN 0 7295 1410 2.
1. Health promotion. 2. Health promotion — Australia. I. Title.
613

Edited by Graham Grayston
Cover photographs by Judi Kuepper (except man and child)
Typeset in Palatino by Brad Turner
Printed in Australia by Southwood Press

CONTENTS

ACKNOWLEDGMENTS

This book has developed in response to the need for a text for Health Education and Promotion, a unit offered at the University of New England, Armidale. Thanks are due to Lyn Backhouse, with whom I have taught this unit, for her on-going contribution to the development of many of the ideas presented in this book, and to all those students who have responded to the topic with enthusiasm and challenged my ideas along the way.

A number of other people have contributed importantly to the development of this book. Firstly, and most importantly, grateful thanks are due to Pamela Griffith, who critically reviewed drafts of most chapters, and added much to the depth of the material presented. Thanks are also due to Rod Menere, who reviewed a number of chapters and ideas, Jane Dixon who provided a critical review of the community development chapter and offered some valuable suggestions, and Garth Ritchie, who reviewed the health education chapter. Lyn Backhouse provided an important draft of the health education chapter, and Fran White prepared the section on working with people from other cultures.

Margaret Dunlop, Julia Sunderland, Sue Dean, Donna Wetherspoon and Elizabeth Ruse all provided critical comments on the final manuscript and helped refine some of the ideas presented. Particular thanks are due to Donna and Elizabeth, whose attention to detail helped clarify some of the material from a student's perspective.

Editorial staff at Harcourt Brace and Company also provided support and assistance. Thank you to Janet Healey for coordinating the editorial process and guiding both author and book to completion, Amanda Kennedy for editorial assistance and Graham Grayston for editing the manuscript.

As with any major project, though, this book would not have been completed without the sustenance and encouragement of those friends who have lived with the project almost as though it was their own. Special thanks are therefore owed to Nicola Wass, Rod Menere and Robert Edwards, for providing friendship and good cheer at times when it was really needed. Finally, a very heartfelt thank you is due to Pamela Griffith and Garry Griffith, whose continuing friendship, support and endless cups of tea helped me to stay sane (well, almost!) and enabled this book to happen.

The authors and the publishers wish to thank the following for permission to reproduce copyright material.

Extract, p. 17, from Health Targets and Implementation ('Health For All') Committee, *Health for all Australians: report to the Australian Health Ministers' Advisory Council and the Australian Health Ministers' Conference,* Australian Government Publishing Service, Canberra, 1988, p. 9, Commonwealth of Australia copyright reproduced by permission; Extract, p. 12, from S. Rifkin and G. Walt, "Why health improves: defining the issues concerning 'Comprehensive Primary Health Care' and 'Selective Primary Health Care'", *Social Science and Medicine,* 23(6), 1986, pp. 559-66; Figure 2.1, p. 41, from V. Brown, "Towards an epidemiology of health: a basis for planning community health programs", *Healthy Policy,* 4, 1985, pp. 331-40; Figure 2.2, p. 44, from S. Arnstein, "Eight rungs on the Ladder of Citizen Participation", in E. S. Cahn and B. A. Passett (eds), *Citizen participation: effecting community change,* Praeger Publishers, New York, 1971, p. 70; Extract, p. 47-9, from J. Dwyer, "The politics of participation", *Community Health Studies,* 13(1), 1989, pp. 59-65; Extract, p. 65, from M. Mies, "Towards a methodology for feminist research", in G. Bowles and R. Duelli Klein (eds), *Theories of women's studies,* Routledge and Kegan Paul, London, 1983, pp. 124-7; Extract, p. 75, from A. Twelvetrees, *Community work,* Macmillan, London, 1987, pp. 25-6; Extract, pp. 81-2, from P. Henderson and D. N. Thomas, *Skills in neighbourhood work,* Allen and Unwin, London, 1987, pp. 57-68, Reproduced with permission from HarperCollins Publishers Limited; Extract, p. 102, from Australian Community Health Association, *Manual of standards for community health,* Australian Community Health Association, Sydney, 1993, pp. 1, 8, 16, 24, 33, 37, 43, 50, 59, 68; Extract, p. 107, from the Victorian Health Promotion Foundation, "Quit smoking" and "Active at any age" billboard posters, Victorian Department of Health; Extract, p. 116, from "Martin St residents' unhappy anniversary", *Armidale Express,* 15 January 1991; Extract, p. 131, from P. Butler and S. Cass (eds), *Case studies of community development in health,* Centre for Development and Innovation in Health, Northcote, Victoria, 1993, p. 10; Poem, p. 133-4, from J. H. T. Chabot, "The Chinese system of health care", *Tropical Geographical Medicine,* 28, 1976, pp. 87-134; Figure 6.1, p. 136, from K. Tones, S. Tilford and Y. Robinson, *Health education: effectiveness and efficiency,* Chapman and Hall, London, 1990. p. 251; Extract, p. 137, from D Werner, "The village health worker: lackey or liberater?", *World Health Forum,* 2(1), 1981, pp. 46-68; Extract, p. 159, from "Inquiry into Suicide in Rural New South Wales", *Sydney Morning Herald,* 26 February 1994, Reprinted by permission of the *Sydney Morning Herald;* Extract, P. 159, from "National Approaches to Ecologically Sustainable Development and the Greenhouse Effect", *Sydney Morning Herald,* 4 July 1992, p. 17, Reprinted by permission of the *Sydney Morning Herald;* Extract, p. 159, from "Inquiry into the Implementation of the Recommendations of the Royal Commission into Aboriginal Deaths in Custody", *Sydney Morning Herald,* 5 March 1994; Extract, p. 161, from Consumers' Health Forum, *Guide-lines for consumer representatives: suggestions for consumers or community representatives working on public committees,* Consumers Health Forum of Australia, Curtin, Act, 1994; Extract, p. 168, from D. W. Johnson and F. P. Johnson, *Joining together: group theory and group skills,* Prentice Hall, Englewood Cliffs, New Jersey, 1987, p.8; Extract, p. 174, from The Conflict Resolution Network, *Rules for fighting fair,* The Conflict Resolution Network, Chatswood, NSW, Australia, Copyright the Conflict Resolution Network, PO Box 1016 Chatswood NSW 2057 Australia; Extract, p. 189, from L. Ewles and I. Simnett, *Promoting health: a practical guide to health education,* John Wiley and Sons, Chichester, UK, 1985, p. 28; Appendix 1, pp. 217-19, from the World Health Organisation, "Declaration of Alma-Ata", *World Health,* August/September 1988, pp. 16-17; Appendix 2, pp. 221-5, from the World Health Organisation, *Ottawa Charter for Health Promotion: an International Conference on Health Promotion: the move towards a new Primary Health,* November 17-21 1986, Ottawa, Ontario, Canada.

While every effort has been made to contact copyright holders or their agents, a few have remained untraceable. The publisher would be interested to hear from any copyright holders who have not already been acknowledged.

CONTRIBUTORS

Trish Abbott
Generalist Community Nurse, Taree Community Health Centre, 22 York St, Taree New South Wales 2430

Judy Aiello
Director, Health Promotion, Flinders Medical Centre, Bedford Park South Australia 5042

Bob Berry
Clinical Nurse Consultant (Alcohol and Other Drugs Service), Taree Community Health Centre, 22 York St, Taree New South Wales 2430

Jennifer Brett
Coordinator, Community Health, Moree Plains Health Services, Alice St, Moree New South Wales 2400

Pat Brodie
Manager, Team Midwifery Project, Westmead Hospital, Westmead New South Wales 2145

Sandy Brooks
Clinical Nurse Specialist (Mental Health Promotion), Taree Community Health Centre, 22 York St, Taree New South Wales 2430

Margaret Brown
Chairperson, Murray Mallee Health and Social Welfare Council, PO Box 346, Murray Bridge South Australia 5253

Joan Byrne
Consumer and arthritis activist, 2 Shirley Ave, Syndal Victoria 3150

Margaret Carroll
Coordinator, Rural Women's Network, New South Wales Agriculture, Locked Bag 21, Orange New South Wales 2800

Judyth Collard
Director of Nursing, Blue Nursing Service, Tablelands, Atherton Queensland

Pamela Griffith
Lecturer, School of Health, University of New England, Armidale New South Wales 2351

Sue Lauder
Community Health Worker, PO Box 1211, Geelong Victoria 3220

Jenny MacParlane
Senior Lecturer, School of Health, University of New England, Armidale New South Wales 2351

Liz Meadley
Health Education Officer (HIV/AIDS), Lower North Coast District Health Service, Forster Community Health Centre, PO Box 448, Forster New South Wales 2428

Lorna Neal
Clinical Nurse Consultant (Women's Health), Lower North Coast District Health Service, c/- Taree Community Health Centre, 22 York St, Taree New South Wales 2430

Northcote Hydrotherapy and Massage Group
c/- Northcote Community Health Centre, 42 Separation St, Northcote Victoria 3070

Leonie M. Short
Senior Lecturer, School of Health, University of New England, Armidale New South Wales 2351

Anna Treloar
Clinical Nurse Specialist (Mental Health), Kempsey District Hospital, River St, Kempsey West New South Wales 2440

Karen Williams
Paediatric Clinical Nurse Specialist, Griffith Community Health Centre, 39 Yambil St, Griffith New South Wales 2680

INTRODUCTION

This book examines the Primary Health Care approach to health promotion. It does so from the position that health promotion is an important component of Primary Health Care, and that health promotion is a more potent force if it is driven by the Primary Health Care philosophy.

Primary Health Care was formally recognised as an important framework for improvement of the world's health in 1978, when the Declaration of Alma-Ata provided the blueprint for Primary Health Care and 'Health for All by the year 2000'. This Declaration, supported by representatives from 134 nations, emerged from international concern that health care systems had developed with a focus on costly high technology care, usually at the expense of the provision of even basic health services for the majority of the world's people.

Primary Health Care was seen as a solution to the inadequate illness management systems which had developed. By providing a balanced system of treatment and disease prevention, through affordable, accessible and appropriate services, it was hoped that Primary Health Care would address some of the major inequalities in health observed both within countries and between countries. At the same time, though, there was recognition that new health services alone were not the answer, and that a major reorientation was needed in the way in which we both think about and act on issues which impact on health.

Primary Health Care is therefore about much more that the provision of new health services. Central to Primary Health Care is the Primary Health Care philosophy or approach, which should guide all action on health issues. It is the Primary Health Care philosophy which tells us how we should do what we do. The Primary Health Care philosophy emphasises social justice, equity, community participation and responsiveness to the needs of local populations. It emphasises the need to work with people, in order to enable them to make decisions about which issues are most important to them and which responses are most useful. This Primary Health Care philosophy, to be effective, needs to be applied at all levels of the health system and in every interaction between health workers and community members.

Following on from the development of Primary Health Care, and its application in varying degrees in different countries, has come a focus on health promotion. One key reason for this is that greater emphasis on health promotion is needed if we are to develop the more balanced health system required in Primary Health Care. The Ottawa Charter for Health Promotion, developed in 1986, reflects the same principles seen in the Declaration of Alma-Ata, and very much builds on the Declaration, by providing a clear framework for action by health workers. It recognises that action to promote health must work to change the environment, as well as to help individuals to change those things over which

1

they have control. Health promotion is defined within the Ottawa Charter for Health Promotion as 'the process of enabling people to increase control over, and to improve, their health' (WHO 1986).

The broad range of actions required to achieve this is perhaps best captured in Green's definition of health promotion:

> *Health education **and** related organisational, political and economic interventions that are designed to facilitate behavioural and environmental changes to improve health.*

(Green 1979, cited in Fisher et al., 1986: 96)

This book focuses on those strategies which are emerging as central to health promotion practice, but which have been largely neglected in the education of health workers to date. It is designed to provide both a theoretical introduction and practical strategies for action.

Throughout this book, the term 'health worker' is used to refer to the person working to promote health. There are two reasons for this. Firstly, while the book has been written primarily with nurses in mind, it may also be useful for other health workers or community members learning about health promotion. Health promotion is not the responsibility of any one professional group or even of the health professions as a whole. As an inclusive term, 'health worker' describes the broad range of people who may be working to promote health. Secondly, the term first came to be extensively used in the women's health movement, because it was regarded as a term which implied a more equal relationship between professional and 'patient'. The use of the term 'health worker', rather than professional titles, was hoped to be part of the process of breaking down the way in which professional groups related to women, and enabling the establishment of a more equitable health worker–client relationship. It is in this spirit of greater equality and partnership that the term health worker is used in this book.

Health promotion draws on many areas of expertise. This means that it is difficult to make the hard choices about what to examine, and what not to, in a text of this size. In deciding which skills and issues need to be addressed in a book such as this, consideration has been made of what topics are already examined in undergraduate nursing education. As a result, those topics which seem to be most in need of including in education for a Primary Health Care approach to health promotion have been included. Thus some topics which are an important part of this area have not been included because it can reasonably be expected that they are covered elsewhere. For example, it is expected that readers will already have a grounding in sociology, psychology, social ecology, and health and disease. Hence, a number of topics, including the structural basis of ill health, communication skills and health and disease processes, while referred to, are not examined in any great depth. Readers who are using this book without having previously examined these issues are encouraged to supplement their reading in these areas.

Included throughout this book are a number of examples of how some of the concepts presented in the book have been put into practice. These examples will add to the growing list of case studies being presented in recent Australian publications which address health promotion and Primary Health Care. It is hoped that these examples will add to your understanding of the issues of relevance in health promotion work. It is also hoped that they will encourage budding health promoters to become involved, by demonstrating that health promotion is already a meaningful part of a great many health workers' practice.

However, these examples are not meant to be definitive; rather, they represent part of an evolving practice. Many of the more difficult areas of health promotion, including dealing with the root causes of ill health, are not as well represented as health education designed to prevent specific diseases, because we are still coming to grips with how to address these issues. You are encouraged to read widely and examine the great many other examples currently available, and to work with your colleagues to develop your own ways of working.

Chapter 1 examines the development of Primary Health Care and the new public health movement, internationally and in Australia. In chapter 2, a number of related issues, notably the values which drive Primary Health Care and the new public health movement, are discussed. These are by no means simple issues, and the chapter raises a number of questions for readers to consider. Chapter 2 includes an examination of definitions of health and health promotion.

Chapters 3 and 4 introduce the reader to research in the area of health promotion. These chapters are built on the premise that any research in health promotion involves either assessing needs or evaluating action and that the line between these two is often blurred.

Chapters 5 to 9 then explore a number of strategies useful in promoting health — working with the mass media, community development, work for public policy change, group work and health education. Although these issues are examined in different chapters, the lines between these different strategies are often not clear and any number of permutations and combinations are possible should the need arise in practice.

Chapter 10 then makes a number of suggestions about how to incorporate the range of material presented in this book into your own practice and into developing health promotion activities. Finally, the conclusion briefly examines where to go from here if you wish to continue developing your skills in health promotion.

The emergence of Primary Health Care and the new public health movement has provided us with a strong frame work for health promotion, within which health and welfare workers, policy makers, and members of the wider community can work together. It is only when we accept fully the responsibilities of working in such a broad health promotion framework that we will be able to say that we are working fully for the health of our communities. It is hoped that this book reflects the spirit of Primary Health Care, and that it will contribute to our growing understanding of how to work for health promotion.

CHAPTER 1

Health promotion in context: Primary Health Care and the new public health movement

Health and ill-health patterns and the current illness management system

In the last 80 years Australia has seen quite dramatic improvements in the overall health of its inhabitants, and is now regarded as one of the healthiest countries in the world. However, this image hides the fact that there are major inequalities in health between different groups in the population, some groups having considerably poorer health status than others (Health Targets and Implementation Committee 1988).

Despite popular misconceptions, there is now a wide range of evidence that illness is as much a result of social and economic conditions as it is of individual pathology. It is apparent that inequalities in health, based on such differences as social class, gender and ethnicity, determine the sorts of life chances that many people have all over the world, and Australians are not immune to this process (Bates and Linder-Pelz 1990; Health Targets and Implementation Committee 1988).

We know that poor socioeconomic status is the single biggest determinant of ill health and death (National Health Strategy 1992: 10). We know that males and females of all ages in the lower socioeconomic groups have higher rates of death and reported illness than their better-off counterparts, with unemployed people faring worst of all (Australian Institute of Health and Welfare 1992: 184, 194). These inequalities have been noted in the statistics for sudden infant death syndrome, accidental drowning, motor vehicle accidents, other accidents, suicide, cardiovascular disease, respiratory disease and cancers, for example (National Health Strategy 1992: 11). We know that there are marked differences in prevalence rates of diseases between different cultural groups (Sax 1990: 24), although it

5

is not always the case that Australia's recent migrants have poorer health than Australian citizens, despite the impression given by the mass media. Indeed, many migrants have better, not worse, health than the average Australian citizen, although this advantage disappears the longer they have been in Australia (Bates and Linder-Pelz 1990: 36–8). We also know that men's mortality rates are higher than women's for all major causes of death (Australian Institute of Health and Welfare 1992: 177–80). At the same time, however, women's reported morbidity rates are worse than men's (Australian Institute of Health and Welfare 1992: 180), and women's experience of the health system is often negative.

However, it is Australia's Aboriginal people who have the most serious health inequalities, with infant mortality rates three times as high as Australia's overall rate and life expectancy up to 21 years less than for the population overall. As a result, Aboriginal hospitalisation rates are two to five times higher than for other Australians (Thomson 1991: 73). This statistic may underestimate the prevalence of illness among Aboriginal people, since the poor treatment they have received in the past, coupled with equally poor staff attitudes, may well delay future decisions to seek treatment.

To date, however, structural issues such as the above have been largely ignored, attention having remained focused on individual medical cure of disease. As figure 1.1 demonstrates, by far the majority of Australia's health spending is on health institutions, including hospitals and nursing homes, and the provision of non-institutional treatment services such as medicine, dentistry and pharmaceuticals. In the year 1989-90, the latest year for which figures are available, just 4.4 per cent of total health expenditure was on community and public health, with health promotion and illness prevention accounting for 32 per cent of this category — that is, just 1.4 per cent of health expenditure (Grant and Lapsley 1993: 113). This figure represents a small increase on previous years, with health promotion accounting for 1.2 per cent of health spending in 1988-89 (Grant and Lapsley 1992: 106), 1.1 per cent in 1987-88 (Grant and Lapsley 1991: 108), 1.0 per cent in 1986-87 (Grant and Lapsley 1990: 94) and 0.9 per cent in 1985-86 (Grant and Lapsley 1989: 92). It is therefore quite apparent that health promotion has so far played a relatively minor role in the health care system in this country. For this reason, critics have considered it more appropriate to refer to the system as an illness management, rather than a health care, system.

However, calculation of health promotion expenditure is not quite as simple as consideration of the annual funds allocated within the health system, for much of the money spent to promote the health of the community is spent from budgets other than health (Sax 1990). For example, money spent on safe roads, public transport systems and basic services such as water supply has a positive impact on health yet is not counted as part of health promotion expenditure. Indeed, it is now widely accepted that action in the field of public health has had a much greater impact on health than action in the field of medicine (see McLachlan and McKeown 1971, McKeown 1965, and Eckholm 1977 for early examples). Nevertheless, even after such things have been taken into consideration, the proportion of government funds spent on health promotion remains small. In comparison, public expenditure continues to support ill health in Australia. Subsidies to cigarette and alcohol companies provide two examples of this unhealthy expenditure (see Sax 1990: 37).

□ TOTAL INSTITUTIONAL   □ TOTAL NON-INSTITUTIONAL

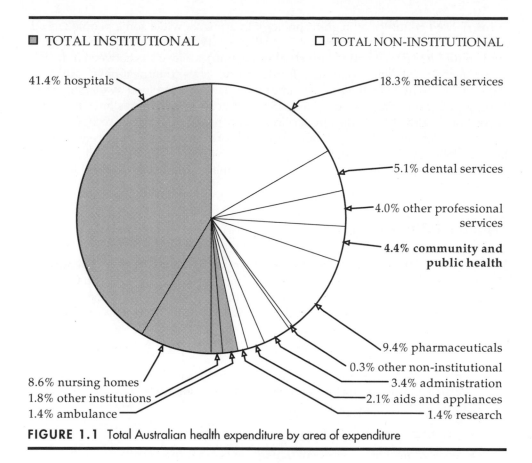

41.4% hospitals

18.3% medical services

5.1% dental services

4.0% other professional services

4.4% community and public health

9.4% pharmaceuticals

0.3% other non-institutional

3.4% administration

2.1% aids and appliances

1.4% research

8.6% nursing homes
1.8% other institutions
1.4% ambulance

FIGURE 1.1 Total Australian health expenditure by area of expenditure

The World Health Organization's response to health problems

The World Health Organization (WHO) was established in 1948. Included in its constitution were two important statements about health. The first was WHO's definition of health: 'Health is a complete state of physical, mental and social well-being, and not merely the absence of disease or infirmity'. This definition has been criticised by some (for example, Sax 1990: 1) as unrealistic and unmeasurable. Nonetheless, it is important because it defines health not merely as the lack of medically defined problems, but in much broader terms. Moreover, it provides a goal towards which we can aspire. The second important statement was about the role which WHO saw governments playing in health promotion: 'Governments have a responsibility for the health of their peoples, which can be fulfilled only by the provision of adequate health and social measures' (WHO 1958, cited by Roemer 1986: 58).

Despite those statements, however, there was growing concern in the 1970s that all was not well with the world's health and health care systems. There had been a rapid growth in the international health care industry without an increase in the health status of some people. Vast amounts of money were being spent in industrialised countries on high-technology treatments, while some people lacked access to even basic health care services (Roemer 1986). These disparities existed (and continue to do so) within industrialised countries as well as between industrialised and developing countries. Furthermore, few countries have acted to improve health by reducing poverty, improving housing and food availability, and ceasing political oppression, despite evidence that social conditions have a greater impact on health than do health services. As a result of growing recognition of these concerns, WHO and UNICEF held a major international conference in the former USSR, in 1978, attended by representatives from 134 nations. This conference is now regarded as an important milestone in the promotion of world health.

Primary Health Care

The outcome of the conference was the Declaration of Alma-Ata (see appendix, p. 217). Contained in its ten principles was the blueprint for Primary Health Care, including the goal of 'an acceptable level of health for all the people of the world by the year 2000' (WHO 1978 reproduced in WHO 1988: 16). This has become known as Health for All by the year 2000.

A number of concepts stand out in the Declaration of Alma-Ata:

- equity;
- participation and maximum community self-reliance;
- socially acceptable technology;
- health promotion and disease prevention;
- involvement of government departments other than health;
- political action;
- cooperation between countries;
- reduction of money spent on armaments in order to increase funds for Primary Health Care;
- world peace.

Attempts to provide a brief definition of Primary Health Care often do not capture what is illustrated by the above concepts. For example, the commonly cited definition of Primary Health Care is contained in one section of the Declaration of Alma-Ata:

> Primary Health Care is essential health care based on practical, scientifically sound and socially acceptable methods and technology made universally accessible to individuals and families in the community through their full participation and at a cost that the community and country can afford to maintain at every stage of their development in the spirit of self-reliance and self-determination. (WHO 1978 reproduced in WHO 1988: 16)

This definition, however, fails to reflect the whole spectrum of Primary Health Care and the fact that it is more than just a particular type of health service.

Indeed, WHO states that 'primary health care should be a philosophy permeating the entire health system, a strategy for organising health care, a level of care and a set of activities' (WHO, cited by Chamberlain and Beckingham 1987: 158), and it is in its entirety that Primary Health Care has the most potential to be revolutionary in its impact on the health of the world.

Primary Health Care as a philosophy permeating the entire health system

All health workers and components of the health care system should be guided by the principles of Primary Health Care. No matter where in the health system consumers find themselves, the principles of equity, consumer and community participation in decision making, the use of socially acceptable and affordable technology, the provision of services on the basis of the needs of the population, the provision of health education and work to improve the root causes of ill health should be present. Central to work aimed at addressing the root causes of ill health is a commitment to social justice and equity. These principles reflect the Primary Health Care philosophy or Primary Health Care approach. Given the recognition of the need for intersectoral action to improve health and the impact of social services on health, this facet of Primary Health Care should be expanded so that it becomes a philosophy permeating the entire social system.

Primary Health Care as a strategy for organising health care

When the philosophy of Primary Health Care is implemented, a particular strategy for the organisation of health care becomes apparent. A balanced system of illness treatment, disease prevention and health promotion should be developed, with the entire system built to meet the goals of Primary Health Care.

Primary Health Care as a level of care

The term 'Primary Health Care' is often used to refer to primary-level health services — that is, the first point of contact with the health system for people with health problems. In a Primary Health Care system, this level of care should be the most comprehensive. In this way, problems can be dealt with where they begin. Primary-level services include community health centres, domiciliary nursing care and general medical practitioners. Non-government organisations and community groups can also be an important part of Primary Health Care services. However, these services can only be regarded as Primary Health Care services if the Primary Health Care philosophy underpins the way in which those first-level services are provided. That is, Primary Health Care practitioners' work is guided by the principles of consumer control over decision making; collaboration with other health and welfare workers to deal effectively with health issues in their local area; equity and social justice (reflected in part by bulk-billing or salaried medical officers attached to community health centres, in the case of general medical practitioners); and incorporation of health promotion into their work.

Because of the now common use of the term 'primary health care' to refer to community or first-level services, I will use 'Primary Health Care' to reflect the Primary Health Care approach or philosophy.

Primary Health Care as a set of activities

The Declaration of Alma-Ata (WHO 1978) highlights a minimum set of activities that need to occur if Primary Health Care is to be implemented. These are:

- education concerning prevailing health problems and the methods of preventing and controlling them;
- promotion of food supply and proper nutrition;
- provision of an adequate supply of safe water and basic sanitation;
- provision of maternal and child health care, including family planning;
- immunisation against the major infectious diseases;
- prevention and control of locally endemic diseases;
- appropriate treatment of common diseases and injuries;
- provision of essential drugs.

What Primary Health Care is not

Many people confuse Primary Health Care with a number of other concepts. Some of these are listed below, together with an explanation of what they are.

1. Primary medical care (or primary care)

Primary medical care (or primary care) is medical care provided for individuals at their first point of contact with the health system. It may be provided in the outpatients section of a hospital, or by a general medical practitioner.

2. Primary nursing

Primary nursing is a system of nursing in which an individual nurse takes primary responsibility for particular patients. The focus is still on illness care rather than health promotion, and the individual, not the whole environment, is the target for change. (For a more detailed comparison of primary nursing and Primary Health Care, see Dowling et al. 1983.)

3. Third World nursing

Contrary to what some people believe, Primary Health Care is applicable to all countries of the world, not just developing ones. Firstly, there are major inequalities in health between different groups of people within wealthy countries. Secondly, much of the poverty and ill health in developing countries is actually there because of the actions of industrialised countries. For example, the siting of dangerous industries and the dumping of wastes in developing countries, the use of land in developing countries to produce cash crops rather than provide food for local people and the destruction of the habitats of people in developing countries to provide raw materials for industrialised countries all have a potent impact on developing countries for the benefit of industrialised countries. Moreover, many developing countries are locked into repayment of loans from industrialised countries, which requires them to sell off their own natural resources, often just to keep up with the interest payments. The Primary Health Care approach recognises these interconnections between developing and industrialised countries, and the inequities within industrialised countries, and is therefore extremely relevant to developing and industrialised countries alike.

Other potential priorities are also acknowledged by WHO — for example, mental health and priorities set by local communities themselves.

Clearly, the movement for Primary Health Care is pushing for more than just changes in health services. 'It is a movement calling for new democratic actions, major health system changes and social equity' (Roemer 1986: 63).

Implementation of Primary Health Care

Implementation of the Declaration Of Alma-Ata has been slow, particularly in industrialised countries such as Australia. One reason for this is the lack of understanding of the concept of Primary Health Care and the belief that it is relevant to developing countries only (WHO 1982: 2). Another reason is the complexity of the definition. A third major reason, and arguably the most potent, is the resistance to the concept from those who profit from the current system. Primary Health Care requires a balanced system of health promotion, prevention of ill health and an accessible source of illness treatment (WHO 1982: 4). The impact of Primary Health Care represents a real threat to the current illness management system of industrialised countries, since the system would have to redistribute its resources, and companies reduce their profits, if health promotion became an important priority. The 'medico-industrial complex' is an extremely powerful force in Australia, and indeed in the whole world (Davis and George 1988: 174).

Primary Health Care would also require a major shift in the focus of many health workers' roles, away from the provision of acute, high-technology treatments to a greater focus on the provision of low-technology community services, health promotion and advocacy for health. Because of the challenge which Primary Health Care presents to the current illness management system, a less threatening form of Primary Health Care has been suggested. This has become known as selective Primary Health Care.

Comprehensive versus selective Primary Health Care

It is widely acknowledged by those involved in Primary Health Care that its expectations are huge, and that some priorities for action need to be set. This is the kind of argument that was used to suggest the more limited form of Primary Health Care which has become known as selective Primary Health Care. Although the rationale seems reasonable, it is argued that it has been used to support a vision of Primary Health Care whose philosophy is diametrically opposed to that proposed at the Alma-Ata conference. The issues surrounding this debate are by no means simple. While many people regard the Declaration of Alma-Ata as reflecting comprehensive Primary Health Care, some writers argue that the Declaration of Alma-Ata embraces both approaches (Taylor and Jolly 1988), while others suggest that its intent has supported selective Primary Health Care (Navarro 1984). Discussion of the debate on these two forms of Primary Health Care is important because the philosophical differences between the two approaches have broad implications for how we view and implement Primary Health Care and health promotion. It is important to understand those differences and be able to locate yourself and your practice within them.

Comprehensive Primary Health Care emphasises community-controlled social changes which impact on health and in which medicine may play a minor role, whereas selective Primary Health Care concentrates on providing 'medical interventions aimed at improving the health status of the most individuals at the lowest cost' (Rifkin and Walt 1986: 560). Thus, while comprehensive Primary Health Care focuses on the process of empowerment and increasing control over all those influences which impact on health, selective Primary Health Care operates in a way which ensures that control over health is maintained by health professionals. Selective Primary Health Care might be seen in the short term to reduce prevalence rates of specific diseases, but in the longer term it does not deal with the root causes of ill health, nor does it generate community control over health service provision. Conversely, it is argued that the greater benefits of comprehensive Primary Health Care are apparent in the longer term and are likely to be more sustainable.

Rifkin and Walt (1986: 561–2) identify four key areas in which the differences between comprehensive Primary Health Care and selective Primary Health Care become apparent.

1. By focusing on the eradication and prevention of diseases, selective Primary Health Care assumes that health is the absence of disease rather than, in the broader WHO definition, a state of complete physical, mental and social well-being. This then locates action for health almost solely within the realms of specialists trained to treat disease.

2. Through its emphasis on those diseases and problems most likely to respond to treatment, selective Primary Health Care ignores the need for Primary Health Care to address issues of equity and social justice, which are at the root of many health problems.

3. In establishing medical interventions as the most important part of Primary Health Care, selective Primary Health Care ignores the importance of all those non-medical interventions, such as the provision of education, housing and food, which may have a greater bearing on health than health services themselves.

4. Selective Primary Health Care limits the value of community development as a strategy for improving health. Within it, community development is seen solely as a technique to be used to increase community acceptance of medically defined solutions. It thus identifies expertise as residing with medical workers and denies the great expertise which people have with regard to their own lives and the issues which affect them.

Rifkin and Walt (1986: 563) point out that although the philosophical differences between these two definitions of Primary Health Care are clear-cut, this may not be immediately apparent when they are examined in practice. That is not to suggest that the distinction between the two is unimportant — on the contrary.

What it does suggest is that health promotion practitioners need to be quite clear about their values and how best to implement them before they start. Otherwise, they may find it difficult to explain their actions to people who do not share their perspective, or they may find that their actions do less to effectively promote the health of their clients than they had hoped.

Nurses and Primary Health Care

Nurses currently make up almost 70 per cent of the paid health workforce in Australia (Grant and Lapsley 1988, cited by Palmer and Short 1989: 124). By virtue of their numbers alone, the impact they can have, if they embrace health promotion and the philosophy of Primary Health Care, is immense. Both the International Congress of Nurses and the Australian Nursing Federation have pledged their support for Primary Health Care and the Health for All movement. Australia's nursing workforce is therefore formally committed to Health for All. WHO is very supportive of nurses acting as change agents in the Health for All movement. Indeed, Halfdan Mahler, Director-General of WHO from 1973 to 1986, saw nurses as 'more than ready' to take up the challenges of Primary Health Care (Mahler 1987: 23), and urged:

> If the millions of nurses in a thousand different places articulate the same ideas and convictions about primary health care, and come together as one force, then they could act as a powerhouse for change. (1987: 23)

Of course, many nurses are still working out how they see their role in Primary Health Care and health promotion, and many others are still unaware of Primary Health Care and its implications. It remains to be seen how many nurses will take up the challenge to work as health activists, to promote health in a way which enables communities and individuals to live their lives to the full. It is vital that nurses take up this challenge if our work is to have a positive impact on the health of those we are meant to serve. If we choose to ignore the shift to Primary Health Care and continue to support a burgeoning illness management system, the costs to the health of the community will be immense.

If, on the other hand, this challenge is taken up by all nurses and others whose work impacts on health, as well as by community members who find their health being jeopardised by the circumstances in which they live, the effect could be quite profound.

The Ottawa Charter for Health Promotion and the new public health movement

As part of the development of Primary Health Care for industrialised countries, the first WHO International Conference on Health Promotion was held in Ottawa, Canada, in 1986 (see appendix, p. 220). The outcome of this conference was the Ottawa Charter for Health Promotion, which set out the action required to achieve Health for All by the year 2000. It builds on the Declaration of Alma-Ata, and states, in part:

The fundamental conditions and resources for health are peace, shelter, education, food, income, a stable eco-system, sustainable resources, social justice and equity. Improvement in health requires a secure foundation in these basic prerequisites. (WHO 1986)

How are we to achieve this? The Ottawa Charter (WHO 1986) states that health promotion action must occur on five fronts:

1. We must promote health by *building healthy public policy*. It is not health policy alone that influences health: all public policy must be examined for its impact on health, and where policies have a negative impact on health, we must work to change them. For example, if a state or local government has a policy of allowing industrial complexes near residential areas, this would need to change if it was having a negative impact on residents' health. Through building healthy public policy, it is hoped to make healthy choices easier for people.

2. We must promote health by *creating environments which support healthy living*. For example, we need living, work and leisure environments organised in a way that does not create or contribute to poor health. These will come through the establishment of healthy public policy.

3. We must promote health by *strengthening community action*. Communities themselves should determine what their needs are and how they can best be met. Thus greater power and control remains with the people themselves, rather than with the 'experts'. Community development is one means by which this can be achieved.

4. We must promote health by *helping people develop their skills* so that they can work for more control over their own health and the environment in which they live, and so that they have the skills necessary to make healthy choices. They also need the skills to deal effectively with illness and injury should they occur.

5. We must promote health by *reorienting the health care system* so that there is a much greater balance between health promotion and curative services, and so that the health care system works more closely with other sectors whose work impacts on health. One prerequisite for this reorientation is a major change in the way in which health care workers are educated.

To ensure effective work in those five areas, the Ottawa Charter highlights the need for health workers to be effective in *advocacy* and *mediation* in order to *enable* people to gain greater control over their lives (WHO 1986). The need for advocacy and mediation is particularly important in order to reorient the system towards Primary Health Care and health promotion, and achieve greater equity in health.

The Ottawa Charter for Health Promotion is regarded as the formal beginning of the new public health movement, a term which is gaining widespread recognition. The approach to health promotion established by WHO through the Ottawa Charter differs from traditional public health as it has been practised in

The Ottawa Charter for Health Promotion's action framework

- Build healthy public policy
- Create supportive environments
- Strengthen community action
- Develop personal skills
- Reorient health services

recent years in three important ways. Firstly, it recognises the intersectoral nature of health promotion, and the need to work with other sectors of government and private institutions whose work impacts on health. Secondly, it recognises the need to increase community participation in and control over issues which affect health, and to demedicalise the control of health care. Thirdly, it recognises the primacy of people's environments (both physical and socioeconomic) in determining their health, and thus acknowledges the need to work to change them, rather than focusing only on the medical elements of a problem (Tones et al. 1990: 3–4). This means that many of the changes acknowledged as vital to the new public health movement may challenge existing ways of doing things. Indeed, WHO acknowledges the need for political action in the new public health movement in order to achieve the required changes.

The new public health movement is based on a social model of health and challenges the narrow approach of the medical model. This social model of health sets very wide parameters for health promotion practice. This is exciting because it means we can actually start dealing with health problems at the point of their root cause. Indeed,

> *a social view of health implies that we must intervene to change those aspects of the environment which are promoting ill health, rather than continue to simply deal with illness after it appears, or continue to exhort individuals to change their attitudes and lifestyles when, in fact, the environment in which they live and work gives them little choice or support for making such changes. (South Australian Health Commission 1988: 3)*

Issues of social, political and environmental origin are largely ignored in the medical model of health, and this severely limits the ability of medical model responses to get at the root causes of ill health. This is not to suggest that a medical model approach should be disregarded. Clearly, people will continue to get sick and require medical treatment. What is required, however, is a more balanced combination of medical model and social health approaches (Sax 1990: 36–7). This is the Primary Health Care approach.

The view of health presented by the Ottawa Charter for Health Promotion has also been referred to as an ecological view of health, because of the recognition of the importance of the environment and ecological sustainability in promoting world health. This social and ecological emphasis can be seen reflected in recommendations of the second and third international conferences on health promotion.

The Second International Conference on Health Promotion — Adelaide, Australia

WHO's Second International Conference on Health Promotion was held in Adelaide in 1988. Its theme was healthy public policy, the key action area set out in the Ottawa Charter, and its recommendations built very much on the spirit of Primary Health Care and the Ottawa Charter. Participants reaffirmed their commitment to the latter, and urged everyone else to do so. In addition to making clear the importance of healthy public policy and the responsibility of all who produce public policy to observe and be responsive to the health impact of their policies, the conference urged industrialised countries to develop policies which reduce the growing disparity between rich and poor countries.

Furthermore, the conference identified four priority areas for action: support for the health of women, in recognition of their often unequal access to health and their role as health promoters within their own families; the elimination of hunger and malnutrition through action which takes account of agricultural, economic and environmental issues; the reduction of tobacco growing and alcohol production; and the creation of more supportive environments, in particular through the alliance of the public health, peace and ecological movements (WHO/Commonwealth Department of Community Services and Health — Australia 1988).

The Third International Conference on Health Promotion — Sundsvall, Sweden

The Third International Conference on Health Promotion was held in Sundsvall, Sweden, in 1991. Its theme was supportive environments for health, and it made four recommendations for action to create such environments. These were:

- strengthen advocacy through community action, particularly through groups organised by women;

- enable communities and individuals to take control of their health and environment through education and empowerment;

- build alliances to strengthen cooperation between health and environment campaigns;

- mediate between conflicting interests in society in order to ensure equitable access to a supportive environment for health

(WHO 1991, cited by Tassie 1992: 28).

Australia's response to the Health for All movement: the *Health for all Australians* report and beyond

As a signatory to the Declaration of Alma-Ata, Australia formally committed itself to Health for All by the year 2000 in 1981. However, it was not until the mid-1980s that action started becoming apparent. Even so, most of the action to date has been in the formulation of policies. The way in which these are translated into action will become more apparent, it is to be hoped, over the next few years.

The Better Health Commission was established by the federal government in 1986. It identified national health goals for Australia in its report *Looking forward to better health* (1986). These were then examined in greater detail by the Health Targets and Implementation ('Health For All') Committee, which released the *Health for all Australians* report in 1988. This is essentially Australia's plan of action to achieve Health for All by the year 2000. A number of Australian states have gone on to produce their own health goals and targets based on the *Health for all Australians* report, and a number of health regions and zones have applied it at a more local level.

In its report, the Health Targets and Implementation Committee (1988) set national goals and targets in a range of areas, under three general categories of population groups, major causes of illness and death and risk factors (see below). It set five priorities for action in the areas of control of high blood pressure, improved nutrition, injury prevention, the health of older people and the prevention of cancer (notably lung, skin, breast and cervical cancers). In addition, it noted a number of barriers to better health and recognised the need for structural change in the health system if we are to promote the health of all Australians.

Areas in which goals and targets were set in the *Health for all Australians* report

Population groups

The socioeconomically disadvantaged, Aborigines, migrants, women, men, older people, children, adolescents.

Major causes of illness and death

Heart disease and stroke, cancers (including lung, breast, cervical and skin cancers), injury, communicable disease, musculoskeletal diseases, diabetes, disability, dental disease, mental illness, asthma.

Risk factors

Drugs (including tobacco smoking, alcohol misuse, pharmaceutical misuse or abuse, illicit drugs and substance abuse), nutrition, physical inactivity, high blood pressure, high blood cholesterol, occupational health hazards, unprotected sexual activity, environmental health hazards.

Health Targets and Implementation Committee 1988: 9

The *Health for all Australians* report represented a quite important shift in Australian health policy development. It was the first time that the federal government had formally recognised the role played by social inequalities in causing ill health. It was also the first time that a national health strategy document setting goals and targets for the health of Australians had been drawn up (Health Targets and Implementation Committee 1988: 8), quite a remarkable fact given the large amounts of money which the health system consumes each year. Furthermore, in defining the quest for better health for Australians, the report acknowledged the existence of barriers to that quest, both those outside the health system such as economic and social factors, and those within the system, which it acknowledged is geared to illness rather than health (Health Targets and Implementation Committee 1988: 8).

However, the *Health for all Australians* report has been criticised on a number of grounds. Firstly, although it acknowledges that health inequalities exist between different groups in Australian society, it is built primarily on a biomedical, rather than a social model, of health. Although setting goals for population groups, major causes of illness and death, and risk factors, the report focuses largely on medical problems in the priorities for action which it sets. Furthermore, targets are set for disease categories, yet none are set for population groups or for conditions which severely limit people's health but which have not been categorised as a disease — for example, chronic back pain and the health consequences of sexual assault (Brown 1988: 33). Therefore, the solutions which the report suggests are somewhat limited. One of the main reasons for this is that the Health Targets and Implementation Committee (1988: 6) chose to identify changes which could be made within the health system, rather than also looking at what could be done in a comprehensive intersectoral approach to health. This was quite an unfortunate choice, since the document was meant to implement Primary Health Care, and could have been an important first step in the formal establishment of intersectoral action for health in Australia.

Furthermore, the committee chose as its priorities those problems where action was likely to be effective (1988: 11). Other issues may have been ignored because they were difficult to address, although they may have been urgent. It has also been suggested that the committee chose as priorities those areas where well-defined goals and targets were already available, rather than the areas which were most important (Consumers' Health Forum 1988, cited by McPherson 1992: 128). Such an approach has been criticised elsewhere for ignoring the most serious health problems which people face, and thus achieving less for people's health in the longer term (Rifkin and Walt 1986). Therefore, although the *Health for all Australians* report represents an important beginning for Australia's health, it does not embrace the principles of Primary Health Care to the extent that it could have.

Following on from the *Health for all Australians* report, the National Better Health Program was established in order to implement its recommendations. It provided funding for health promotion activities, particularly those which addressed the five priority areas outlined in the *Health for all Australians* report (Australian Institute of Health 1990: 81). The program was funded until June 1992, when it was evaluated. The evaluation was released in March 1993.

Towards Health for All and Health Promotion (1993) included recommendations for the establishment of a national Health for All Strategy, supported by legislation, and for the continuation of a strong national health promotion program as part of this strategy.

With the completion of the National Better Health Program, funding for health promotion programs is now administered through the National Health Advancement Program.

Goals and targets for Australia's health in the year 2000 and beyond

The goals and targets set in the *Health for all Australians* report were for the five-year period following the report's release. The second set of goals and targets were developed in 1992, and released in February 1993. These built on the lessons learned from the first set. In particular, they recognised the importance of moving beyond a mainly medical model focus, and beyond the marginal approach to the necessary changes to the health system. *Goals and Targets For Australia's Health in the Year 2000 and Beyond* (Nutbeam et al. 1993) revised and refined the targets set in the *Health for all Australians* report in the areas of preventable morbidity and mortality and healthy lifestyles and risk factors, and established additional targets in the areas of health literacy, health skills and healthy environments (see p. 16). It recognised the need for the whole health system to be involved in achieving health goals and targets and, in order to help achieve this, identified the need to establish specific goals and targets for the health system (Nutbeam et al. 1993: 13–14). It also urged a stronger intersectoral approach to health issues. As a result, this second set of goals and targets are broader, less medically defined and therefore much more in line with the Ottawa Charter for Health Promotion's broad

---

Areas in which goals and targets have been set in *Goals and targets for Australia's health in the year 2000 and beyond*

Preventable mortality and morbidity

Cardiovascular disease, preventable cancer, injury, communicable diseases, HIV/AIDS, sexually transmitted diseases, maternal and infant (including perinatal) health, asthma, diabetes mellitus, mental health problems and disorders, physical impairment and disability, developmental disability and oral health.

Healthy lifestyles and risk factors

Diet and nutrition, overweight and obesity, physical activity, high blood cholesterol, high blood pressure, smok-

ing, alcohol misuse, illicit drug use, quality use of medicines, healthy sexuality, reproductive health, sun protection, oral hygiene, safety behaviours, immunisation and mental health.

Health literacy and health skills

Health literacy, life skills and coping, safety skills and first aid, self help and self care and social support.

Healthy environments

The physical environment, transport, housing, home and community infrastructure, work and the workplace, schools and health care settings.

framework. A separate set of Health Goals and Targets is also being developed for Aboriginal and Torres Strait Islander people.

The establishment of health goals and targets represents something of a two-edged sword for advocates of the Primary Health Care approach. On the one hand, they finally set goals to direct the issues which the entire health system should be addressing, and so provide an opportunity for the health system to make a bigger difference to health status in Australia. On the other hand, they are prescriptive and amount to some quite narrow goals being imposed from above. This limits communities being able to set their own goals relevant to their own needs, and so is in some contrast to a Primary Health Care approach, where community control and responsiveness to local issues is a priority.

Improving Australia's health: The role of Primary Health Care

In 1991, the National Centre for Epidemiology and Population Health was commissioned by the National Better Health Program to examine the role of Primary Health Care in health promotion in Australia. Despite concern expressed by a number of those consulted that the role of health promotion in Primary Health Care should have been examined, the approach remained unchanged. In October 1992, after a year-long consultation process, the final report — *Improving Australia's health: the role of Primary Health Care* — was released. A range of issues were studied, including how Primary Health Care currently looks in Australia, how it might address the issue of more efficient, effective and equitable health promotion and how it could be strengthened. The report recommends the establishment of Primary Health Care reference centres in each state and territory, greater education for and funding of innovative Primary Health Care activity, greater support for 'Healthy Cities' (see p. 149) and the development of a national Primary Health Care Policy and Implementation Plan. Furthermore, it acknowledges two alternative attitudes towards health promotion in Primary Health Care: health promotion as a developmental process in partnership with community members, and health promotion as a planning process imposed by a central health promotion agency. These often opposing approaches have been of concern to a number of health workers for some time and their acknowledgment in the report is valuable. However, the report does not deal with the many barriers to the implementation of Primary Health Care in Australia, a vital issue if Primary Health Care is to move beyond being token.

It remains to be seen what impact this review of the role of Primary Health Care in health promotion will have on the way in which health services are structured, funded and supported. As discussion of the National Health Strategy demonstrates below, it is likely that the development of a comprehensive Primary Health Care system will require continued action on the part of community members and concerned health workers.

However, a number of Australian states have been in the process of developing their own Primary Health Care policies. South Australia has produced *A Social Health Strategy* (1988), *Primary Health Care in South Australia: a discussion paper* (1988) and an implementation plan, *Strategic Directions for Primary Health Care* (1993). Similarly, Queensland has released *A Primary Health Care Policy* (1992) and a draft *Primary Health Care Implementation Plan* (1992). It is to be hoped that other states will follow suit. The real challenge, of course, will come in the implementation of these policies.

The *National Health Strategy*

In 1991, the Australian health ministers commissioned the *National Health Strategy*, a two-year examination of the structure and funding of the Australian health system. Development of the *National Health Strategy* provided an excellent opportunity to reorient the system to a Primary Health Care approach. Unfortunately, the strategy focused on making the current system more efficient without making the major changes required of a reorientation to Primary Health Care. Indeed, the National Health Strategy considered health promotion and Primary Health Care towards the end of its life and after issues of funding and restructuring had been considered, so this opportunity for major change was lost. This seems to reflect a continued belief that health promotion and Primary Health Care are marginal to the Australian health system. However, the National Health Strategy paper which considered health promotion, *Pathways to Better Health* (1993), drew on previous Australian health promotion and Primary Health Care work (including *Towards Health For All and Health Promotion* (1993) and *Improving Australia's health: the Role of Primary Health Care* (1992)). Quite a comprehensive document, it made a number of recommendations about continuing support for health promotion within the health system, including the establishment of a National Health Promotion Authority, further development of education for health promotion, the development of a stronger intersectoral approach to health promotion and the further strengthening of health promotion action by community health centres, schools, general medical practitioners, hospitals and workplaces.

A number of other more specific recent national policy and strategy documents have implications for Australia's health. These are the *National Aboriginal Health Strategy*; the *National Women's Health Policy: Advancing Women's Health in Australia*; the *National Non-English Speaking Background Women's Health Strategy*; the *National Mental Health Policy*; and the *National Rural Health Strategy*. It is worthwhile briefly examining these and the approaches they take.

The *National Aboriginal Health Strategy*

Of all the current national policy documents, it is the *National Aboriginal Health Strategy* that most reflects a social health approach. This is perhaps not surprising, given the extremely poor state of health of Aboriginal people as a whole. The strategy was prepared by a working party, with a consultation process which involved seeking the opinions of a large number of Aboriginal communities, groups and individuals, as well as a number of non-Aboriginal people. The National Aboriginal Health Strategy is grounded in the recognition of the importance of the structural basis of health, and it describes the inextricable link between Aboriginal health, land rights and domination of Aboriginal people by non-Aboriginal culture. Within this framework, it considers the roles of government in dealing with Aboriginal health, the necessary changes to the structure of the health system, the role of intersectoral collaboration in promoting Aboriginal health, a wide range of specific health issues, and Aboriginal health research and evaluation.

In particular, the strategy argues for Aboriginal community control of health services and research into issues related to Aboriginal people and their health. It also argues for Aboriginal women's control of specific women's issues — that is, matters related to childbearing, family planning and gynaecological health. This is vital because Western medical control of childbearing and related issues ignores the fact that they are regarded as 'women's business' and also ignores the spiritual importance of many of them. In suggesting strategies to deal with the specific ill health problems facing Aboriginal people, the strategy acknowledges cardiovascular disease, diabetes, chronic lung disease, pneumonia, asthma, kidney diseases and renal failure, ear disease, diarrhoeal diseases, trauma and injury, contagious diseases of childhood, hepatitis B, sexually transmittable diseases, ocular diseases, dental health, mental health, domestic violence and child abuse as serious problems. In addition, it examines abuse of alcohol and other substances, and the health impact of such things as housing, food supply and education.

Concern continues to be expressed by Aboriginal people and a number of other groups that the *National Aboriginal Health Strategy* has still not been implemented, despite the fact that it is four years since it was developed. Given the urgency of Aboriginal health issues, this raises serious questions about whether the Australian government's commitment to it is anything more than lip-service.

National Women's Health Policy: Advancing Women's Health in Australia

The National Women's Health Policy was presented to the Australian health ministers in 1989. The development of this policy included extensive consultation with women's groups throughout Australia. It highlights seven priority health issues for women, which are not limited to standard medical classification of illness, but reflect the social health basis of the policy. These issues are reproductive health and sexuality, the health of ageing women, women's emotional and mental health, violence against women, occupational health and safety, the health needs of women as carers and the health effects of sex role stereotyping on women.

The policy also recognises that issues of concern to women and their health are not limited just to specific health issues, and so it highlights five issues related to the structure of the health system that require action. These are the need for improvements in health services for women, the need to provide relevant health information for women, the need for more research into women's health issues, the need to increase women's participation in health decision making and the need to train health workers to deal more appropriately with women and their health concerns. Of course, the next step is for greater intersectoral work on issues which impact on the health of women. However, the National Women's Health Policy does go some way to incorporating a social health approach into the way women's health issues are viewed.

National Non-English Speaking Background Women's Health Strategy

In 1991, the *National Non-English Speaking Background Women's Health Strategy* was released. It complements the National Women's Health Policy by focusing on the particular needs of women from non-English speaking backgrounds. It focuses on occupational health and safety as it relates to women from non-English speaking backgrounds, the needs of carers from non-English speaking backgrounds, the need for better language services, the need for better access and choice for a range of health services for women from non-English speaking backgrounds, and the need to improve the quality of a number of health services required by women from non-English speaking backgrounds (Alcorso and Schofield 1991). Like the National Women's Health Policy, the *National Non-English Speaking Background Women's Health Strategy* recognises the impact of the environment on health. Many of the issues it raises will require action in a number of sectors in order to be addressed.

The *National Mental Health Policy*

The *National Mental Health Policy* and the *National Mental Health Plan* were both released in April 1992. The *National Mental Health Policy* recognises the importance of promoting the mental health of the Australian community, although overall its focus is on better quality services for individuals with mental health problems and for their carers. It emphasises the importance of a 'community oriented approach to the provision of mental health services' (Australian health ministers 1992: 2), although, as previous deinstitutionalisation policies have noted, community-based care without sufficient funding can have disastrous consequences. Furthermore, the policy recognises the need for better access to such services as transport, accommodation and community services, and the need for better education for the community as a whole about mental health problems. It identifies the need for greater support for the carers of people with mental health problems, including greater financial support and involvement in decision making (Australian health ministers 1992: 4). Unfortunately, despite their aim of improving the mental health of the community as a whole, the policy and the plan focus on provision of services for people with mental health disorders, in particular those with serious mental health problems, and place little emphasis on mental health promotion. Consequently, this latter area appears to remain largely unrecognised.

The *National Rural Health Strategy*

Following government recognition that the health needs of people living in rural areas of Australia are different to those of their urban counterparts, the (then) federal Department of Community Services and Health hosted the first National Rural Health Conference in February 1991. The aim of this conference was to develop a national Rural Health Strategy.

The strategy recommends the establishment of a national body to direct and coordinate rural health policy and practice, the funding of research into the particular needs of rural dwellers and approaches to address those needs, the development of support and education for rural health workers, improvement of current equity and access problems for rural dwellers, the promotion of health for rural dwellers and effective planning to address the particular health needs of vulnerable groups (including Aboriginal and Torres Strait Islanders, older people, people with chronic illness or disabilities, women, children, adolescents and people with HIV/AIDS or at risk of contracting the virus (National Rural Health Strategy 1991: 1–2). Following on from the strategy, a Rural Health Alliance was established, funds have become available through the Rural Health Support Education and Training Program, and a National Rural Health Unit has been announced.

Unfortunately, the *National Rural Health Strategy* and its implementation to date have not taken a Primary Health Care approach to addressing health issues, and action to promote the health of rural Australians has been somewhat limited.

As these various documents demonstrate, a great deal of policy and planning work has recently been developed with reference to health promotion in Australia. It is to be expected that we will see at least some of the recommendations of these reports implemented in the not-too-distant future.

Health promoting hospitals

By far the largest amount of health promotion work conducted by the health system in Australia is done within the community health sector, a sector which receives just 4.4 per cent of the health budget. Clearly, greater funding for that sector is an important part of effectively implementing Primary Health Care. However, if we are to effectively reorient the current health system towards a greater emphasis on Primary Health Care and health promotion, we need to do more than shift the spending priorities within the health system. Primary Health Care and health promotion cannot work effectively if they are established in opposition to the hospital-based system. The hospital system itself needs to become an integral part of the Primary Health Care system, working in direct response to community needs and promoting the health of the community as a whole. This is clearly quite a different approach from the one currently prevailing in most hospitals, although there are some important exceptions, particularly in some rural areas of Australia. We need to ensure that we maximise the role of health promotion within the present health system by increasing the role that hospitals play in health promotion, and increasing their commitment to the Primary Health Care philosophy. This approach has been urged by WHO (WHO 1987; Ebrahim and Ranken 1988: 85).

The federal Department of Human Services and Health recently funded a research project examining ways in which the role of hospitals in health promotion can be strengthened. A number of hospitals are already working to increase their health promotion work. The major challenge in this process is for hospitals to adopt the health promotion philosophy in a meaningful way, rather than merely 'add on' health promotion activities in order to increase their credibility without actually changing their responsiveness to community needs. The extent to which they can do this will depend on the barriers which exist in each hospital and the level of commitment which health workers and health administrators have towards this reorientation. What can be achieved in large teaching hospitals, for example, may differ greatly from what can be achieved by smaller rural hospitals who may already have close contacts with their community.

Health workers, however, do not have to wait for major policy changes within hospitals to occur before increasing their individual health promotion action. In particular, they can lobby their employing organisations to take a greater role in health promotion. They can also choose to increase their commitment to health education in the hospital setting; they can use their rights as community members to write to their Members of Parliament and lobby for changes to unhealthy public policy; and they can join community groups and work for a healthier community. Such actions recognise that health workers are part of their community and that they have a right and responsibility to protect their health and that of their community.

Health promotion at Flinders Medical Centre

Flinders Medical Centre, established in 1976, is a public teaching hospital of approximately 500 beds in the southern metropolitan area of South Australia. In 1983 a small group of staff from a range of disciplines formed a steering group to address the lack of patient information services available at the hospital. The result was the establishment of a health information centre in August 1984, initially staffed by a registered nurse with a background in health education. The establishment of this centre marked the beginning of a long, challenging process that sought not only to provide a service which complemented the existing clinical work of the hospital, but also to facilitate a change in the hospital culture towards health promotion.

The centre is situated in the hospital's consulting clinics, easily accessible from the main hospital entrance and by public transport from the city and southern suburbs. Its initial function was to provide an information service, with a particular emphasis on lifestyle issues, to patients, staff and the general public. In 1992 the centre, now a designated health promotion department, was providing a wide range of services developed in response to demand from both the hospital and the wider community.

Administration of the Health Promotion Department

The initial steering group formed the basis of a management committee representative of nursing, medical, allied health, administrative and media staff. This committee met quarterly to consider major policy and finance decisions and was co-chaired by the Director of Nursing and the Professor of Primary Health Care. As the role, function and organisational relationships of the department evolved, the management committee was disbanded and a consultative group established, representing a range of health promotion expertise and interest from the hospital and other agencies.

Although in the early stages of its development the Health Promotion Department was part of the Nursing Division, it is now an independent department reporting directly to the hospital's Chief Executive Officer. Day-to-day functions, policy development, staffing and budget control are the responsibility of the department's director.

Funding

The cost of running the Health Promotion Department was initially borne by the hospital's Nursing Division. Since

1986 a specific department cost centre, including a salary line and minimal goods and services budget, has been allocated from the hospital's global budget.

The financial viability of the department is a source of constant pressure. Providing the range of services currently demanded of it necessitates seeking sponsorship, grants and donations from a variety of sources, particularly private enterprise. Progressively, the department has developed a range of marketable health education resources which assist in generating income and providing a degree of financial independence. The networking required to advertise the department's work and gain sponsorship widens its sphere of influence, facilitating valuable alliances for community-based health promotion strategies.

Staffing

The department is staffed by four health educators and a clerical officer. Other professional staff are appointed on a sessional or contract basis according to specific programs being conducted. The department has access to the staff of the hospital Media Unit, who assist with the design and production of many of its educational resources.

The role of the Health Promotion Department

Apart from providing a wide range of specific services, a health promotion department within a public hospital can, by its presence, influence the social and professional culture of the institution. The process of encouraging cooperation and collaboration with both clinical and non-clinical staff has been a large component of this department's activities, particularly contributing to educational programs to assist in changing staff attitudes, and developing new knowledge and skills.

Strengthening links with community services and other government and non-government agencies has been an important process not only for the Health Promotion Department but also for the hospital as a whole. Providing an information service to clients in person, by mail or by telephone continues to be a major component of the department's activities, together with health education, counselling and selected courses.

Major health promotion projects are conducted to address a range of health issues using a multiple strategy approach directed to specific target groups. Issues addressed are selected because of their local relevance or to complement statewide initiatives. Opportunities are sought to involve key staff members from hospital departments or community services in the planning and implementation of these projects.

Smaller-scale activities and displays with a specific health focus are also conducted throughout the hospital, helping to make health messages more accessible to the community.

All services are free of charge, require no referral, and are available to any member of the public, hospital patients and their families, and hospital staff. For many clients, the department is the first contact with the health system. Often confused by the range of services and how to access them, clients will discuss their particular problem and can be assisted by staff who have rights of referral to hospital departments and to other professionals in the community.

A major source of clients, both inpatients and outpatients, is referral from medical staff and other health professionals from the hospital and the community. Reasons for referral vary widely but may include nutrition advice, weight loss, smoking cessation, stress management and advice about community support groups.

The department maintains close liaison with the South Australian Health Commission and other government departments and community agencies. This helps create a wide resource network to assist clients and also ensures a profile which facilitates consultation regarding service delivery and policy development at all levels.

Current and anticipated changes in Health Service organisation, planning and resourcing in South Australia will have an impact on the future of the Health Promotion Department. It is envisaged that an integrated and collaborative approach to planning at a regional level will evolve, with emphasis on disease prevention and health promotion as well as clinical and community-based services. Flinders Medical Centre and the Health Promotion Department will have a central role in contributing to this process, initiating further opportunities for reorienting hospital services consistent with Primary Health Care principles.

Judy Aiello
Director, Health Promotion
Flinders Medical Centre

How can we promote health along the lines recommended by the Ottawa Charter?

Further action is required to reorient the Australian health care system to greater emphasis on health promotion and Primary Health Care. This is going to take a great deal of effort by many people, committed to working at it for some time.

The challenge for you, then, is to put into practice the principles of Primary Health Care and health promotion using a social health perspective. There are a growing number of strategies that you can use to do this. In the remainder of this book you will be introduced to those strategies, and you will be able to examine some examples of how health workers have implemented them. It is important to remember, however, that we are still exploring how best to put the Ottawa Charter into practice, and so your own endeavours in this area may contribute to our understanding of how best to use these strategies to give effect to the principles outlined in this chapter and the next one. You may be able to come up with other strategies which can help further develop our approach to the issues which face us in promoting the health of our communities.

Conclusion

The last 15 years have seen the development of a number of international and national documents designed to reorient health systems towards Primary Health Care and health promotion. These developments occurred as a result of recognition of inequities in health and social development throughout the world.

Within Australia, we are slowly seeing action based on these calls for a reorientation of our approach to health issues. It remains to be seen, however, to what extent these changes will result in a reorientation to the Primary Health Care approach, because of the extent to which it challenges the current health system. Health workers are encouraged to take up this challenge by incorporating the principles of Primary Health Care into their daily practice and to develop their skills in health promotion.

REFERENCES AND FURTHER READINGS

Aiello, J., Barry, L., Lienert, L. and Byrnes, T. 1990. Health promotion: a focus for hospitals, *Australian Health Review*, 13(2), 90–4.

Alcorso, C. and Schofield, T. 1991. *The National Non-English Speaking Background Women's Health Strategy*, Australian Government Publishing Service, Canberra.

Anderson, I. 1988. *Koorie health in Koorie hands: an orientation manual in Aboriginal health for health care providers*, Koorie Health Department, Health Department Victoria, Melbourne.

Australian Community Health Association (eds). 1990. *Making the connections: people, communities and the environment: papers from the first National Conference of Healthy Cities Australia*, Australian Community Health Association, Sydney.

Australian health ministers. 1992. *National Mental Health Policy*, Australian Government Publishing Service, Canberra.

Australian Institute of Health. 1989. *Australia's health: the first biennial report of the Australian Institute of Health 1988*, Australian Government Publishing Service, Canberra.

Australian Institute of Health. 1990. *Australia's health 1990: the second biennial report of the Australian Institute of Health*, Australian Government Publishing Service, Canberra.

Australian Institute of Health and Welfare. 1992. *Australia's health 1992: the third biennial report of the Australian Institute of Health and Welfare*, Australian Government Publishing Service, Canberra.

Australian Nursing Federation. 1990. *Primary Health Care in Australia*: strategies for nursing action, Australian Nursing Federation, Melbourne.

Bates, E. and Linder-Pelz, S. 1990. *Health Care Issues*, Allen and Unwin, Sydney.

Bechhofer, F. 1989. Individuals, politics and society: a dilemma for public health research?, in Martin, C. J. and McQueen, D. V. (eds), *Readings for a new public health*, Edinburgh University Press, Edinburgh.

Better Health Commission. 1986. *Looking forward to better health*, Australian Government Publishing Service, Canberra.

Broadhead, P. 1985. Social status and morbidity in Australia, *Community Health Studies*, 9(2), 87–98.

Brown, S. 1988. Health for all Australians, *Health Issues*, 14, June, 33–4.

Chamberlain, M.C. and Beckingham, A.C. 1987. Primary health care in Canada: in praise of the nurse?, *International Nursing Review*, Nov-Dec 34(6), 158-60.

Commonwealth Department of Community Services and Health. 1989. *National Women's Health Policy: advancing women's health in Australia*, Australian Government Publishing Service, Canberra.

Commonwealth Department of Health, Housing and Community Services. 1993. *Towards Health For All and Health Promotion: the evaluation of the National Better Health Program*, Australian Government Publishing Service, Canberra.

Davis, A. and George, J. 1988. *States of health: an introduction to health and illness in Australia*, Harper and Row, Sydney.

Dowling, M., Rotem, A. and White, R. 1983. *Nursing in New South Wales and Primary Health Care: a survey of perceptions*, University of New South Wales Centre for Medical Education, Research and Development, Sydney.

Ebrahim, G.J. and Ranken, J.G. 1988. *Primary Health Care: reorienting organisational support*, Macmillan, London.

Eckholm, E. P. 1977. *The picture of health*, W. W. North and Co., New York.

Grant, C. and Lapsley, H. M. 1990. *The Australian health care system 1989*, Australian Studies in Health Service Administration No. 69, School of Health Services Management, University of New South Wales, Kensington.

Grant, C. and Lapsley, H. M. 1991. *The Australian health care system 1990*, Australian Studies in Health Service Administration No. 71, School of Health Services Management, University of New South Wales, Kensington.

Grant, C. and Lapsley, H. M. 1992. *The Australian health care system 1991*, Australian Studies in Health Service Administration No. 74, School of Health Services Management, University of New South Wales, Kensington.

Grant, C. and Lapsley, H. M. 1993. *The Australian health care system 1992*, Australian Studies in Health Service Administration No. 75, School of Health Services Management, University of New South Wales, Kensington.

Hancock, T. 1985. Beyond health care: from public health policy to healthy public policy, *Canadian Journal of Public Health*, supplement to vol. 76, May/June, 9–11.

Health Issues Centre. 1988. *Where the health dollar goes*, Health Issues Centre, Melbourne.

Health Targets and Implementation ('Health For All') Committee. 1988. *Health for all Australians*, Australian Government Publishing Service, Canberra.

Hill, S. 1989. 'Health For All': bureaucracy unravelled, *Health Issues*, 19, 14–15.

Illich, I. 1975. *Limits to medicine*, Penguin, Harmondsworth, UK.

Leeder, S.R. 1989. Public health as an alternative path to better health in Australia, *Australian Health Review*, 12(1), 5–14.

Legge, D. 1989. Towards a politics of health, in Gardner, H. (ed.), *The politics of health*, Churchill Livingstone, Melbourne.

Lennie, I. 1988. Do health departments promote health? If not, what do they do?, *Community Health Studies*, 12(4), 400–7.

Mahler, H. 1987. A powerhouse for change, *Senior Nurse*, 6(3), 23.

McKeown, T. 1965. *Medicine in modern society*, George Allen and Unwin, London.

McLachlan, G. and McKeown, T. (eds.). 1971. *Medical history and medical care*, Oxford University Press, London.

McPherson, P. 1992. Health for all Australians, in Gardner, H. (ed), *Health policy: development, implementation, and evaluation in Australia*, Churchill Livingstone, Melbourne.

National Aboriginal Health Strategy Working Party. 1989. *A National Aboriginal Health Strategy*, Department of Aboriginal Affairs, Canberra.

National Health Strategy. 1992. *Enough to make you sick: how income and environment affect health*, Research Paper No. 1, September.

National Health Strategy. 1993. *Pathways to better health: National Health Strategy Issues Papaer No. 7*, Commonwealth Department of community Services and Health, Canberra.

National Centre for Epidemiology and Population Health. 1991. *The role of Primary Health Care in Health promotion in Australia: interim report*, National Centre for Epidemiology and Population Health, Australian National University, Canberra.

National Centre for Epidemiology and Population Health. 1992. *Improving Australia's health: the role of Primary Health Care: final report of the review of the role of Primary Health Care in Health Promotion in Australia*, National Centre for Epidemiology and Population Health, Australian National University, Canberra.

Navarro, V. 1984. A Critique of the ideological and political position of the Brandt Report and the Alma-Ata Declaration, *International Journal of Health Services*, 14(2), 159–72.

Nutbeam, D., Wise, M., Bauman, A., Harris, E., and Leeder, S. 1993. *Goals and targets for Australia's health in the year 2000 and beyond*, Department of Public Health, University of Sydney, Sydney.

Palmer, G., and Short, S. 1989. *Health Care and Public Policy*, Macmillan, Melbourne.

Queensland Health. 1992. *A Primary Health Care Policy*, Queensland Department of Health, Brisbane.

Queensland Health. 1992. *A Primary Health Care Implementation Plan*, Queensland Department of Health, Brisbane.

Rifkin, S. and Walt, G. 1986. Why health improves: defining the issues concerning 'comprehensive primary health care' and 'selective primary health care', *Social Science and Medicine*, 23(6), 559–66.

Research Unit in Health and Behavioural Change. 1989. *Changing the public health*, John Wiley and Sons, Chichester, UK.

Roemer, M.I. 1986. Priority for primary health care: its development and problems, *Health Policy and Planning*, 1(1), 58–66.

Russell, C. and Schofield, T. 1986. *Where it hurts: an introduction to sociology for health workers*, Allen and Unwin, Sydney.

Saggers, S. and Gray, D. 1991. *Aboriginal health and society: the traditional and contemporary Aboriginal struggle for better health*, Allen and Unwin, Sydney.

Sax, S. 1990. *Health care choices and the public purse*, Allen and Unwin, Sydney.

South Australian Health Commission. 1988. *A Social Health Strategy for South Australia*, South Australian Health Commission, Adelaide.

South Australian Health Commission. 1988. *Primary health care in South Australia: a discussion paper*, South Australian Health Commission, Adelaide.

South Australian Health Commission. 1993. *Strategic directions of primary health care*, South Australian Health Commission, Adelaide.

Tassie, J. 1992. *Protecting the environment and health: working together for clean air on the Le Fevre Peninsula*, Le Fevre Peninsula Health Management Plan Steering Committee, Port Adelaide.

Taylor, C. and Jolly, R. 1988. The straw men of primary health care, *Social Science and Medicine*, 26(9), 971–7.

Thomson, N. 1991. A review of Aboriginal health status, in Reid, J. and Trompf, P. (eds), *The health of Aboriginal Australia*, Harcourt Brace Jovanovich, Sydney.

Tones, K., Tilford, S. and Robinson, Y. 1990. *Health education: effectiveness and efficiency*, Chapman and Hall, London.

Williams, D. M. 1989. Political theory and individualistic health promotion, *Advances in Nursing Science*, 12(1), 14–25.

World Health Organization. 1978. Declaration of Alma-Ata, reproduced in *World Health*, August/September 1988, 16–17.

World Health Organization. 1982. *Primary Health Care from theory to action*, World Health Organization, Copenhagen.

World Health Organization. 1986. *The Ottawa Charter for Health Promotion*, World Health Organization, Geneva.

World Health Organization. 1987. *Hospitals and health for all: Report of a WHO Expert Committee on the Role of Hospitals at the First Referral Level*, Technical Report Series 744, World Health Organization, Geneva.

World Health Organization/Commonwealth Department Of Community Services And Health — Australia. 1988. Healthy public policy — strategies for action, in Australian Nursing Federation 1990. *Primary Health Care in Australia: strategies for nursing action*, Australian Nursing Federation, Melbourne.

CHAPTER 2

Values and health promotion

No matter how we act, whether in health promotion or any other field, our actions are never value-free. Our values determine to a large extent how we will decide what health promotion action is appropriate, and other people's values will reflect how they respond to our actions. Moreover, much health promotion work has ethical implications, and health workers must consider these before planning any action. An examination of values and how they affect our approach to the promotion of health forms the basis of this chapter.

Defining health

Health within a political context

No examination of health promotion is possible without first considering what health is. In our predominantly Western culture, we tend to think automatically of health only as an individual responsibility and an individual phenomenon. However, the health of individuals is strongly influenced by the social, cultural, political and economic conditions of the society in which they live, and it can never be considered outside that context.

Indeed, in many respects the whole notion of health is politically constructed. In Western capitalist society, with its emphasis on consumption and profit making, attempts are made to define health as a consumable product. Emphasis is then placed on individual choices about which products to buy, rather than on people's unequal access to health.

Furthermore, because of the relationships between politics and industry, particularly in capitalist countries such as Australia, decisions about health are often the result of political agendas and are determined more by these than by need. In turn, decisions about health issues can have a substantial impact on political agendas both locally and internationally, as the discussion of the potential of Primary Health Care in chapter 1 demonstrates. The key reason why health and politics are so related is that access to health is inextricably linked to access to power (Benn 1981: 266–7), and access to power forms the basis of politics. While ever health is defined only in individual terms, these issues of power and control, and the unequal access to life chances due to socioeconomic status, ethnicity and gender, are ignored. One stark Australian example of these links is provided by the interconnection between the health of Aboriginal people and the struggle for Aboriginal self-determination (reflected in part by the land rights movement).

In defining health, then, it is not sufficient to consider only the health of the individual. People live and work in groups, communities and societies, which have lives of their own and impact on each other quite profoundly. Any examination of health must consider the health of individuals, families, communities, societies and even the world. Remember, as you examine health on each of these levels, that the interrelationships between them are very strong, and that none of them can be considered in isolation from the others.

Individual health

Health can mean many different things to many different people. Probably the main distinction between definitions of individual health is between those who define health as the absence of disease and those who define it more broadly as a sense of wellness. WHO's definition of health as 'a complete state of physical, mental and social wellbeing, and not merely the absence of disease or infirmity' — while being criticised as unrealistic and unmeasurable (Sax 1990: 1) — is important in that it recognises the broad scope of health. Consider the following examples. Whom would you regard as healthy?

- a person who is free from disease but experiencing long-term grief;
- a person who has a serious chronic illness but is happy and lives an active life;
- a person who is free from disease but engages in risky behaviours;
- a person who is free from disease but culturally isolated and depressed;
- a person who is living in poverty.

As the above examples show, defining health is not an easy task. Indeed, it has kept some people busy for years! How health is defined is very important, however, because it determines what will be regarded as health problems and therefore what will be regarded as the work of health promotion. We touched on this issue briefly in chapter 1. If we define health as merely the absence of disease, we see health promotion as disease prevention, and ignore many issues which may make people's lives uncomfortable but which are not medically classified as diseases or risk factors for disease. There are some major problems with this approach.

Ignoring those problems which do not necessarily create disease — chronic back pain and domestic violence, for example — may leave people suffering from conditions which limit their abilities or reduce their quality of life. Indeed, medical knowledge of what causes disease is still in its infancy in many respects. It is quite possible that, if we address only medically defined problems, we could be ignoring today issues which do not seem to be related to diseases only to discover in a few years that they do, in fact, play an important role in disease causation. For example, cigarette smoking was a socially acceptable habit until recently, and it is not all that long ago that sunbaking was regarded as a normal healthy activity. Furthermore, many environmental health issues are ignored on the grounds that there is no 'evidence' of a problem, when epidemiological evidence may take 20 years to surface and people may have already suffered greatly during this time.

Defining health only on a physical level ignores a great many factors in people's lives which may impact on their sense of wellness and how they make sense of their lives. In turn, their psychic, or mental, health may impact on their physical health. Knowledge about the inextricable relationship between physical and mental health is growing all the time, but we still have a great deal to learn in this area (see, for example, Kennedy et al. 1988; Gelman 1988).

It is important to note that many people may not consider a definition of their own health outside the context of how they define their lives, and what things are important to them. It is, after all, within this context that most individuals consider their own health and its relative value. Carlyon (1984) recognises this when he points out that health promotion is as much the realm of social philosophers as health workers because of the centrality of how people make meaning of their lives in their feelings of health or ill health. For these reasons, quality of life is inextricably linked to health.

Quality of life

One very important element of how people value their lives which has gained much recognition in recent years is quality of life. The philosophical elements of health discussed above demonstrate its importance. Johnstone (1989: 277–9) describes the range of attempts to define quality of life, which she points out is an extremely complex, perhaps indefinable, concept. She concludes that quality of life judgments can properly be made only by the individual, because quality of life may be defined quite differently by different people and because only the individual is in a position to judge his or her own quality of life. This is significant because it alerts us to the importance of enabling people to make the decisions about their own quality of life, rather than imposing judgments on them.

At the very least, health workers need to acknowledge the philosophical element in any consideration of health and health-promoting activities. This is particularly so when they have had a tendency to focus on the biological elements of life. Physical health is not necessarily a positive end in itself. Indeed, the Ottawa Charter for Health Promotion states that health is 'a resource for everyday life, not the objective of living' (WHO 1986). The extent to which people value their health depends on how they feel about their life as a whole. This has been described as asking the question 'health for what?' (Marsick 1988: 112).

Family health

There are two key themes worth noting when considering the concept of family health. The first of these is that it is through the family that individuals may be exposed to, or protected from, aspects of the social, economic and physical environment. Families may be the source of domestic violence, for example. Also, it is within the context of the family that many occupational hazards are transmitted between individuals (for example, family members exposed to asbestos particles brought home on a worker's clothes) (Jackson 1985: 4), and individuals absorb the human cost of occupational injury. Further, it is within the family that the burden of most human caring is borne. There is now growing recognition of the health impact of caring for a dependent person on the carer, who is usually a woman. This also provides one example of the impact of sex role stereotyping on health, and much of this is transmitted through the family.

The second theme is that most people live much of their lives as members of a family, and it is within the context of family life and dynamics that they learn much about how people respond to life experiences and relate to each other. Families can influence the life of an individual quite profoundly.

The notion of family is a value-laden concept, and definitions of it vary across cultures; consequently, there are different definitions of what a healthy family might be. The popular notion of family presented in the Australian press — two parents with two children — represents just one form of family currently existing in Australia, and should not be assumed to represent the optimally healthy family. Moreover, many people live not in family groups, as they are popularly imagined to do, but in other household groups. For example, groups of friends share a house and partners who do not regard themselves as a 'family' share living space. These groups effectively function as families, even though they are not structured as we expect families to be. The dynamics of these groups can impact on the health of the people living in them in the same way as in a traditional family.

The fundamental element which defines family life is interdependency (Sokalski 1992, cited by Edgar 1992: 3), and it is this element which demonstrates the similarity between family dynamics and group dynamics. To a certain extent, then, family health can be considered to be reflected in the degree to which the family operates as an effective group (Douglas 1983). (The principles which help make a group effective will be discussed in greater detail in chapter 8.)

Henryk Sokalski, coordinator of the International Year of the Family (1994), has suggested eight aspects of family life which we should aim for in encouraging a more egalitarian family life than many people experience now. These key elements are 'shared responsibility; mutual respect; trust and support; nonthreatening behaviour; honesty and accountability; negotiation and fairness; economic partnership; and responsible parenting' (Sokalski 1992, cited by Edgar 1992: 3).

Community health

Health at the level of the community is also vital to any consideration of health. However, in order to examine the notion of community health, we need first to clarify what is meant by the term 'community', and this is by no means a simple task. Firstly, the term is value-laden, and its use often gives the impression that the thing to which it refers is necessarily good (as in, for example, 'community care') (Bryson and Mowbray 1981). Secondly, the term has been defined in a variety of ways, and is used to refer to a variety of things, some specific and others more general (Goeppinger and Baglioni 1985: 518). Indeed, some suggest that it is used in so many different ways as to be useless (Dalton and Dalton 1975: 1). At the very least it is a slippery concept, and a number of points are worthy of discussion.

Dalton and Dalton (1975: 2) suggest that the term community can appropriately be used only to refer to 'a relatively homogeneous group within a defined area, experiencing little mobility, interacting and participating in a wide range of local affairs, and sharing an awareness of common life and personal bonds'. While this definition is rather prescriptive, it does reflect some of the commonly held perceptions about communities and raises a number of important questions. For example, is it realistic to expect a large group of people to be homogeneous? What are the costs to the community if homogeneity means lack of diversity? How does this definition account for the conflict which occurs in communities due to competing interests and unequal access to power?

There has also been much recognition that linking the concept of community to geographical location may be somewhat limited. In order to overcome this limitation, the term 'community of interest' has been coined. A community of interest has been defined as a group of people who share beliefs, values or interests regarding a particular issue (Clark 1973: 411). Communities of interest include such people as residents of a housing estate, groups of single parents or unemployed people, members of particular ethnic groups, and global communities, such as religious groups which span nations or social movements such as the women's movement or the environmental movement.

In addition to freeing communities from geographical boundaries, by organising a community of interest around 'a particular issue', this definition allows more scope for heterogeneity amongst people and recognises that those who share an interest in one issue may have no other common interests or beliefs, and may even be sharply divided on other issues. Communities are very rarely, if ever, characterised by harmony and shared values on all issues, and are more likely to reflect elements of conflict and competing interests.

One useful differentiation is between a community as 'an *inter-relating* and *acting* group of people with shared needs and interests' and a population as 'a statistical aggregate of separate individuals with similar or the same characteristics' (Wadsworth 1988: 16, author's emphasis). For our purposes here, the issue of overriding importance is the need to consider the health of relatively large groups of people within a social environment.

Consideration of what makes a healthy community and how this can be measured raises more questions than it answers. Moreover, Hayes and Willms (1990: 165) point out that definitions of a healthy community may vary between communities, depending on the values espoused by each community, and it is most appropriate for each community's definition of its health to be considered separately.

One important element of a healthy community is community competence. There have been a number of recent attempts to define what makes a competent community, but the notion is not yet a clear one. One suggested definition is that a competent community is 'one in which the various component parts of the community: (1) are able to collaborate effectively in identifying the problems and needs of the community; (2) can achieve a working consensus on goals and priorities; (3) can agree on ways and means to implement the agreed upon goals; and

(4) can collaborate effectively in the required actions' (Cottrell 1976, cited by Goeppinger and Baglioni 1985: 508).

Community competence is likely to be just one element of what makes a healthy community. Other elements may vary depending on the community in question, including its cultural and political values. While the question of community health may continue to be raised for some time yet, one important issue is worth reiterating: that health, at the level of the community as well as at that of the individual, relates to much more than the absence of disease, and any attempts to measure community health which focus solely or primarily on epidemiology and illness indices will not reflect the notion of community health as it is currently conceptualised.

World health

The Declaration of Alma-Ata alludes to the importance of world health in referring to the need for world peace and cooperation between countries if we are to achieve health for all. It makes it quite clear that people cannot experience health if they are living in a war-torn country and are subjected to the deprivation, suffering and fear that goes with this.

The concept of world health is also extremely important because without it some communities or societies may achieve health at the expense of others, through the exploitation of resources or lack of consideration for the global environment. For example, the Western world's use of a large proportion of the world's oil and other non-renewable energy sources is creating a situation in which there will soon be little left for anyone to use, while the uncontrolled use of these energy sources is creating a worldwide pollution problem impacting on everybody's health.

Furthermore, as Western countries introduce laws to protect their environments and residents from the dangers of illness-producing substances, many of the industries and products concerned are being transferred to the Third World. For example, tobacco products are now being aggressively marketed in the Third World, as public opinion and public policy make them less acceptable in industrialised countries (see Chapman and Wong 1990). Dangerous industries, too, are increasingly being transferred to developing countries.

The question 'health for what?' also needs to be raised at the level of world health. Rifkin and Walt cite a measles immunisation program which, although it reduced the number of deaths from measles, did not actually reduce the number of deaths overall. Those children who might have died from measles died from some other cause because the root cause of the problem — poverty — was not addressed (Kasongo Project Team 1981, cited by Rifkin and Walt 1985: 563). Those who implemented this program do not seem to have considered to what end they were working for health; they seem to have assumed that the reduction in the number of people with measles is an inherently good thing. Certainly, on face value, many people would agree that it is. However, if one recognises that those saved from measles may die from something else if that is all that is done, this highlights the importance of seeing the whole picture and considering 'health for what?'. Turshen (1989: 24) argues that the eradication of smallpox had the same impact in the Third World: people are simply dying of other illnesses, and mortality and morbidity rates remain approximately the same. One great advantage

A developing country pays the price of improved standards of living in the West

In December 1984, an accident at the Union Carbide factory at Bhopal in India left at least 2850 people dead and some 200 000 injured, many of them permanently disabled. The deaths and injuries occurred as a result of a toxic cloud of methyl isocyanate, caused by a water leak in the factory, which spread over a populated area around Bhopal (Turshen 1989: 260–1). Many large companies from industrialised countries site dangerous industries in Third World countries because of the cheaper labour costs and lower worker and environmental safety requirements. The result is that these poor countries and their people are the ones who bear the brunt of the risks and human costs of injury in industries which often benefit industrialised nations more than developing ones.

of comprehensive Primary Health Care over selective Primary Health Care (see pp. 11–13) is that it takes account of the question 'health for what?'.

The other important element of consideration in world health is that the health of human individuals and groups cannot be considered in isolation from the physical environments in which they live. In order to attempt to capture the importance of the inter-relationship between people and their environments, Honari (1993) has defined health as 'a sustainable state of well-being, within sustainable ecosystems within a sustainable biosphere'.

What is health promotion?

Having briefly reviewed the issues of concern in any discussion of health, we are in a better position to consider what health promotion is. It is already clear that it relates not just to the health of individuals, but also to the health of groups and communities and the world, and that it relates to more than the absence of medically defined problems. One popular definition which fits comfortably with the preceding discussion is that health promotion is:

> health education **and** related organisational, political and economic interventions that are designed to facilitate behavioural and environmental changes to improve health. (Green 1979, cited by Fisher et al. 1986: 96)

This definition recognises the importance of health education in promoting health, but also acknowledges that health promotion is so much more than health education — it also requires structural changes on a number of levels in order to produce environments which are supportive of health. This is clearly a huge task and a political process.

The Ottawa Charter for Health Promotion recognises this approach to health promotion, as the discussion in the previous chapter demonstrates. It notes the central importance of increasing people's control over their health and issues which impact on it, and also notes the structural changes and community building required for that to be achieved.

In considering health promotion action, Labonté (1989b: 236) urges us to ask the question 'exactly what is a health problem, and who gets to define it?'. He argues that issues defined by communities as health problems should be regarded as such, and should therefore be the work of health promotion.

A question often raised is whether there is any difference between health promotion and disease prevention. Certainly many people seem to assume that they are the same thing. People may talk about health promotion, but all their activities may be in the area of disease prevention. Some people even talk solely of 'prevention', while others talk of 'health prevention', when in fact they mean disease prevention (I hope!). This distinction between health promotion and disease prevention is worth examining.

Disease prevention has been described as occurring on three levels: primary disease prevention refers to activities designed to eradicate health risks; secondary disease prevention refers to activities which lead to early diagnosis of disease; and tertiary disease prevention refers to rehabilitation work which helps people to recover from illness. While primary, secondary and tertiary disease prevention make an important contribution to health care overall, they do not encapsulate health promotion as it has been developed through the Ottawa Charter for Health Promotion. Rather, disease prevention tends to focus on activities which prevent particular diseases, and is therefore very specific to illness and disease. More often than not, disease prevention focuses on alleviating symptoms, reducing risk factors and changing individual behaviours.

Health promotion incorporates disease prevention but extends beyond it to address broader issues of health. Brown (1985: 332) suggests the development of a health promotion framework to complement that of disease prevention. This is extremely important because it helps to make visible those broad aspects of health promotion ignored by disease prevention. In this schema, primary health promotion refers to those activities which eradicate health risks; secondary health promotion refers to activities which improve people's quality of life; and tertiary health promotion refers to activities which result in social changes which are conducive to health. The relationship between disease prevention and health promotion is demonstrated in figure 2.1.

There is a real danger, however, that discussions of health promotion and disease prevention may excessively simplify any differences between the two. Perhaps more important than whether an activity is aimed at preventing disease or addressing health is whether the approach which is taken is reductionist or holistic. Both specific disease prevention or more general health promotion can be carried out in a way which is either simplistic and focuses on superficial change or holistic and addresses the problem on a number of levels. For example, recent work in the area of smoking prevention has highlighted the political dimension of Australian and Third World tobacco sales and attempted to address these issues. On another level, attempts have been made to break the social acceptability of smoking by severing the ties between smoking and culture, sport and success (see 'The Victorian Health Promotion Foundation' p. 147 and 'Tobacco sponsorship replacement at the local level — a success story' pp. 154–6).

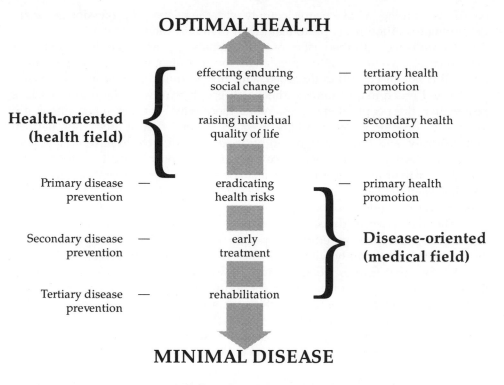

OPTIMAL HEALTH

Health-oriented
(health field)

	effecting enduring social change	— tertiary health promotion
	raising individual quality of life	— secondary health promotion
Primary disease prevention —	eradicating health risks	— primary health promotion
Secondary disease prevention —	early treatment	**Disease-oriented (medical field)**
Tertiary disease prevention —	rehabilitation	

MINIMAL DISEASE

FIGURE 2.1 A continuum of health promotion and disease prevention (developed from Brown 1985: 332–3)

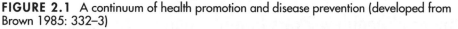

Such activity challenges the profit base of tobacco companies and their role in Australian society.

Similarly, some work has been done to raise awareness of the control of the international agriculture and food industries by a small number of multinational companies, and to address issues of improving nutrition by working to free availability of healthy food and challenge advertising of manufactured, largely unhealthy, food, rather than focus solely on educating individuals about how to choose a healthy diet. These, then, represent broad approaches to what can be regarded as 'disease prevention' issues.

The aim of health education: compliance or liberation?

As the definition presented above demonstrates, health education is an integral part of health promotion. Indeed, as Green and Kreuter (1991: 14) point out, education should play a central role in health promotion, because not only is it a part of work for individual behaviour change or values clarification, but it also plays a vital role in any public policy or environmental changes, since as often as possible these should be made with the informed consent of the community, rather than imposed on it. Having recognised the central role of health education in health promotion, we need also to examine what the aim of any health education should be. Are we aiming to have people comply with the wishes of professionals, or are we aiming to empower people to make their own informed decisions?

Compliance with the wishes of professionals appears to be the reason for a great deal of early health education, and many people continue with this aim in mind. But health education designed with this in mind does little to empower people and much to disempower them: it keeps control with the health workers rather than the people themselves. While there may be times when this is unavoidable, on the whole workers need to ensure that it does not happen unnecessarily, and that, through education, people are able to have greater control over the things which influence their lives. If people are to keep or gain control over their lives, education needs to be an enabling or liberating force. This idea has been developed by Paolo Freire (1973), who first developed the concept of empowerment education.

The line between education as compliance and education as liberation is not always clear-cut. If we are educating people in order to liberate them, are we not expecting them to comply with our wishes and liberate themselves? And can we ever be sure that in presenting all sides of an issue our own biases are not reflected in how we present the argument and the emphasis we place on different points? Determining the extent to which we are working for compliance rather than empowerment is something that all health educators must do in order to evaluate the way in which they practise and further to develop their approach so that they are working *for* and *with* people rather than *on* them.

Attitudes of health workers towards community members

How we see control over health will determine how we work to promote health and whether we see ourselves working *with* people or working *on* them. The approach which health workers have towards the people they are employed to work for can have quite a marked impact on the way in which health promotion is achieved and how community members feel about the experience. Their approach will influence how much control they give up and enable community members to have. It can also stifle or encourage the development of those skills which will allow people to work more effectively for what they need in the future.

The authoritarian approach. People with the authoritarian approach believe that the experts and power holders know best, and are right in imposing their decisions on their 'target', whether this is an individual, a group or a community. They believe that, because of their expertise and status in the community, these people do not need to involve community members in the decision-making process.

The paternalistic approach. The paternalistic approach is very similar to the authoritarian approach, except that decision makers believe it is important to consult with the community to find out what it wants or believes. However, there is a strong sense of the decision makers being wiser than the community, and if people's wishes do not match professional opinion, it is assumed that they do not understand, and so efforts are made to explain the decision makers' views before they are imposed.

The partnership approach. In the partnership approach, it is assumed that members of the community have a great deal of expertise regarding their own lives and the issues of concern to them. Workers therefore involve community members actively in the decision-making and implementation process, so that instead of merely being consulted, community members become joint decision makers. Generally, people who use this approach believe that the process of involving people in the decision making is just as important as the actual decision made. They also believe that the decision made is likely to be more valuable because of the involvement of the people themselves in the process. Workers are regarded as having expertise in their particular field, rather than expertise in all aspects of their clients' lives.

Participation

The importance of community participation in all stages of planning, implementing and evaluating policies and services which impact on health is recognised in both the Declaration of Alma-Ata and the Ottawa Charter for Health Promotion. Since the publication of those documents and the development of the Health for All movement, community participation has been increasingly accepted into the rhetoric of health policy documents. Health workers are being urged to incorporate participation strategies into their practice. However, the notion of participation is not value-free, and should not be accepted uncritically and without evaluation because it can be used just as much to control people as to enable them to empower themselves. Some discussion of the different ways in which participation can be used is therefore necessary.

Rifkin (1985: 42) suggests three questions that we can ask about participation to determine the extent to which it is likely to strengthen or deny people's access to power in any one instance. They are: '1) Why participation? 2) Who participates? 3) How do they participate?'

Why participation?

There are a number of reasons why participation by members of the community may be supported, and not all of these may actually benefit those being encouraged to participate. Before we start working to increase people's participation, we need to clarify just why we want them to participate. What approach do we take to participation, and are we intending to empower people through their participation or have them support our own ideas for health improvement?

The first reason participation may be encouraged is that there is recognition that community members bring their own perspective and their own expertise to issues, and these may contribute a great deal to the quality of decisions made by health workers. However, not all reasons for the encouragement of participation are driven by a recognition of community members' expertise. People may be made to feel that they are playing an important role even when their ideas are not being given serious consideration, in the hope that the feeling of involvement will 'make them feel better'. People may be encouraged to participate because of the likely health benefits of the participation itself, rather than a belief in the value of what they may contribute. For example, members of a local support group may be permitted to have a representative on a committee looking at mental health services in the region, but this may be because it is considered to be 'good for' the members of the support group, and no real heed is taken of their opinions and ideas. This, then, is a fairly manipulative use of participation.

Participation may also be used to 'buy' people's acceptance of a preplanned change. There is evidence that people are less likely to resist a change if they have contributed to its development. Thus, in some instances, people may be encouraged to participate, not because their ideas are highly regarded and will be implemented, but because it is hoped that their involvement will prevent them from complaining about the final result.

Sherry Arnstein (1971) has suggested that there are at least eight types of participation, ranging from forms of manipulation and cooption to more 'true' participation. It is worthwhile examining her Ladder of Citizen Participation (figure 2.2) because it provides quite a useful framework of the forms of participation which can operate. Although other models of participation exist, Arnstein's provides the most useful one for the purposes of this discussion, and will be used throughout this book.

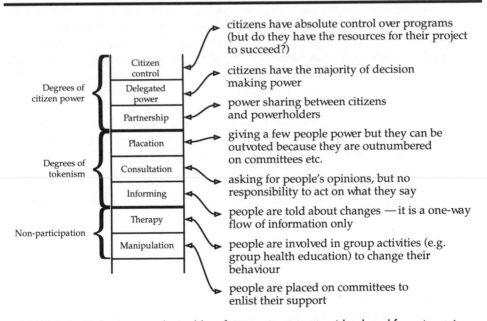

FIGURE 2.2 Eight rungs on the Ladder of Citizen Participation (developed from Arnstein 1971: 70)

Arnstein describes manipulation and therapy as non-participation because at this level there is no attempt to enable community members to participate; rather, they are attempts to 'educate' or 'cure' participating community members. Informing, consultation and placation are described as forms of tokenism because, while people may be heard, there is no guarantee that their ideas will be acted upon, because they have no power. It is only at the levels of partnership and above that people have decision-making power. There is delegated power when citizens have most of the decision-making power, while with citizen control citizens have total control (Arnstein 1971: 73). Using Arnstein's ladder as an analytical tool, it is possible to see that a great many instances of participation are actually non-participation or tokenism and few cases of participation actually result in shared power or power being handed over to community members. However, it is this power sharing which we are aiming for in a Primary Health Care approach. In many instances, power sharing will result only from the decentralisation of decision making.

Who participates?

Although there are strategies to enable people to participate in the current health system (see below), it is of some concern that they may in reality enable only the most articulate to participate. This may mean that many people for whom services are supposedly planned may have little real opportunity for participation. Examination of participation processes to see exactly who is involved provides an opportunity to consider what avenues for participation currently exist and whether they are enabling people to participate fully.

How do they participate?

In 1989, Dwyer (1989: 60–1) outlined five forms of participation in common use in Australia. They are client feedback and evaluation, volunteerism, consultation and public discussion, representative structures, and advocacy and public debate. With the recognition of a Primary Health Care approach, it was clear that more innovative models of participation were required, and many health workers have been working at the local level to provide opportunities for community members or consumers to participate more fully in issues which are of concern to them.

Client feedback and evaluation

The most basic form of participation is client feedback and evaluation, which occurs when clients are asked for their opinions on how effective a service or policy is. On the basis of their responses, changes may or may not be made. The extent to which the feedback received is useful will depend in part on what feedback is sought and how it is sought.

Volunteerism

Volunteerism means that community members are actively involved in the running of a service, but as volunteers. The extent to which this includes input into how things are done varies greatly between agencies. The value of volunteerism is a matter of contention. On the one hand it can be a form of cheap (free!) labour, while on the other hand it is an opportunity for volunteers to develop skills and contribute their own expertise. It is also often used as a mechanism to change the system so that it better meets the needs of its users. Self-help groups provide some examples of how this may be done. Volunteerism has been used successfully in a number of areas, for example the women's health movement. Health workers working with volunteers should be mindful of the potential for exploitation, and should reflect critically on their own relationships with volunteers.

Consultation and public discussion

It is argued that all members of Australian society have the right to respond to calls for public discussion on issues of relevance to them. Government departments advertise in the major Australian newspapers when they call for public comment on draft policy documents, and, so it is argued, everyone has the opportunity to respond and therefore participate in the policy-making process. However, not everyone has the confidence or the skills to respond in the format required, and the fact that calls for public response are often published only once, and only in the more prestigious newspapers in each state, means that this avenue for public participation is not as available to all community members as it might at first appear. Further development of this approach, so that it becomes more universally accessible, is needed.

Representative structures

Management committees responsible for the day-to-day running of centres such as refuges, Aboriginal health centres and women's health centres are said to enable their members to contribute quite closely to the way in which services are delivered. In reality, because of the way many of these organisations are funded, committee members may find that they become caught up in the responsibilities of administrative work and have little opportunity to seriously affect the direction the organisation is taking or make an impact on public policy relevant to their areas of concern. People on management committees may have responsibility without the corresponding authority to influence the direction the service or its guiding policies take, and may find little scope to implement any innovative ideas they have. That said, community-controlled services, such as community-controlled Aboriginal health services, are often very responsive to the needs of the community they are serving and provide an excellent model which could be better incorporated into the health system.

Involving people in the management of a particular service can be very valuable because the quality of the service which results may better meet the needs of its consumers if potential consumers are amongst those on the management committee. However, because of some of the shortcomings of the management committee approach, described above, people may be unwilling to commit themselves to a management committee, be unable to attend enough committee meetings to affect the direction that the organisation takes, or be 'burnt out' by the work required of management committee members before they have been able to implement their ideas for improvement of the service. For these reasons, establishing an advisory committee may be very worthwhile. Such a committee can act in the same way as a management committee, except that it does not have responsibility for administrative management of the service. It may focus on establishment and implementation of policy for the service, strategic planning and development of any new ideas, and response to public feedback. In this way, members are able to focus their energies on the elements of the service with which they want to be involved. This approach is likely to work

best if the advisory committee has the authority to decide on the matters it dis-
cusses, rather than simply advising another committee which may or may not
take its advice.

One way in which this idea has been implemented in recent years has been
through the establishment of community advisory bodies which take up this role
at district or regional level. District Health Councils in Victoria, Health and Social
Welfare Councils in South Australia and District Health Forums in Tasmania provide structures through which community members are able to influence the
direction of local health care and encourage an emphasis on equity and a broad approach to health (National Health Strategy 1993: 59–62). They provide a useful
model for community control of health care direction; though to be effective they
need to be representative of the community and, as mentioned above, they do need
some power to have their decisions acted upon if they are to make an impact.

Advocacy and public debate

Relatively powerful representatives of groups can lobby for changes on their behalf, usually involving them in the process. The Office for the Status of Women is
one example of this approach. Similarly, a number of smaller groups can join together to form an umbrella group under which they lobby together, pressuring
the system to change. The Consumers' Health Forum of Australia is one such
group. It is a national health consumer organisation which any consumer group
with an interest in health issues can join. Its aim is to increase the voice of consumers and community members in the health-policy-making process. The
Australian Council of Social Services (ACOSS) is another such group.

Process and outcome in participation

It is often argued that the *process* of participation is just as important as the *outcome*
of the activity, and sometimes even more so. Through the process of involvement,
it is argued, people gain skills in such things as negotiation, submission writing,
organisation, working with the media and working as part of a group. This process is meant to give people greater confidence and improve their sense of being
able to make an impact on their world, resulting in greater self-esteem. These
things, it is further argued, make participation important even if the participants
do not achieve what they set out to achieve. While these skills are certainly valuable, such an approach risks being patronising to people, who may regard
themselves as successful only if they achieve their objective.

Encouraging effective participation

Dwyer (1989: 62) suggests that there are three prerequisites for effective community participation. These are skills and resources, power sharing and appropriate
agendas.

Skills and resources

In many respects, Australians are not adequately prepared to participate effectively. Although Australia is regarded as a democratic society, we do not learn
that we should actively participate or how we should do it. Therefore, if people
are to be encouraged to participate, they need to be provided with an opportunity

to develop the skills and resources they will need. One program, which has been adapted for use in Victoria, South Australia and Tasmania, attempts to prepare people to participate more effectively in the health system. Known as Healthwise, it provides an opportunity for participants to reflect critically on their experiences with the health system and how they can work to improve these (Sinclair 1990; Carr et al. 1991).

Power sharing

Unless people feel that they are likely to have an impact, they may decide it is not worth the effort of trying to participate. Organisations which decide they want to encourage participation must therefore decide to prevent manipulative tactics which exclude community members from effective decision making and to instigate affirmative action techniques in meetings and decision making so that everyone has a fair say. Otherwise, only those people who are most comfortable with meeting procedure, and are therefore the most dominant within the group, may have their voices heard and their ideas acted upon. As Sherry Arnstein (1971: 72) has said, 'participation without redistribution of Power is an empty and frustrating process for the powerless'.

Being a community representative

In the South Australian Mallee community where I live, there has always been a need for volunteers, especially in the health and welfare fields. I have always had an interest in health and welfare and started off years ago on the local hospital auxiliary and board. I also gained valuable insights into the needs in, and workings of, the mental health field through confrontation with the system about the welfare of my own son. Opportunities and challenges have arisen over the last three years and I am now representing consumers at regional, state and national levels.

Consumers have a right to participate in decision making processes which may ultimately affect their health and well-being. They are the people who really count, but their voice is too often not heard, and their comments are quite often not taken seriously or accepted other than at the level of a token gesture.

I feel that consumer representatives have a really important role to play. They have the opportunity to put forward the 'grass roots' issues and concerns, but they must have a mandate to ensure that documents, vision statements, workshop reports and implementation plans reflect lay needs, and in terminology that can be understood by consumers.

Their voice acts as a balance to the views of government and professionals. To enable this to happen, information and sufficient time must be made available to allow consumers to participate in whatever arena they are placed. There must also be continuing opportunities for consumer input, and there must be support systems to enable community members to continue in these roles. Consumer representatives cannot be expected to give, and have to pay to give, hence they need to be given allowances, for travel and child care, for example, especially in rural areas.

What being a consumer representative has meant to me

Being a consumer representative means making a big commitment. In my case it has meant spending many hours on the road travelling to various towns and centres and therefore time and energy have to be accounted for as well. One needs to have an understanding and supportive family, otherwise problems could occur.

There have been times when I have felt very alone, particularly when the support mechanisms are not there. I have had to acknowledge that in the area of community representation one is often left to 'fight it alone', and I have had to work to make sure that it doesn't floor me.

I have also gained a lot from being a consumer representative, and I would like to share some of the gains, hopefully to assist and encourage other people to participate. The positives of being a consumer representative have included:

1. The building up of one's self-esteem (especially if one hasn't worked for quite a while) allows one to feel confident enough to step out into the public forum.

2. Various programs such as 'Health Wise' in South Australia provide the opportunity to learn the fundamental steps of public speaking and facilitating.

3. Acceptance of the consumer voice by Australia-wide professionals and service providers, through chances for input at policy, planning and implementation levels, is a definite plus.

4. The commencement of networking, between other consumers and service providers, is important in the learning process about the 'who and where' of seeking assistance and action.

5. Meeting some very genuine and warm people in my travels. Yes, I do enjoy what I do!

Margaret Brown
Chairperson,
Murray Mallee Health
and Social Welfare Council
PO Box 346
Murray Bridge SA 5253

Appropriate agendas

If people are going to participate, then obviously the agendas of the organisations concerned must be relevant to them. This has an added advantage: if organisations adjust their agendas so that they are more relevant to the community and people are therefore more willing to participate, it is likely that their activities will more effectively meet the needs of their community. Consequently, organisations are made increasingly accountable to the public, which goes hand in hand with the power sharing discussed above.

It is quite apparent that the five forms of participation described above need to be put into effect more often than they currently are, as do the three prerequisites for community participation. We also need to establish more effective participation and decision-making processes if we are to enable people to participate meaningfully in the decisions which affect their lives. Health workers are currently endeavouring to develop more innovative participation strategies, and you may be able to develop some yourselves.

Responsibility for health and the problem of victim blaming

The key impetus for the recent encouragement of community participation in Primary Health Care and health promotion has been the Declaration of Alma-Ata's call for action 'in the spirit of self-reliance'. Encouraging people to take responsibility for their own health, both individually and at the levels of the community and the country, is part of the Primary Health Care approach.

Encouraging people to take responsibility for their own health on an individual level has been gaining momentum as part of health promotion strategies since the 1970s. As the relationships between individual behaviours and illness were researched, and then affirmed, calls for change in individual behaviour became more and more popular as more and more diseases were labelled as lifestyle diseases.

This has been important work. Individual behaviours have a strong impact on health, and people need to recognise the key role they have in influencing their health. However, this needs to happen within recognition of the social context in which people live their lives and the barriers which may constrain the choices they are able to make. As the discussion in chapter 1 points out, a great many of the determinants of health are the result of the social, economic and political structures in which people live their lives. There are some real dangers, therefore, in focusing only on the role of individual behaviours in disease. People may be blamed for ill health, and for some of the determinants of ill health, when they do not have control over the factors which are affecting their health. This has become known as victim blaming.

Victim blaming occurs when the structural causes of ill health are ignored and attention to deal with the issue is focused on the individual or individuals affected by the problem, with the aim of changing their behaviour (Crawford 1977). Victim blaming is a subtle process. Ryan (1976: 8) has described it as 'cloaked in kindness and concern'. It occurs not only when people fail to see the structural causes of deprivation and ill health, but also when they see them but still seek to solve the problem by working to change the individual (Ryan 1976: 8–9).

One of the real strengths of the Ottawa Charter's five-pronged approach to health promotion action is that it minimises the chance of victim blaming occurring: if health promotion action occurs at the level of working for healthier public policy as well as at the level of further developing the skills of the individual, the structural barriers to ill health are likely to be addressed. It is vital, therefore, that the broad approach to health promotion action described in the Charter is not watered down to the point where structural action disappears and is replaced by more 'blame the victim' approaches.

The issues surrounding individual responsibility for health versus social responsibility for health are complex and interrelated. It is not a case of choosing one over the other, but of what balance there is between the two. Unfortunately, because they have come to represent opposing philosophical viewpoints, many discussions present them as opposite to each other, and this does not help individual workers clarify how they will address health issues and assist individuals in making changes in their lives. It is up to individual workers to clarify for themselves how to work with the tension between these two aspects of health promotion, to be aware of their biases, and to keep clear in their minds how both aspects of a problem need to be addressed in whatever balance is appropriate for the issue in question.

The influence of labelling

The concept of labelling is very much related to the notion of victim blaming. Our response to issues and problems which arise may well be influenced by our beliefs and expectations about particular groups of people, stages of life or illness experiences. The labelling of people, often because of their ethnicity, gender, age or socio-economic status, can have a powerful impact on the way in which they are treated. For example, an older person who suffers pain when walking may be told that it is just part of getting old and is to be tolerated, while a younger person may not be treated in the same way. Similarly, stories of the development of labels such as 'Mediterranean back' demonstrate that health workers do not always respond to a migrant working in a factory who develops back pain in the same way as they respond to non-migrants with a similar problem. Many such stories demonstrate the assumptions which some people make about the behaviour of others and the seriousness of their symptoms. For example, some researchers have found evidence that people's reported pain is regarded quite differently by health workers depending on the class, gender and ethnicity of the sufferer (Davitz and Davitz 1980).

Working with people from other cultures

It is not surprising that health workers may spend much of their time working with people from cultures different from their own, given the diversity of backgrounds from which Australians come. Indeed, work to improve the health of people from non-Anglo cultures is a high priority for many health workers, due to the poor health of many Aboriginal people and Australian immigrants and the fact that these groups tend to be of low socioeconomic status. Consideration of some of the general principles guiding work with people from different cultures is therefore in order given the important role that culture plays in determining values and meanings. You are encouraged to read further on this topic if you have not already examined it in some depth.

As we have discussed previously, the notion of working in partnership with people is central to the Primary Health Care approach. This partnership approach really comes to the fore when working with people from cultures different from your own, since the expertise which they bring in relation to the norms and values of their own culture is vital to the communication process and the promotion of health.

However, this awareness of the norms and values of the culture with which we identify does not come automatically to health workers or community members. Culture develops within a social, political and historical context and expresses a group's preferred ways of thinking about the world. These world views permeate all social structures, and are reflected in the policies and procedures that govern the system itself. 'Culture presents a way of perceiving, behaving and evaluating one's world. It provides the blueprint or guide for determining one's values, beliefs and practices' (Boyle and Andrew 1989: 11–12). It defines relationships and roles within society, by describing rights and obligations. In some instances, culture constrains individual behaviour, while in others it results in shared meanings and understandings, leaving room for the beliefs and interpretations of individuals. As a result, the culture of a society, community or group is integrated into the daily lives of individuals and groups, and is largely hidden from our awareness.

Because culturally driven beliefs and practices are so unconscious, we are often unable, unless we make a conscious effort, to recognise the culturally influenced values and behaviours we portray to others. Furthermore, because our own culture is so familiar to us, we tend to believe that the way we think, act and judge our world is shared by all others, and tend to judge unfavourably others who do not portray similar values. Our upbringing, our education and our own enculturation make it difficult for us to reflect on and challenge notions that are considered common sense or traditional in our culture. If we are going to work effectively with others, we need to ensure that we reflect on those beliefs and values which we take for granted, so that we can respond effectively in the face of differing values.

Language plays a key role in transmitting and reproducing the dominant culture, and can be a major barrier to effective communication. This can be the case even when you are communicating in English with people from another culture, since meanings and nuances can be culture-specific even when the same language is apparently being spoken. In addition, non-verbal communication is just as much culturally driven as verbal communication and so greater awareness of your own non-verbal communication and that of others is vital. Be mindful of the fact that other people's non-verbal communication may not mean what it appears to, and that your own non-verbal communication may be misinterpreted.

When people discover they will need to work with someone from another culture, their initial reaction is often to begin to find out about the other culture, and people usually attempt to do this by reading. Certainly, reading can be an important beginning, but it is by no means the only way to learn. Books and articles are a limited way of finding out about another culture. Firstly, they tend to portray a static picture of a culture, when in fact culture is dynamic and constantly changing. Secondly, because they provide little or no room to individualise cultural beliefs and interpretation, books present an image of a culture as uniformly shared by all its members. Just as members of your own culture vary widely in the acceptance of its values, so too do members of other cultures vary in their acceptance of the values of their particular culture. Thirdly, books often represent a very limited view of the cultures they discuss. For example, many anthropological accounts of cultures ignore women's roles, and present a one-sided picture of cultural life. Therefore, reading about other cultures may be useful, but your investigation of them will be strengthened by listening to the people themselves and coming to conclusions tentatively.

While the particular issues of relevance to communities may vary across communities and according to the issue at hand, common issues of which you may need to have an understanding are time orientation, personal space, the interrelationship between culture and religion, family practices (such as avoidance conventions), status rules according to gender and age, and philosophies of health and illness.

Perhaps the most useful skill for a health worker working with people from other cultural backgrounds is sensitivity, including, but certainly not limited to, intercultural sensitivity. Intercultural sensitivity is built on a recognition of the value base of our own and others' cultures. It is reflected by preparedness to listen and to learn from those with whom you are working. Being culturally sensitive includes not attributing all difference to 'culture' as such, but recognising that there is scope within culture for individual difference. Indeed, there is as much variety and conflict within communities from other cultures as there is within communities generally. Being culturally sensitive therefore includes recognising the need to canvass the opinions of as many people as possible, rather than assuming that the opinions of one small group of people reflects the opinions of the community overall. This sensitivity to the people with whom you are working provides a basis on which trust can develop and effective communication can occur.

Working with people from other cultures presents a challenge for a variety of reasons. The health problems which they face are often quite urgent, and the challenges of intercultural communication quite strong. The challenges to their own values can also often present a personal challenge for health workers. Nonetheless, the principles of effective intercultural work provide important guidance for health workers, both for working with individuals and groups from other cultures and for working with individuals and groups from subcultures different from their own.

Dealing with opposing values and conflicts of interest

In many respects, how people view health and health promotion reflects their broader views on the way the world works. As a result, many of the issues which underpin discussions of health promotion reflect the world views which people hold. It is therefore not surprising that some of the issues raised by health promotion create conflict between people with opposing views; after all, the difference is often not simply about an issue itself but also about the underlying philosophical framework. This is particularly so where health promotion action challenges profit making or power holding.

As we discussed in chapter 1, Primary Health Care and the new public health movement represent a move to shift the emphasis from illness management to health promotion. This move does not sit comfortably with everyone, and will necessitate some shifts in power. The multimillion dollar medico-industrial complex, in particular, is likely to lose a great deal if health promotion is successful. Moreover, many conventional health workers may have built careers around illness management and are reliant on research funds and high-technology institutions to achieve their ends.

Belief in the primacy of the illness management system is not limited to health workers. Because it has been part of the dominant ideology, all members of society have come to expect that high-technology individual sickness care will be relatively readily available. For many people, this includes a belief that science and medicine will come up with a medical solution to just about any problem. We have come to expect this and to see it as more important than the prevention of illness and the promotion of health. The mass media's use of individual emotive cases where the state does not deliver theoretically available high-technology care supports the expectation that it should always be available, no matter the cost. In few of these instances is the opportunity cost of high-technology care mentioned.

Conflict can also occur with industries whose work has a negative impact on health, and for which profit has a higher priority than health. Because health promotion in many instances directly challenges these industries, the conflicts created may be intense. It is therefore not surprising that conflict can be an inherent part of health promotion work. Health workers need to develop skills to deal positively with potential conflict situations so that conflict is not created unnecessarily, and to deal constructively with conflict should it arise. This requires effective communication and negotiation skills, and skills in assertive communication.

Vic Health struggles with political opposition

The promulgation of the *Tobacco Act 1987* and the establishment of the Victorian Health Promotion Foundation are excellent examples of what can be done at a social level to work for health promotion (see pp. 154–6). They also provide excellent examples of the sort of opposition and political pressure which can surface when practices which are profit-making, but which have a negative impact on health, are challenged. In this case, the advertising practices of tobacco companies in Victoria were curtailed by legislation prohibiting advertising of tobacco products. The implications of this for tobacco company profits are clear.

In 1990 the Victorian government announced that under the *Tobacco Act 1987*, tobacco advertisements could not be displayed at the Phillip Island motorbike races. This was a major challenge to the tobacco companies, and one which the Victorian government seemed determined to see through. However, as the tobacco company concerned was trying to have this decision overturned, the New South Wales government announced that it would allow the races to be held in New South Wales, tobacco advertising being no problem. As a result, Victoria now risked losing the races. Since it was in some financial difficulty and the races were an income-generating event, the Victorian government was backed into a corner. In October 1990, the premier of Victoria announced Parliament's decision that the races were exempt from the Tobacco Act.

In 1991, when the Victorians succeeded in winning the event back to Victoria, the New South Wales Minister for Sport, Recreation and Racing publicly denounced the Victorian government for backing off its 'moral high ground'. The minister in question seemed oblivious to the fact that it was the actions of the New South Wales government some 12 months earlier that had led to this situation. We can only speculate whether the Victorian government would have won its stand against the tobacco industry if the New South Wales government had not interceded.

Since then, other states have adopted the idea of the Victorian Health Promotion Foundation, with some variation in how each state's health promotion foundation is actually implemented. Considerable opposition continues to come from tobacco companies, through the Tobacco Institute of Australia, which sees 'the introduction of Health Promotion Foundations as destructive of the free market economy which we understood existed in Australia . . . We're very concerned about the future' (J. Welch, Spokesperson, Tobacco Institute of Australia, ABC TV, 30 October 1991).

The importance of collaboration

It is not suggested, however, that all communication in health promotion is always adversarial. Effective communication with many individuals and groups is an important part of working for health promotion, and the greater part of this is, or can be, positive and collegial rather than confrontational.

Health promotion requires communication and joint action with individuals, health workers from a variety of backgrounds, workers from a range of other areas (for example, local council workers, education workers, environmental workers, road and safety workers) and community groups. Much of this communication can involve building bridges between people. It is very important that barriers not be created unnecessarily between groups, and that people collaborate as much as possible.

Personal value conflicts in health promotion

Value conflicts in health promotion do not occur just at the level of conflicts between individuals or institutions. They can also occur, and indeed do occur quite regularly, within individual practitioners as they make choices and adopt priorities as part of their normal working lives. Different aspects of health promotion may compete for priority, and choices made to support one aspect of health promotion may result in a worker feeling uncomfortable about the implications of this choice for other aspects of health promotion. These value conflicts can occur regularly in health promotion work, and you need to be able to recognise them and reconcile them within yourself in order to continue working effectively in health promotion.

Similarly, as we change and our ideas develop through experience, it is quite possible that actions which seemed acceptable in the past no longer seem appropriate. However, the past cannot be changed, and health workers may have to come to terms with their previous decisions.

Working with change: the costs of healthy choices

Although making healthy choices does not always result in conflict, it can sometimes result in groups or individuals feeling ostracised or left out of a group which is important to them. This has been reported by people who have tried to give up smoking, and find that they do not fit in well with their smoking friends, and by people on diets who are not able to find anything to eat in restaurants they might previously have gone to. The same sort of thing can happen to groups of people when they make a healthy choice. These costs need to be acknowledged, and prepared for as much as possible. Unless action is taken to overcome any barriers created by the costs of these healthy choices, people may well not be able to keep to their decision, and may revert to their old behaviour.

For example, in 1992, the teachers at Quakers Hill Primary School made the decision, supported by parents, that school sport in the summer would be played only in the mornings, before 11 o'clock, in order to protect the children from the risks of skin cancer. The cost of this was that the children were unable to play in summer competitions with children from other schools, as these competitions are held in the afternoons, when the power of the sun is at its strongest (Mulcahey 1992, personal communication). If it had not been for the strong support which this policy received (and continues to receive) from parents, the cost of this healthy choice might well have been too great, and the decision might have been reversed. Of course, as other schools adopt a similar policy, support for schools which first made this decision is increasing.

Value conflicts: 'Life. Be in it with a cat'

As part of its ongoing 'Life. Be in it' program, the New South Wales Department of Sport, Recreation and Racing runs a television and radio campaign encouraging pet ownership. 'Life. Be in it with a cat' is one part of this program. Certainly the health effects of companionship from pets are now well recognised, and 'pets as therapy' programs continue to blossom and report success. However, 'Life. Be in it with a cat' highlights the value conflicts which can arise between health promotion programs which develop as a result of a focus on different aspects of health. For at the same time as cat ownership is being encouraged through the 'Life. Be in it' program, we are becoming increasingly aware of the damage that feral cats are doing to our natural environment. Many native animals are extinct, or severely threatened, as a result of the activities of feral cats. However, cats do not need to be dumped and left to fend for themselves in order to threaten Australian wildlife. The night-time hunting activities of domestic cats, no matter how well fed they are, is also severely threatening our wildlife. So, while cat ownership is being encouraged as a way of providing companionship and support for lonely people, an idea which is assumed to be health-promoting, it is also potentially very health-damaging because of its impact on the fauna in our environment.

A more critical perspective on the 'Life. Be in it with a cat' and 'Life. Be in it with a dog' campaigns raises the question of why the government is encouraging this stopgap measure to address the alienation of people within our society, rather than dealing more directly with the problem by working to encourage a greater sense of community and breaking down the oppressive structures which put barriers between people and lead to alienation.

The above example demonstrates that even within health promotion work, value conflicts arise and need to be dealt with by health workers almost on a daily basis, and that even seemingly innocuous programs can present value conflicts which need to be considered and addressed.

Weighing up the good of the community versus the rights of the individual

In the discussion so far, we have examined the importance of people being actively involved in deciding what they want and health workers acknowledging the expertise that people have in the things which impact on their lives. Unfortunately, there are times when this principle alone cannot guide health workers in their judgments. In many situations there are competing interests at stake, and health workers must choose between the wishes of different individuals, as well as between the wishes of individuals and their own professional judgment about what is 'best' for the community. At such times, health workers who are attempting to work by the principles of empowerment and community participation may experience intense personal conflicts.

One related question that needs to be asked here is, who decides what is for the good of the community, and on what basis? As the discussion has demonstrated, imposition of decisions from above is problematic, but it is not always practical or possible to involve the whole community in decision making and prepare them with all the necessary information so that they can make informed decisions. When is it acceptable for decisions to be made on behalf of the community? Do health workers have the right to manipulate the environment 'for the good of the community'? Should current manipulation of the environment (for example, by companies) be counteracted by health workers? When different parts of the community have conflicts of interest on particular issues, whose interests should take precedence? These are just some of the ethical questions raised by community-wide health promotion.

Facing the differences between health promotion and illness management

One of the biggest value shifts facing workers when they move from an illness management philosophy to a health promotion philosophy is in how they see themselves and their role. A common reason which health workers give for enjoying their work is that they are 'needed'. Unfortunately, there is a real trap in this, since if we are really to care for those who are sick or whose health we are hoping to promote, we would hope for them that they do not need us — that they can live their lives to the full without outside interference, or in an interdependent relationship with those around them. After all, this is what we would hope for ourselves. If we really are working for health promotion, then we are working to do ourselves out of a job! Working to do yourself out of a job is not an easy thing to come to grips with, but without awareness that that is what we are trying to achieve, it is easy to get caught in *not* doing that. We may be unconsciously encouraging people to be dependent on us rather than independent of us, and while this might make us feel better, it does little to really help those we are meant to be working for.

The shift from illness management to health promotion philosophy needs to occur on more than the individual level. The most important changes are those which need to occur at the level of the health system, and it is here that the notion of 'doing yourself out of a job' is most powerful. Currently, the Australian health care system is one of the biggest public sector employers in the country, employing approximately half a million people (Grant and Lapsley 1990, cited by Hill 1991: 7). The impact of this system on other related industries also accounts for a great many workers. Vast resources in bureaucracies, infrastructure and industry are tied up in the delivery of illness care. If the system is to change its emphasis and work to 'do itself out a job', much of it will need to be changed quite dramatically.

Promoting your own health

It is not possible to survive for very long as a health promoter if you do not ensure that you promote your own health at the same time. As obvious as this may sound, it is often very difficult to do. Firstly, it can be difficult to take time out when you are working on an issue that is of great importance to other people's lives. This can be particularly so for community work campaigns. Secondly, health as an issue is never neutral, and at times this can make health promotion work stressful. Nevertheless, it is a challenge we must take up. Indeed, Baum urges us to remember that conflict is an inherent part of health promotion work (1990a) and urges us to be 'troublemakers for health' if we want to really be successful in health promotion (1990b).

It is therefore up to all health workers or community members involved in health promotion to develop healthy strategies to look after themselves and to support other members of the team with whom they are working. Unless we look after ourselves and each other, our impact on health promotion will be short-lived and more limited than we had hoped for when we first decided to take up the challenge.

Conclusion

This chapter has examined a number of key philosophical issues in health promotion. These issues are complex, and there are no easy answers. As health promoters, you are urged to examine the questions raised in this chapter, and to be mindful of their implications for your daily practice.

REFERENCES AND FURTHER READINGS

Abramson, L. Y., Seligman, M. E. and Teasdale, J. 1978. Learned helplessness in humans: critique and reformulation, *Journal of Abnormal Psychology*, 87, 49–74.

Arnstein, S. 1971. Eight rungs on the Ladder of Citizen Participation, in Cahn, E. S. and Passett, B. A. (eds), *Citizen participation: effecting community change*, Praeger Publishers, New York.

Baum, F. 1990a. The new public health: force for change or reaction?, *Health Promotion International*, 5(2), 145–50.

Baum, F. 1990b. Troublemakers for health?, *In Touch*, 7(1), 5–6.

Becker, M. H. 1986. The tyranny of health promotion, *Public Health Review*, 14, 15–25.

Benn, C. 1981. *Attacking poverty through participation: a community approach*, PIT Publishing, Melbourne.

Bennett, M. 1986. A developmental approach to training for intercultural sensitivity, *International Journal of Intercultural Relations*, 10, 179–96.

Brown, V. 1985. Towards an epidemiology of health: a basis for planning community health programs, *Health Policy*, 4, 331–40.

Bryson, L. and Mowbray, M. 1981. Community: the spray-on solution, *Australian Journal of Social Issues*, 225–67.

Carlyon, W. H. 1984. Disease prevention/health promotion: bridging the gap to wellness, *Health Values: Achieving High Level Wellness*, 27–30.

Carr, M., Kuo, H., Fong, A., Jones, L. and Taylor, P. 1991. *Healthwise Tasmania: a handbook for facilitators*, Tasmanian Department of Health, Hobart.

Chapman, S. and Wong, W. L. 1990. *Tobacco control in the Third World: a resource atlas*. International Organization of Consumers' Unions, Penang, Malaysia.

Clark, D. B. 1973. The concept of community: a re-examination, *The Sociological Review*, 21(3), 397–415.

Crawford, R. 1977. You are dangerous to your health: the ideology and politics of victim blaming, *International Journal of Health Services*, 7(4), 663–80.

Dalton and Dalton. 1975. *Community and its relevance to Australian society: an examination of the sociological definition*, Australian Government Publishing Service, Canberra.

Davitz, L.J. and Davitz, J.R. 1980. *Nurses' responses to patients' suffering*, Springer, New York.

Douglas, T. 1983. *Groups: Understanding people gathered together*, Tavistock, London.

Downie, R. S., Fyfe, C. and Tannahill, A. 1991. *Health promotion models and values*, Oxford University Press, Oxford.

Dwyer, J. 1989. The politics of participation, *Community Health Studies*, 13(1), 59–65.

Eckermann, A. K., Dowd, T., Martin, M., Nixon, L., Gray, R. and Chong, E. 1992. *Binan Goonj: Bridging cultures in Aboriginal health*, Department of Aboriginal and Multicultural Studies, University of New England, Armidale.

Edgar, D. 1992. Changing families in changing societies, *Family Matters*, 31, April, 3–4.

Ewles, L. and Simnett, I. 1985. *Promoting health: a practical guide to health education*, John Wiley and Sons, Chichester, UK.

Ferguson, B. and Browne, E. (eds). 1991. *Health care and immigrants: a guide for the helping professions*, MacLennan and Petty, Sydney.

Fisher, K., Howat, P.A., Binns, C.W. and Liveris, M. 1986. Health education and health promotion: an Australian perspective, *Health Education Journal*, 45(2), 95–8.

Fisher, R. and Ury, W. 1983. *Getting to yes: negotiating agreement without giving in*, Hutchinson, London.

Freire, P. 1973. *Education for critical consciousness*, Sheed and Ward, London

Gelman, D. 1988. Body and soul, *Newsweek*, November, 92–8.

Goeppinger, J. and Baglioni, A. J. 1985. Community competence: a positive approach to needs assessment, *American Journal of Community Psychology*, 13(5), 507–23.

Green, L. W. and Kreuter, M. W. 1991. *Health promotion planning: an educational and environmental approach*, Mayfield Publishing Company, Mountain View, California.

Hayes, M. V. and Willms, S. M. 1990. Healthy community indicators: the perils of the search and the paucity of the find, *Health Promotion International*, 5(2), 161–6.

Hill, S. 1991. *Who controls where the health dollar goes?*, Health Issues Centre, Melbourne.

Honari, M. 1993. Advancing health ecology: where to from here?, paper presented at the 'Health and Ecology: a Nursing Perspective' conference, 25–26 March, Melbourne.

Jackson, T. 1985. On the limitations of health promotion, *Community Health Studies*, 9(1), 1–9.

Johnstone, M. J. 1989. *Bioethics: a nursing perspective*, Harcourt Brace Jovanovich, Sydney.

Kennedy, S., Kiecolt-Glaser, J. K. and Glaser, A. 1988. Immunological consequences of acute and chronic stressors: mediating role of interpersonal relationships, *British Journal of Medical Psychology*, 61, 77–85.

Labonté, R. 1989a. Commentary: community empowerment: reflections on the Australian situation, *Community Health Studies*, 13(3), 347–9.

Labonté, R. 1989b. Community health promotion strategies, in Martin, C. J. and McQueen, D. V. (eds), *Readings for a new public health*, Edinburgh University Press, Edinburgh.

Labonté, R. 1989. Community empowerment: the need for political analysis, *Canadian Journal of Public Health*, 80, 87–8.

Marsick, V. 1988. Proactive learning in primary health care: an adult education model, *International Journal of Lifelong Education*, 7(2), 101–14.

National Health Strategy. 1993. *Healthy participation: achieving greater public participation and accountability in the Australian health care system*, Background paper 12, March, National Health Strategy, Canberra.

Reid, J. and Trompf, P. (eds). 1990. *The health of immigrant Australia: a social perspective*, Harcourt Brace Jovanovich, Sydney.

Reid, J. and Trompf, P. (eds). 1991. *The health of Aboriginal Australia*, Harcourt Brace Jovanovich, Sydney.

Research Unit in Health and Behavioural Change. 1989. *Changing the public health*, John Wiley and Sons, Chichester, UK.

Rifkin, S. 1985. *Health planning and community participation: case studies in South-East Asia*, Croom Helm, London.

Rifkin, S. and Walt, G. 1985. Why health improves: defining the issues surrounding 'comprehensive primary health care' and 'selective primary health care', *Social Science and Medicine*, 23(6), 559–66.

Rodin, J. and Langer, E.J. 1977. Long-term effects of a control-relevant intervention with the institutionalized aged, *Journal of Personality and Social Psychology*, 33(12), 897–902.

Ryan, W. 1976. *Blaming the victim*, Vintage Books, New York.

Sax, S. 1990. *Health care choices and the public purse*, Allen and Unwin, Sydney.

Seligman, M. E. 1975. *Helplessness*, W. H. Freeman and Company, San Francisco.

Sinclair, A. 1990. *Health Wise South Australia: a handbook for facilitators*, South Australian Health Commission, Adelaide.

Turshen, M. 1989. *The politics of public health*, Rutgers University Press, New Brunswick, New Jersey.

Wadsworth, Y. 1988. *Participatory research and development in primary health care by community groups: report to the National Health and Medical Research Council*, Public Health Research and Development Comittee, Consumers' Health Forum, Deakin, ACT.

World Health Organization. 1986. *The Ottawa Charter for Health Promotion*, World Health Organization, Geneva.

CHAPTER 3

Assessing Needs

In the next two chapters, needs assessment and evaluation will be examined. These two areas have a great deal in common, being areas in which research skills form the basis of the work. Because of this, they have a certain mystique for many health workers, and people may feel that they do not have the skills to conduct needs assessments or evaluations. However, the idea that research is out of the reach of ordinary people is misleading. As you read through the next two chapters you will see that you already have a great many research skills, and that with the ideas presented here, you should be able to formalise them and develop additional ones. This will enable you to develop the research base of your practice in a way which both strengthens the relevance of the work you are doing and helps you to be accountable for it. Before we examine the issues specific to needs assessment and evaluation, it will be useful to have a brief overview of some of the issues involved in research.

A common assumption made about research is that it requires health workers to set aside specified periods for going out and 'doing' research, and that it is thus a separate or additional part of health workers' work. People often use this assumption as a reason for not doing research, since if it is correct, research requires other work to be put aside, and people may feel they do not have the luxury of doing that.

However, research is a process that needs to be an ongoing, integrated part of practice if it is to be meaningful to health workers and the community. Unless it is such a process, a number of problems can arise for health workers and the community alike. Firstly, health promotion work may not be built around the needs of the people for whom it is designed. It must, however, be responsive to those needs and be based on a recognition that they are dynamic rather than static, and therefore change over time. Secondly, without a grounding in community needs, health workers may implement programs which do not meet these needs and thus become an expensive mistake. Thirdly, those two things together can lead the community to lose confidence in health workers (Griffith 1992, personal communication). This loss of confidence can take some time to repair and may result in further damage as community members ignore future health promotion work.

The inextricable relationship between research and practice means that the additional resources required to carry out research may not be as great as people often think. When research is an integral part of practice, it is as much a state of mind and an approach to working as anything else. Certainly there are times, for example, when a major needs assessment may be required, and this may necessitate an additional commitment of time and resources. However, not researching and improving practice may result in wasting the resources that are being allocated to health promotion.

A Primary Health Care approach to research

A primary health care approach to health promotion emphasises the importance of health promotion work being socially relevant and conducted *with* people, rather than working on them. Research conducted as part of health promotion needs to meet this criterion also. If research is to reflect a Primary Health Care approach to health promotion, our emphasis must be on working with people as equal partners, involving them in the research process and acknowledging their expertise in it. This will ensure that the research conducted is relevant to their needs and therefore useful.

There are two research methodologies which offer a great deal to health promotion, because their approach corresponds to a Primary Health Care approach. These are action research and feminist research. It is worthwhile examining them briefly in order to understand how they can be utilised in health promotion.

Action research

Action research is a dynamic process which is built on a foundation of working with people, enabling them to be the key developers of problem solving and change. It is a continuing, cyclical approach to work which involves an ever-developing 'self-reflective spiral of cycles of planning, acting, observing and reflecting' (Carr and Kemmis 1986: 162).

Because action research is built on a recognition of the inextricable links between research and practice (Carr and Kemmis 1986), it has a great deal to offer health workers. It can be used in health promotion in two ways. It is ideal as an approach to working with community members, enabling them to reflect on their own experiences, plan how they can act to change their situation, act and then evaluate the impact of the changes in order then to re-plan, re-act and re-evaluate in a continuing cycle of change, development and learning. Action research can also be used to provide a framework for health workers to continually analyse and develop their own practice. That is, it provides a framework for good reflective practice.

Feminist research

While feminist research developed originally for work with women as an oppressed group, its potential for use with other groups, in particular other oppressed groups, is great. It has been defined as:

> research that relates to an understanding of women's position as that of an oppressed social group, and which adopts a critical perspective towards intellectual traditions

rendering women either invisible and/or subject to a priori categorizations of one form or another. (Oakley 1990: 169–70)

Feminist research is therefore conducted in a way which is not oppressive to those involved in it and care is taken to ensure that the research findings can be used by the research participants (Acker et al. 1983; Roberts 1981, cited by Oakley 1990: 169–70).

Feminist methodology is built on a recognition of the expertise of the people affected by a particular issue. Mies suggests a number of key issues to guide feminist research. These are:

1. We need to recognise that research is not value-free. Therefore, rather than attempting to remain totally distant from and uninvolved with research participants, we need to identify with them sufficiently to see the problem from their perspective as well as our own.

2. We need to work with research participants in an equal partnership, not setting up a situation where researchers are the 'experts' and the people being researched are mere subjects. This is reflected in the use of the term research 'participant', rather than 'subject'. Unless we work in an equal partnership, we contribute to the oppression of women and other groups.

3. Research is inseparable from the wider actions for improvement of women's position in society. Therefore, researchers are also engaged in *'active participation in actions, movements and struggles* for women's emancipation' (Mies 1983: 124, author's italics).

4. The interrelationship between action and research indicates that an inherent part of feminist methodology is *'change of the status quo'* (Mies 1983: 125, author's italics). In particular, feminist methodology is built around changes to women's position in society and the fight for emancipation.

5. 'The research process must become a process of "conscientization"', or critical consciousness raising, for both researchers and research participants (Mies 1983: 127). That is, through the research process, people must come to see the social, political and economic constraints on their lives and therefore recognise the context in which their lives are lived. This process also results in recognition of the experiences which individual women share with each other; consequently, the power of the group becomes recognised and can thus be used for collective action (Mies 1983: 127).

Towards a Primary Health Care approach to research

It is quite apparent that there are links between feminist research, action research and the process of conscientisation or critical consciousness raising. Together these form a powerful basis for dynamic, relevant research which promotes the health of the people for whom it is designed. This Primary Health Care approach to research can be described by the following elements:

1. Research is a dynamic, cyclical process, inextricably intertwined with action. Its aim is to improve the conditions under which people live.

2. The research process is guided by critical self-reflection on the part of the 'researcher' and the research participants. The values of researcher and research participants are acknowledged up front and are the subject of critical self-reflection as part of the research process. Conscientisation is a key feature of this process.

3. The relationship between researcher and research participants is a partnership, which itself acts to change the status quo by breaking down the traditionally 'top down' approach of researchers. Thus, all people involved in the research process are best described as research partners.

This Primary Health Care approach to research is based on principles which have been recognised in research only relatively recently. The Consumers' Health Forum, in particular, has urged the adoption of these principles, which it believes form the basis of true community research (Matrice and Brown 1990). Their importance in research into Aboriginal health has also been acknowledged (Houston and Legge 1992: 114–15). In addition, a growing number of international reports urge the acceptance and development of participatory research (see Oakley 1989: 70), which is another term for the process described above. However, such research may still not be recognised by all researchers and funding bodies as 'true' research, although this is slowly changing. One consequence of this is that you may need to clearly explain to funding bodies or management committees your reason for using these approaches. In addition, you need to be aware that you may experience some uncertainty as you work with a process that does not fit a traditional description of research.

Other research methods: what they offer Primary Health Care

Although what I have described here as a Primary Health Care approach to research is a vital part of any research in health promotion, it may not always be sufficient for every purpose for which research is conducted. In addition to informing practice, research may be required to meet the needs of the funding body for information or to demonstrate whether particular health promotion action has been successful. Similarly, community members themselves may want to investigate an issue in order to find out more than they already know, and so they may want to use other methodologies within a Primary Health Care approach. For example, they may decide they want to find out how other communities have responded to problems similar to the ones they are addressing, or they may want to find out the extent of dissatisfaction with health services in their community. For these reasons, it is worthwhile examining other approaches to research and what they have to offer health promotion. It is important to note, however, that while they may contribute to our understanding of health promotion issues, they do not necessarily incorporate Primary Health Care principles into their approach to problems. It is therefore up to each practitioner to ensure that he or she uses these approaches in a way which supports Primary Health Care and health promotion.

Traditionally, research methodology has been described as belonging to two groups — the quantitative approach and the qualitative approach.

Quantitative methods

Quantitative methods stemmed from the positivist approach, of which the basic philosophy was that researchers must examine the world as objectively as possible, as uninvolved observers. The positivist approach has developed from the sciences, and is synonymous with scientific method.

Quantitative methods utilise statistical calculations to determine issues of significance and relationship. For example, how many people are experiencing respiratory difficulty? Is there a relationship between the number of people experiencing respiratory diffculty and the number of factories in the area? Has there been a significant improvement in respiratory illness since the closure of a particular industry in the area?

A number of methods can be used to gather quantitative information. These include experiments (epitomised by the randomised clinical trial), epidemiological surveys and surveys of self-reported illness. The information collected is then collated, and numerical and statistical calculations may be carried out to establish whether significant differences between groups exist, or whether relationships exist between such factors as environmental stressors and health outcomes. These methods can also be used to infer characteristics of a population from what you might find out about a sample of it.

Qualitative methods

Qualitative methods, on the other hand, have stemmed from the interpretive approach, which is based on a recognition of the interpretation that people make of the things they see and experience, and the sense they make of them. As such, it acknowledges the power of people's subjective experience of their world, and their power in constructing that world. It is based on a recognition that research can never be value-free, and that researchers need to acknowledge the values which they bring to their work.

Qualitative methods enable us to find out something about the quality of people's experiences and their interpretation of them. For example, how do people respond to living near so many factories? Do they have any concerns for the health of their children, and if so, what are they?

Useful methods for collecting qualitative information include interviews, focus groups, participant observation and open-ended questionnaires. This information is then collated to construct a picture of people's experiences and their interpretations of them.

However, there is growing recognition that quantitative and qualitative methods are not exclusively linked to the approaches from which they developed, and that they can be effectively used to address questions asked from a variety of philosophical perspectives. The important issue is that the method used is appropriate to the question being asked.

Each of these approaches to research enables us to find out slightly different things, and to see the issues from a different angle. Thus, as in the case of the proverbial six blind men and the elephant, answers provided by each method present only part of the story, but together all the answers increase our chances of seeing the whole picture. Depending on the reason for our research and the resources available for it, it is possible to maximise the number of approaches used in order to strengthen the complexity and utility of the research conducted. That is, you can use a number of research methods to find out about different aspects of the issue you are addressing, and combine them to provide a more detailed examination of the issue. This is known as triangulation, and is becoming increasingly popular as people recognise that the value of quantitative research and qualitative research is not as restricted by the bases from which they have developed as was originally thought.

Research in practice

Two pictures of research emerge from the previous discussion — one in which it is an inextricable component of practice and the other in which it is conducted separately from practice, in order to address certain questions. These two pictures are by no means contradictory. Indeed, they reflect more a continuum, and it is often difficult to determine where one ends and the other begins. As we move towards the second part of the continuum, where research is more easily recognised as discrete from practice (though still essential because of the way in which it informs practice), two key reasons for conducting research emerge. These are to assess the needs of the community in order to convince a funding body or management committee of the relevance of the work being planned, or to evaluate the work of the agency in order to report back to the community, an external funding body or accreditation committee. In order to examine some of the details of relevance in needs assessment and evaluation, needs assessment will be discussed in the remainder of this chapter, and evaluation will be examined in the following chapter.

Need: what is it?

Any examination of needs assessment should start with an examination of just what need is, and a review of some of the issues surrounding the definition of something as a need. The 1987 edition of the *Longman dictionary of contemporary English* defines need as 'the condition in which something necessary, desirable or very useful is missing or wanted'. This definition highlights the fact that the very concept of need itself is value-based and socially constructed. That is, it is through the way in which issues are defined at a social and political level that individuals, groups and societies come to decide which issues are of concern to them and which things they need. Which issues are constructed for us as needs depends on the particular values which are in place in our society or group. In addition, needs assessment is based and judged on the values of people conducting the assessments and those judging them (for example, funding bodies). For these reasons, critical examination of how we define need is important.

There are a number of different categories into which needs can be classified. Bradshaw (1972) has classified need into four types — felt need, expressed need, normative need and comparative need. The categories of felt and expressed need include need determined by people themselves, while the categories of normative and comparative need represent need determined by consideration of external measures. With an emphasis on equal partnership between professionals and community members in a Primary Health Care approach to health promotion, all these types of need have something useful to contribute to an assessment of need.

Bradshaw's typology of needs

Felt need

Felt need is most easily described as what people say they need. For example, if a local community is surveyed regarding its highest priorities for health promotion action, people may say that they want more intensive-care beds, safer streets in which their children can play or less youth unemployment in the local area. Despite the fact that determining felt need involves asking people what their needs are, it may not give a complete picture of need for a number of reasons. Firstly, people may limit what they tell you they need to what they think they can have (Walker and Dixon 1984: 16–17). If they believe meeting some of their needs is beyond their reach, they may not ask for it. Secondly, people may tell you only those needs which they believe you are interested in. For example, if a health worker asks someone about their health needs, that person may interpret the question as referring to his or her illness problems, and may not think of health in its broad context. Thirdly, you need to consider very carefully what you can conclude about the people who informed you of a need. Whom do they represent — a section of the community, a small subsection or only themselves (Hawe et al. 1990: 19)? A vital component in determining felt need is clarifying who you need to find out from, and how you do it so as to ascertain the needs of that part of the community you are interested in.

Fourthly, powerful groups in the community can have a strong influence in determining how people see their needs. Community members' beliefs about what they need can, in fact, be socially constructed by the dominant groups in society. Groups and communities may 'adopt' certain needs as their own because these have been sold to them through the mass media. One example of this process can be seen in the recent establishment of the need for national mammography services. Because of a concerted media campaign, which actually 'sold' the importance of mammography screening rather than providing a balanced education about the issues, mammography screening units are increasingly seen as something which every community should have. This has happened despite the dangers and limitations of mammography screening, which have not been widely discussed; for example, the risks of mammography screening, the problems of false negatives and false positives, and whether it actually makes a difference to people's lives or merely increases the length of time in which they know they are dying (Browning 1992; Wass 1990). Through the impact of the medical profession and medical insurance companies, which have advertised mammography as 'the only safe way to detect breast cancer', the need for appropriate breast cancer screening has been redefined for many people as the need for mammography.

If we are to take the principles of Primary Health Care seriously, we need to work to promote health based on people's own assessment of their need — that is, felt need must be amongst the types of need present. However, because of the all pervading forces which influence people's felt need, most particularly through the media, people may not have had a real opportunity to decide for themselves. In health promotion as in any other area of health, workers need to ensure that people are able to make informed decisions and that they have access to the information they need to make those decisions. Of course, this process may require more than giving people information; it may require them to examine those forces which influence their decisions. That is, this process of helping people clarify their felt need may well involve the process of conscientisation.

Furthermore, the presence of felt and/or expressed need alone, without the presence also of normative and/or comparative need, raises some questions. What if a group or community wants something, but there is no evidence to demonstrate the need for it? In such a situation, more information may be needed. Does the group or community know that it is comparatively well off in the area concerned? This may change the priorities that the group sets. Conversely, is it the case that there is a lack of formal evidence in this area because of the shortcomings of information collection, rather than that there is no objective need? For example, until relatively recently few statistics on Aboriginal health were collected, and the collection of these statistics continues to be poor (Thomson 1991: 38–9). This means that there may still be inadequate formal evidence of the extent of Aboriginal health problems.

The problems of external funding and felt need

Currently, health promotion funding is available for specific projects, often aimed at particular diseases or risk factors. Frequently, it may be granted, and the project begun, without any prior systematic assessment of the community's felt needs. The particular project being funded may be a long way down the community's list of priorities, and people may not be motivated to participate in the project. It is then imposed on the community, at 'best' with the community being educated about why it should want it. This approach to funding presents some very real dangers, as it encourages health workers and bureaucrats to ignore communities' own assessment of their needs or regard it as a simple 'add on' rather than an integral part of the project. Moreover, it is quite ironic, given that much current health promotion funding has stemmed from Australia's involvement in the international Health for All movement, in which the felt needs of the local community are supposedly paramount. It therefore raises once again questions about the extent to which Australia is truly committed to the international Health for All movement.

Expressed need

Expressed need is need that is demonstrated by people's use of services or demand for new or more services. That is, expressed need can be described as 'felt need turned into action' (Bradshaw 1972: 641). Examples of expressed need include waiting lists for child care or nursing home places, numbers of people using public dental services or lack of use of existing sporting facilities. Needless to say, this demand, or lack of demand, has even more limitations on it than felt need, since people can only add their names to waiting lists for services which already exist or are about to come into existence. Indeed, waiting lists are limited to issues of service provision: it is not possible to put your name on a waiting list for a new public policy, for example (although the number of letters written to a politician on a particular issue may be regarded as another form of expressed need). The constraints on people's choices here are even greater than in felt need, since the specific thing they are demanding must already be there. Moreover, expressed need can easily be misinterpreted. For example, a waiting list at the local dentist might be interpreted as the need for more dental treatment services, when in fact it could reflect inadequate oral health promotion or lack of awareness of school dental therapy services, to give just two examples. Another problem with expressed need is that it is more likely to reflect the needs of the more articulate, because it is they who are most likely to write, demanding new or more services. Indeed, people's beliefs about whether they have a right to particular services, or deserve to have access to them, will influence whether they act to formally express a need.

Naturally, there are strong links between felt need and expressed need. It may seem that expressed need is merely felt need written down. While to a certain extent this is true, there are also particular differences between them, and so they each may tell us slightly different things. However, you may find that some authors use these terms interchangeably.

Community participation or manipulation? The impact of dominant interests on a community's expressed needs

Stephanie Short (1989) has outlined a case study which demonstrates the power of dominant groups in society in structuring community needs. It describes the efforts of the Wollongong community to raise $1.5 million for the purchase of a linear accelerator, a piece of high-tech equipment for use in cancer treatment. The community took up the cause with gusto, and readily accepted that this was the thing that Wollongong most needed, despite the fact that the money could have been spent on a great many other health-related services, such as palliative care, cancer prevention and health promotion. It seems that beliefs about the primacy of high-tech medical care and the desire for all possible medical treatments to be available were dominant, and a lone attempt to question this, and the community's lack of real choice on the issue, was soon quashed.

As Short (1989: 34) argues, '"community needs" are easily manipulated or distorted by interest groups and . . . the political context within which community needs are recognized, articulated and mobilized is the most important issue for community participation in the health policy-making process'.

Normative need

Normative need is need determined by 'experts' on the basis of research and professional opinion. Examples of normative need include safe levels of water pollution, recommended daily allowances of different food groups and unsafe levels of lead ingestion. Normatively determined need is often regarded as immutable because it has been determined by experts. That is, it often carries the assumption that it is value-free and beyond questioning or reproach, but this assumption needs to be called into question. Moreover, professional opinion often changes over time, leaving the public confused (Bradshaw 1972: 641). For instance, Becker (1986) cites the example of professionals' changing views of the dangers of cholesterol, and the consequent confusion among the public. As a result, the public is beginning to develop some healthy scepticism about professional opinion. Normative need may reflect some level of paternalism, and it certainly can provide conflicting information, depending on the values of the experts themselves (Bradshaw 1972: 641).

One crucial issue that influences normative need and that requires examination is the fact that many professional groups act, often unconsciously, as gatekeepers in society. Furthermore, they may be unwilling to acknowledge publicly that something is occurring at an unsafe level if their judgment in this case has political implications. This, then, represents another possible limitation of normatively determined need. Finally, an over-reliance on epidemiological data to provide evidence of normative need is increasingly being called into question as the limitations of epidemiology are recognised (see pp. 76–7).

Comparative need

Comparative need is need that is determined by comparing the services available in one geographical area with those available in other geographical areas. Therefore, either experts or community members may argue that a particular area requires a certain service because other areas with similar demographic characteristics have it. Examples of comparative need are calls for neonatal intensive-care cots or smoke-free workplace policy on the basis of the argument that other areas have them. Comparative need can be problematic because it is based on the assumption that the service provided in the place of comparison was the most appropriate response to the problem (Bradshaw 1972: 641).

'Teeth for Keeps'

The 'Teeth for Keeps' project was funded by the Commonwealth Department of Health, Housing and Community Services through the National Health Promotion Program in 1991 with $40 086. It aimed to promote oral health and prevent dental disease in school communities in the Moree Plains Shire of north-west New South Wales. The shire is a wealthy agricultural area in which 10 per cent of the rural population of approximately 20 000 is Aboriginal.

An oral health survey of about 1000 school children was conducted in 1990 by the New South Wales Department of Health. The resulting report, entitled 'Who caries?', showed a rate of decayed, missing and filled teeth that was 13 per cent higher than the rate reported as the average throughout Australia in 1986 (Carr 1988: 206). Moreover, children in Moree (where the water is unfluoridated) were likely to require dental treatment at a rate 250 per cent higher than children in Tamworth (where the water is fluoridated) (Patterson 1990: 2).

Fortunately, the 'Who caries?' report provided the quantitative data from which to argue a strong case to justify external funding, and this situation was strengthened by the fact that dental disease was a high-priority area and Aboriginal communities were a targeted population for the current round of grant applications. On the other hand, the existence of the relevant dental data and the close fit with the external funding priority areas meant that a community needs analysis was not a requirement for the granting body, and so it is difficult to tell where oral health fitted with the community's list of priorities.

However, the issue of water fluoridation was hotly debated by health professionals, environmentalists, civil libertarians and community members in the Moree Plains Shire between 1985 and 1990. In fact, it could have played a detrimental role in the adoption and success of the 'Teeth for Keeps' project, since many community members associated oral health issues only with the water fluoridation debate. Individuals in the communities were reluctant to discuss oral health promotion, because the long-drawn-out debate over water fluoridation was turning them off the topic completely: *they had had enough!* Therefore, a great deal of effort went into transforming an emotional and divisive issue into a constructive and practical health promotion strategy.

From my point of view, the problems of external funding include working out the aims, objectives, strategies and outcome measures of a particular project well before it begins. This does not allow those working on the project the flexibility to respond to other needs which become apparent once one starts working with different sections of the community. A researcher never really knows what is going to happen during a research project because several factors are completely out of that person's control. It is that aspect which causes anxiety and panic in some researchers, but which makes 'real' research for me so dynamic and exciting!

Community meetings in Moree, Mungindi, Pallamallawa and Boggabilla revealed that community members wanted better access to public dental treatment. On a statewide basis, the New England region has a higher than average number of persons eligible for public dental care (NSW Department of Health 1991). Furthermore, the number of dental therapists in the region is significantly lower than that recommended by the World Health Organization for non-fluoridated areas. Before the project began, only one fixed dental clinic with one dental therapist and one dental assistant was operational in Moree, and so there was clearly a need for more public dental treatment.

However, as the 'Teeth for Keeps' project was funded only for oral health promotion strategies for school children, we were not able to respond directly to the community demands of public dental treatment for adults and children. Fortunately, since one of the project managers was the Principal Dental Officer for the New England Health Region, the community's requests in this regard were addressed by the allocation from regional dental funds for a dental officer, a dental assistant, goods and services ($75 000), a 'Molar Patroller' mobile dental clinic ($90 000) and oral health promotion posters ($18 000). If one of the project managers had not been the Principal Dental Officer, it would not have been possible to address community demands for dental services.

As the project developed, its redeeming feature was that it did not push the 'chemical fix' of water fluoridation but concentrated on activities which were within the control of school communities.

These included classroom-based educational sessions, school 'brush-ins', school 'rinse-ins', healthy school canteens, salivary stimulation and posters promoting oral health.

Most important of all, the work begun by the 'Teeth for Keeps' project did not finish with the end of the research. At the end of the official project, the two coordinators employed for it obtained full-time employment, while the project itself was continued for seven months by the Department of Health and then expanded for a further three years by the Moree Plains Shire Council and the Department of Health at a shared cost of $60 000 per year. The 'Teeth for Keeps' project is now administered by the Moree Dental Health Liaison Committee and remains a part of health services in the Moree area.

Leonie M. Short
Senior Lecturer, University of New
England, and ex-dental therapist

Separating the problem from the solutions

In determining need from each of the above perspectives, it is possible that the need will be expressed in terms of a solution to the problem, rather than the problem itself. Indeed, often when this occurs, the assumption is that the solution presented is the only solution to the problem. This point has also been made elsewhere (Baum 1992: 81). It is really important to develop a vision of the problem as separate as possible from any potential solutions, and so broaden the scope for solving the problem by coming up with a range of possible solutions. This process is one in which community members and workers together can be involved. It provides an excellent opportunity for consciousness-raising to occur. As people discuss the problems in their community, they may, layer by layer, be able to work their way through to alternative conceptualisations of them. This may broaden quite markedly the choices available to them in dealing with those problems.

How can needs be identified?

We can never assume that we know what the needs are in a particular situation. While our hunches about problems can often be sound, we cannot assume that they represent the problems as seen by those directly affected. We can use our hunches as a guide (and they usually lead us to notice particular issues in the first place), but it is vital that we take the time to find out how those affected by a problem interpret the situation and what priorities for action they set for themselves. We also need to determine what the external evidence suggests about the seriousness of the issues facing the community.

Sources of evidence of need can be classified into five key groups (developed from Ewles and Simnett 1985: 61–2). As you read through these, consider how they relate to the categories in Bradshaw's typology of needs, and what sort of need is likely to be found from each source.

Listening to the community

Listening to the community is a vital part of needs assessment, and can be done through both formal and informal means. Firstly, as a health worker, you need to maximise the use of *informal* opportunities to listen to what people have to say. Twelvetrees (1987: 25–6) suggests two ways in which you can do this.

1. *Learn how to listen and take notice.* As obvious as this may sound, so often we do not take full advantage of opportunities to listen to what people have to say. Every interaction that a health worker has with a community member or group is an opportunity to learn something about what that person or group thinks. Leaving space for people to talk and being ready to hear what they have to say enables every interaction with a community member or group to become an informal opportunity to learn about their needs.

2. *Walk, don't ride.* Take the time to walk around your community as a way of meeting people and getting a sense of how the community feels, where the difficult places to live are, and so forth. This is just as relevant if you have responsibility for an organisation rather than a community. For example, for an occupational health nurse, walking around the shop floor provides an opportunity to meet people, to be seen by people (and remind them that you are available) and to notice any potential problem areas or opportunities for implementing some positive change. For a health worker with a responsibility for the health of a geographical community, going along to important community events such as the local show may be useful. Here you can get a sense of some of the issues which are important to people, and possibly meet some key people with whom you could work on health promotion projects. Increasing the number of times you are 'out there' in the community also increases your opportunities to listen to what people have to say. As a general principle, taking steps such as this is a valuable part of getting to know your community and the people in it.

Secondly, you can ask the community for their opinion in more *formal* ways, and use this information to build on your informal assessment. Surveying the community or interest group concerned will enable you to assess people's needs more systematically. It is important that any formal needs assessment be carried out in a way which is supportive of the community and involves people as much as possible in planning, implementing and analysing it. The specific details of how to conduct a needs assessment, although strictly speaking beyond the scope of this book, are discussed below (p. 80).

The importance of backing up requests for services with a needs assessment

I was involved in establishing a support group a few years ago, where I didn't do the ground work I normally do before establishing a support group. I responded to the needs of two people, and I didn't find out whether there was a community need for the group. We went through all the motions of establishing the group, and after five or six meetings it was clear it wasn't working. The attendance was still limited to the two original people that had approached me. It then occurred to me to retrace my steps, and have a look at what went wrong. I realised I had responded to two people's needs, not the community's needs, and I hadn't done my homework. I really learnt from that.

Sandy Brooks, Clinical Nurse Specialist
(Mental Health Promotion)
Taree Community Health Centre

Social and economic indicators

The category of social and economic indicators includes a range of statistical information which helps to construct a picture of your community. Much of it is classified as demographic information. Information such as proportion of people in each age group, income levels, number of people on each type of pension, number of single-parent families, number of single-income families and level of home ownership is useful in helping you to construct a picture of the issues likely to be affecting this community. This information is available from Australian Bureau of Statistics data, which are often held by each local council for its own area and should be available for public viewing. In addition, information on such things as amount of land available for recreation, shopping facilities and availability of public transport will also be useful to access. It should be available from your local council.

Epidemiological data

Epidemiology has been defined as 'the study of the distribution and determinants of disease in human populations' (Christie et al. 1987: 1). Epidemiological data provide information about the levels of death (mortality) and disease (morbidity) in the community, and their distribution according to such things as gender, age and place of residence. They come from a number of sources (Christie et al. 1987: 8):

- death rates;
- cancer mortality and morbidity rates from state cancer registers;
- health surveys and studies, for example those conducted by the Australian Institute of Health and Welfare;
- hospital discharge records;
- reports of notifiable infectious diseases.

Epidemiological data may be useful in telling you about the instances of ill health in your community. This information is available from the Australian Bureau of Statistics and the Australian Institute of Health and Welfare. Many libraries and local councils may keep some of this material if it is relevant to the surrounding area. In addition, local public health units or health promotion units may keep records relevant to their own areas.

By providing information at a population level, epidemiology provides a useful tool against which to confirm or question the hunches of health workers or community members regarding health problems in an area. This can be valuable because assumptions about problems in an area may not always be correct. For example, when staff at Gloucester Soldier Memorial Hospital reviewed injuries to children in the area as part of the Rural Child Accident Prevention Program, they were surprised to discover that horse-related accidents, rather than injuries due to farm machinery, were the major cause of child injury. Epidemiological data and surveys of the local area provided the information which was needed and which in this instance did not support the beliefs of health workers or community members generally (Lower 1992: 10).

Beyond epidemiology: the need for a broader approach to health assessment

Until relatively recently, epidemiology was regarded as the only measuring stick of use in health work. For many workers this remains the case. A number of points are worthy of discussion here. If we were solely interested in preventing disease, rather than being interested in health promotion and a social view of health, we might be happy with the information we can gather from morbidity and mortality data. However, from a social health perspective, morbidity and mortality data are simply not sufficient to enable us to see the problems we are concerned about. Epidemiological data is of limited use in situations where no simple cause and effect relationship exists or where delayed onset of symptoms occurs (Auer 1988: 41; Public Interest Advocacy Centre cited by Brennan 1992: 18). This may particularly be the case, for example, with environmental health issues. Epidemiology also requires a fairly long time frame before there is 'evidence' of a problem, by which time a number of people will have already experienced illness or even death.

Nor is epidemiology sufficient to measure the extent of wellness of a community and of individuals in that community. We therefore need to look at other measures of community health. Valerie Brown (1985) has called for the development of an 'epidemiology of health' in order to overcome the shortcomings of current epidemiological data. This would need to recognise the multifaceted dimensions of health and incorporate them into any analysis of health and health problems. It is important to note that this recognition of the value of measuring health rather than illness is relatively new, and so approaches to measuring community health are still being developed. Your own work in this area can be part of the groundbreaking work that is needed.

Another issue, closely related to this notion of an epidemiology of health, is the need for the development of positive health indicators. If we want to measure more than disease processes or risk factors, we need to consider how we can do this. Lesley King (1990) has suggested one possibility which may provide a useful framework on which others can build. In considering the problem of social isolation, she suggests, we should be examining social participation rather than social isolation. Not only will this enable us to examine the positive aspects of the issue; it may also enable us to see more clearly some of the barriers to social participation. King's framework also focuses on the community picture, rather than just on the individual, so that it enables a person to be seen within the context of the community in which he or she does or does not participate.

The views of professionals

Health workers and other professionals working in areas related to the health of the community may contribute a great deal to the assessment of needs. In particular, other health workers may have themselves listened to community members or may have conducted formal needs assessments in the past, and your use of these can save valuable time and effort. Furthermore, a number of health workers may discuss an issue and each bring to it a slightly different perspective, based on individual experience and professional background (Southern Community Health Research Unit 1991: 52–4). Similarly, they may each notice slightly different issues in the same community. This can all be useful in gaining an understanding of problems and issues facing the community. Your own assessment, and the assessments of your colleagues, can be a valuable adjunct to information gained from other sources.

It is worthwhile briefly examining the relationship between health workers and their communities. Sometimes health workers suggest that since they are a part of their community, there is little need to canvass community need: what they themselves see as problems is an adequate reflection of community need. However, although health workers may be members of the community, they cannot represent all groups in it. Indeed, as a result of their professional education and socialisation, they bring a particular perspective to health issues. Certainly this perspective is a valuable one which contributes much to the debate about health and health promotion. Nevertheless, it is but one perspective, and it should not be substituted for the opinions of other community members. Therefore, while professional opinion offers a great deal, it should not be assumed to reflect the views of the whole community or remove the need for listening to the community or checking external assessments of need.

National and state policy documents

National and state policy or strategy documents often provide material from a combination of sources, particularly epidemiological data, social and economic indicators and the views of professionals. They will also have been developed with varying degrees of community consultation, depending on political will and the 'need' for expediency. It is important to note that national and state policy documents are often reflective more of political priorities and processes than of the needs of the community. The politically determined nature of these documents must be acknowledged. They will also need to be compared with local evidence of need rather than be assumed to reflect the local picture. With a recognition of these issues in mind, such documents can be useful sources of information and should be used wherever possible as one component of identifying needs. Some examples of national and state policy documents of value are given below. Further information about the policy documents relevant to your state or region should be available from the state's health department or the regional office or public health unit.

In addition to national and state documents, some regions or areas may have their own policy and strategy documents. These may be even more useful, because they are one step nearer to your community and so may reflect its needs more closely. However, it is worthwhile finding out about the process by which these documents were developed. Were they simply summarised from state and national documents, or were regional needs assessments carried out? The chances are that if you have not heard of them before, they may have been prepared without consulting the community members in the region. Their value may therefore be limited.

Some useful Australian policy and strategy documents

National — Health for All Australians (1988), Australian and New Zealand Guidelines for the Assessment and Management of Contaminated Sites (1992), A Social Health Atlas for Australia (1992), Australia's Health (1992), National Aboriginal Health Strategy (1989), National Women's Health Policy: Advancing Women's Health in Australia (1989), Researching Women's Health: An Issues Paper (1991), National Non-English Speaking Background Women's Health Strategy (1991), National Food and Nutrition Policy (1992)

New South Wales — Health for All: Promoting health and preventing disease in New South Wales (1989), Providing for the Health of Young People (1991), Overview of Aboriginal Health Status in New South Wales (1991), Public Policy and Older People (1991), Directions on Ageing in New South Wales (1990), Promoting Health in the Workplace (1992)

Victoria — Promoting Health and Preventing Illness in Victoria: A Framework (1991), Achieving Better Health and Health Services (1992)

Tasmania — Building Healthy Futures: The Public's View (1991), Health Goals and Targets for Tasmania (1992), Health Promotion in Tasmania: What Does It Mean for Health Workers? (1992)

South Australia — Social Health Strategy for South Australia (1988), Primary Health Care in South Australia: A Dis-

cussion Paper (1988), Strategic Directions for Primary Health Care (1993), A Child Health Policy for South Australia (1990), Youth for Health for Youth (1991), Overview of Aboriginal Health Status in South Australia (1991)

Western Australia — Our State of Health: an overview of health and illness in Western Australia (1991), Overview of Aboriginal Health Status in Western Australia (1991)

Northern Territory — Corporate Plan (1992), Overview of Aboriginal Health Status in the Northern Territory (1991)

Queensland — National Better Health Program: Queensland Program Outline (1990), Overview of Aboriginal Health Status in Queensland (1991), Rural Health Policy (1991), Corporate Plan 1992–97 (1992), Primary Health Care Policy (1992), Primary Health Care Implementation Plan (1992)

Australian Capital Territory — A health promotion strategic plan, health goals and targets and a number of more specific policy documents are currently being developed. These should be available in 1994.

The above list provides just some examples of policy documents which can prove very useful in helping you assess the needs of your area or interest group. Look around in your own state — what else can you find?

Conducting needs assessments

There are a number of principles which guide the approach taken in assessing the needs of any person, group or community. They reflect the approach taken to any Primary Health Care research.

- Needs assessment reflects the social view of health, which is so much a part of health promotion and Primary Health Care (Baum 1992: 83).

- Needs assessment is an integral part of health promotion work.

- Needs assessment involves both formal and informal assessment of need.

- Needs assessment recognises the partnership between people themselves and health workers in determining their needs, planning action and evaluating any outcomes. Part of this process may involve negotiation between community members and health workers.

- Needs assessment involves a combination of felt, expressed, normative and comparative need.

In preparing to assess the needs of any individual, group or community, it is vital that you keep in mind why you are doing this particular assessment. What is it you are trying to find out, and to what end? This will help you to determine how you will go about finding out. It is rare that the resources, including your time and the time of others involved in the process, are so freely available that you can afford to conduct needs assessment without being clear about what the reasons for it are.

You also need to ensure that you will have adequate resources, or are able to obtain them, to respond appropriately to the findings of any needs assessment. Needs assessments are not an end in themselves, but a guide to action. Unless they are acted on, they are a waste of time and energy (Feuerstein 1986: 153). Needs assessments that leave you with few resources for acting on what you find are likely to do little to help those for whom the needs assessment is purportedly being carried out (Rissel 1991: 30).

Community needs assessment

Presenting a step-by-step guide to conducting a community needs assessment is beyond the scope of this book, but there are a number of excellent resources to help you to conduct such an assessment. Of particular value here is *Planning healthy communities*, issued by the Southern Community Health Research Unit (1991). You are encouraged to refer to this, and to other resources, in order to develop further skills in needs assessment (see also Wadsworth 1984). Only a brief overview of community needs assessment is presented here.

The two key components of a community-wide assessment — a *community profile* and a *community needs survey* — are discussed in the following sections. These descriptions are based on geographical communities but the same principles apply when assessing the needs of a smaller community, such as a workplace or school.

Community profile

Every service which has responsibility to a community will need to have access to a relatively up-to-date picture of it. This is necessary in order to have a sense of what needs there may be and what demographic and social issues are likely to be shaping the lives of people in the community. As a community health worker, you may be part of the team that sets about preparing or updating a community profile. It is worthwhile to examine what sort of information you need to include in a community profile and some of the general principles involved in preparing it.

Henderson and Thomas (1987: 57–68) suggest that a community profile can be considered under six interrelated categories. However, these are meant as a guide only, and if they do not meet the needs of a particular community with which you are working you can adapt the information you collect. The six categories are set out below.

1. *History*. An understanding of the history of an area may help you to understand a great deal about dominant values in the community, and may help explain some of the current attitudes towards contemporary events.

2. *Environment*. The environment in which people live strongly influences the way in which they can interact with each other. It also may be the source of some health problems for the community (Henderson and Thomas 1987: 58). For example, a town which includes a number of dirty industries and is sited in a hollow may face serious environmental pollution; a community may have little recreational space within its boundaries; or a suburb may be designed around the needs of cars, often resulting in lack of access to services for those who do not own cars (as has been seen in new western Sydney suburbs).

3. *Residents*. Obviously, information about the people themselves is extremely valuable. The information you collect here will include information about demography, housing occupation, employment levels, numbers of people receiving single-parent benefits and pensions, residents' perceptions of the area, community networks, and the values and traditions which guide life in the area (many of these may take some time to discover). This will also include epidemiological data and any other information already available about health problems.

4. *Organisations*. A number of organisations may operate in, and influence, an area. Their presence, and the role they play in the community, will be very useful to know about. Organisations can be classified under a number of categories, including local and state government bodies, industrial and commercial organisations, religious bodies and voluntary organisations. It is worthwhile finding out about the roles played by each of these organisations in the community. For example, is there a particular company which is the main employer? Is there a religious organisation which involves itself in a lot of community work?

5. *Communication*. Knowing which mass communication methods are used in the community will help the health worker to keep in contact with many goings-on. For example, what radio and television stations are received in

the area, and which stations seem to be listened to or viewed by which groups of people? Which newspapers are available locally? Is there a local newspaper? However, a number of other effective communications options may also be operating. For example, are there community noticeboards that are well used?

6. *Power and leadership*. Power and leadership can be both formal and informal, and an understanding of both are needed if you are to work in a community. Information of value here includes information about leaders of local political parties, local government and community groups, as well as key influential people within those organisations. It may also include information about people who seem to have a strong voice in influencing public debate or a particular organisation, but who may not necessarily hold a current position of formal power.

Taken together, the information in the above categories will start to give you a picture of the community you are working with. Remember, however, that a community profile is not something which can be completed and then filed away. Communities are dynamic and changing, and so is your understanding of your community. Keep adding to your understanding of it as you live and work there.

Community needs survey

This component of needs assessment examines the needs of the community as they are defined by the community members themselves, as well as by professionals working in the area. However, the line between a community needs survey and a community profile may become quite hazy with the active involvement of community members themselves in planning and organising needs assessment.

Few communities are small enough for it to be possible to ask everyone to define their needs. Therefore, more often than not, a community needs survey will ask only a sample of people. Determining which people to ask in order to obtain an appropriate sample is a key component of planning a needs survey.

An essential part of any needs assessment is reporting back its findings to the people involved (Southern Community Health Research Unit 1991: 257–61). This should be done as a matter of course, to ensure that the information obtained accurately reflects what people said. It will then enable community members to be involved in the priority-setting process discussed below (pp. 86–7).

Conducting a community needs assessment and coming to terms with addressing the issues you find

In 1989 a rural/coastal community health centre was faced with the dilemma of identifying appropriate health promotion strategies to incorporate in its future policy document. The notion of assessing the community's health needs in order to plan action made good sense. This was the beginning of the centre's Health Needs Study.

The centre had expert assistance from a senior research fellow from a nearby university, the 'legwork' being done by one of its community health nurses. The progress of the study was overseen by a steering committee comprising members of the centre's Committee of Management and staff, as well as other local health service providers.

The study comprised four major sections:

1. Community profile

The community profile provided an overview of demographic characteristics, community and health-related services and recreation facilities. In essence, it set the stage for the study's later sections.

2. Community health survey

The second section was prepared by the senior research fellow. A self-report questionnaire, based on one developed by the Southern Community Health Research Unit, was used to survey a random sample of local residents. It asked questions about their recent illness experiences, health behaviours (exercise, weight, diet, alcohol use and smoking), use of health screening (cholesterol, blood pressure, breast self-examination and pap smears), social support and satisfaction with the community health centre's services.

3. Community opinion

The third section of the study was concerned with seeking the opinion of the local community regarding local health needs and concerns. Groups of community leaders were brought together to discuss their ideas about the health needs of the community using the Delphi technique, and groups of people representative of the community discussed their concerns, using nominal group process methods.

4. Patterns of illness and injury

The last section looked at rates of illness and injury using the centre's records, details of hospital admissions and Workcare data.

The role of the community health nurse

The legwork done by the community health nurse encompassed a range of tasks and responsibilities relating to all sections of the study, and required perseverance, persistence and a healthy sense of humour. The following examples (affectionately known as the 'hassles and giggles' of the project) highlight some of the tasks involved:

- gathering data for the community profile, including information from the Australian Bureau of Statistics and interviews with staff from local agencies and service providers;

- finding and coordinating volunteers to deliver the community health survey;

- accessing local community groups to investigate community opinion (it was difficult to access many groups);

- searching for client contact sheets which had been mistakenly 'spring-cleaned' and were required for the retrospective audit.

The findings

Since the study attempted to look at health in its social context, it had the expected outcome of identifying some broad issues which people perceived as affecting their wellbeing, in addition to more traditional ill-health problems.

The major issues identified were as follows:

- poor local public transport;

- inadequate local child care services;

- dissatisfaction with the services offered by the community health centre;

- health and environmental concern regarding local ocean sewerage outfall;

- alcohol consumption by youth and the elderly;

- a significant amount of non-participation in women's health screening (compared to Anti-Cancer Council recommendations);

- lack of social networks;

- concern about additives and chemicals in food;

- concern about the quality of local domestic water.

The next step: tackling the findings

The findings created several dilemmas for the community health centre. They challenged the notion of community health as just a geographical base for clinical services in the community. Some members of the centre's Committee of Management were keen to ignore many of the findings, as they were not seen as relevant to a community health centre. Others now felt some sense of accountability, since the findings were public. The challenge was certainly there to address those broader public health issues which had previously been ignored.

Two years later, despite some changes, many of the issues raised by the study, both traditional health issues and the broader social health problems, remain unaddressed. The difficulty seems to be that staff focus on treating problems, and that little or no time is allocated to preventing or minimising them. Within the centre's medical model of service delivery, ill-health treatment has both prestige and power. The change in approach that is needed will mean a rethinking of the role of the centre's staff.

Another factor to be taken into account by the centre in addressing health needs is not only knowledge of the health issues but also support for staff to take up those issues, and the skills for them to do so appropriately. Poor attendances at some of the programs offered by the centre highlight the need for health promotion strategies to be relevant to the needs of the community and dynamic. Identifying health problems is only the first step—addressing them in a way that is relevant and meaningful to the community is the next.

Sue Lauder
Community Health Worker

Individual needs assessment

You may be working with someone in determining his or her needs. In that case, you are most likely to be useful as an assistant or consultant to the person concerned, rather than being the person making the assessment. As much as possible, you need to work with individuals to enable them to assess their situation, and help them to develop their own skills in assessment. However, remember that even self-assessments can be devised in a way which does not help people to gain control over their lives. Overemphasising medical aspects in a health self-assessment may not be useful for people if they want to assess their health within the context of their whole lives, and may focus attention on individual behaviour changes alone. Individual needs may also be addressed by working for public policy change or other environmental changes, rather than focusing solely on the individual.

Group needs assessment

The principles to be considered when conducting an individual or a community needs assessment also apply when working with a group to assess its needs. An understanding of group dynamics will also help you to work with the group throughout the needs assessment process (see chapter 8).

ORANGESEARCH:
a community view of issues and needs in Orange

ORANGESEARCH was a dynamic process of research and community consultation carried out by a multidisciplinary team in Orange, a regional city of 33 000 people in the Central West of New South Wales. It began in 1989 and formally finished in 1991, although outcomes are still occurring.

The impetus for the study arose from the need for qualitative information on what makes the city 'tick'—the flesh on the bones of the statistical picture. The study took an action research approach using an innovative tool called Rapid Rural Appraisal, more commonly used at that time in agricultural areas of developing countries. It was based on personal interviews with a broad range of people in Orange and a quantitative community profile. The purposes of ORANGESEARCH were:

- to construct an integrated picture of community needs and issues as a basis for future planning, research and debate;

- to consult with a wide range of people in the city as a basis for community involvement, interaction and development;

- to develop an effective team approach as a basis for better intersectoral cooperation and 'ownership'.

The team working on the project was drawn from five local organisations whose decisions make an impact on citizens' lives and health (Orange City Council, Orange Base Hospital, the Regional Housing Department, Orange Community Health Centre and the Central West Regional Health Promotion Unit) and two universities (University of Western Sydney, Hawkesbury Faculty of Agriculture and Rural Development; and Charles Sturt University, Mitchell School of Nursing).

The process involved five different stages:

1. Planning and preparation (four months)

This first stage involved an intensive process of working out 'how to do it' with few guidelines for an urban context; negotiating for team members and training them; selecting respondents and interview techniques; organising 200 respondents and 12 team members to conduct interviews in different pairs each day over five days; and designing methods of analysis, documentation and feedback.

2. Community consultation (one week)

A total of 60 people were interviewed in August 1989—some as key respondents in their field, many in special groups (demographic and occupational) and some as randomly selected householders in contrasting suburbs. The techniques used were focus groups and semistructured interviewing.

3. Collation, analysis and documentation (eight months)

This stage involved a lengthy process of sorting information, insights and ideas from written and tape-recorded material into patterns and themes, developing models and documenting findings in a user-friendly fashion. One full report and five smaller booklets for specific target groups were produced. Over 1300 copies were distributed around Orange, the Central West and other parts of Australia.

4. Community feedback (over a five-month period)

In 1990–91 a number of successful forums were held to feed back findings and develop priority issues and action strategies for youth, young families, older people and the future of Orange. Media coverage also stimulated discussion of issues.

5. Community action (ongoing)

Various organisations and individuals have taken action on a range of issues, including:

- social isolation and loneliness (Friendly Visiting Service);
- youth issues, opportunities and a 'voice' (Youth Coordinator, Youth Council, Newsletter, Activities);
- poor youth nutrition (Fast Foods For Families project with high schools);
- lack of parenting skills (parenting programs);
- health needs of low-income people (health promotion through Housing Department);

- falls amongst the elderly (Slip No More project);
- lack of parks and equipment for young children (Safe Park project);
- treatment orientation of health services (health promotion in health services).

Through its various stages, ORANGE-SEARCH has been a catalyst for people participating in planning to address their own community needs and issues. The process has been used extensively in the Central West and in other regions. Its main difficulties are in analysis of a large amount of qualitative data and organisation of consultation. Its strengths lie in its flexibility and its capacity to involve people, improve understanding of complex issues and stimulate action related to community needs.

Margaret Carroll
(ORANGESEARCH Coordinator)

Setting priorities for action

If you determine a number of needs when doing a needs assessment, it will be necessary to set some priorities, since it is rare to have the time or other resources to be able to deal with all the needs at once. Sometimes a number of needs may be able to be dealt with together if they all share a similar root cause and you have recognised this in your needs assessment, but this will not always be the case.

So, how do you set priorities for action? Some people suggest that you deal with the easiest or most 'winnable' issues first (for example, Minkler 1991: 272), but there are some problems with this approach. The easiest issues to deal with may not be the ones that make the biggest difference in people's lives. Indeed, the most difficult ones may well have the biggest impact if they are acted on successfully. Priority setting done in partnership with community members is most likely to be the most successful approach, because of the community support for, and action on, any decisions made. Of course, there may be times when the health risks involved are great and time for community involvement may be limited. Even then, however, maximum possible involvement by community members should be built into the decision making.

Priorities set by national health documents can be taken up if they are identified also as local health needs. The advantage here is that if they are national priorities, it is likely that funding will be available to support health promotion projects and health workers will be encouraged to take action in this area. Similarly, some areas may be included in the charter of the agency for which you work, and so these may need to be addressed first.

Furthermore, some issues may be able to be dealt with first because the necessary expertise is available in the team with which you are working, or because you have ready access to it (Henderson and Thomas 1987: 101). While it would be a mistake to build an agency's work around the interests of the staff rather than the needs of the community, acknowledging and working with the expertise of the staff and other available expertise is a valuable use of resources.

There are a number of questions worth asking about each identified need in order to help to set priorities for action. Those in the following list are based on Lund and McGechaen 1981 (as cited by Gilmore et al. 1989: 22).

- What type/s of need is/are present? Does the individual, group or community consider this as a need?

- How many people are affected?

- What will the consequences be if this need is not met?

- Is this a critical need that should be met before other needs are addressed?

- How can this need best be met? Is it likely to be affected by health promotion action?

- Does the need coincide with your department's or agency's mission statement or policies? If not, why not? Can you influence the agency's policies?

- With which community members and other agencies do you need to work in order to address the issue?

- Are resources (funds, staff) available?

Determining the most appropriate response to a need

Once you have determined what needs there are and which need (or needs) you are going to address, the next step is to determine what the best response to the latter will be, before you can plan any action. A very useful framework within which to consider this issue is the Ottawa Charter for Health Promotion. Should the need be dealt with by working for healthier public policy and so creating supportive environments; by working to strengthen community action; by working to further develop people's personal skills (through some form of health education); or by working to reorient the health system to a greater emphasis on health promotion? Or should it be dealt with by a combination of some or all of these approaches? You may decide that action will need to occur on some levels in order to address the problem in the short term, while you are attempting on other levels to address it over the longer term. For example, working for public policy change may take some time, and in the meantime you may need to help people to develop some of their own skills to deal with the situation they are in.

Conclusion

Research is an integral part of a Primary Health Care approach to health promotion. In this chapter, we have reviewed the principles which need to underpin research if it is to reflect that approach, and have examined the framework for conducting needs assessment for health promotion.

REFERENCES AND FURTHER READINGS

Alcorso, C. and Schofield, T. 1991. *The National Non-English Speaking Background Women's Health Strategy*, Australian Government Publishing Service, Canberra.

Auer, J. 1988. *Exploring Legislative Arrangements For Promoting Primary Health Care in Australia*, Social Health Branch, South Australian Health Commission, Adelaide.

Australian and New Zealand Environment and Conservation Council and National Health and Medical Research Council. 1992. *Australian and New Zealand Guidelines for the Assessment and Management of Contaminated Sites*, ANZECC and NHMRC, Canberra.

Baum, F. 1992. Researching community health: evaluation and needs assessment that makes an impact, in Baum, F., Fry, D. and Lennie, I. (eds). *Community health: policy and practice in Australia*, Pluto Press/Australian Community Health Association, Sydney, NSW.

Becker, M. H. 1986. The tyranny of health promotion, *Public Health Review*, 14, 15–25.

Bradshaw, J. 1972. The concept of social need, *New Society*, 30 March, 640–3.

Brennan, A. 1992. The Altona Clean Air Project, *Health Issues*, September, 32, 18–20.

Broadhead, P., Duckett, S. and Lavender, G. 1989. Developing a mandate for change: planning as a political process, *Community Health Studies*, 13 (3), 243–57.

Brown, V. A. 1985. Towards an epidemiology of health: a basis for planning community health programs, *Health Policy*, 4, 331–40.

Browning, C. J. 1992. Mass screening in public health, in Gardner, H. (ed.), *Health policy: development, implementation, and evaluation in Australia*, Churchill Livingstone, Melbourne.

Carr, L. M. 1988. Dental health of children in Australia 1977–1985, *Australian Dental Journal*, 33 (3), 205–11.

Carr, W. and Kemmis, S. 1986. *Becoming critical: knowing through action research*, Deakin University Press, Victoria.

Catford, J. C. 1983. Positive health indicators: towards a new information base for health promotion, *Community Medicine*, 5, 125–32.

Christie, D., Gordon, I. and Heller, R. 1987. *Epidemiology: an introductory text for medical and other health science students*, New South Wales University Press, Kensington.

Crowley, V. and Cruse, S. 1992. *Discussion paper on ethics in Aboriginal research*, Aboriginal Research Institute, University of South Australia, Adelaide.

Ewles, I. and Simnett, L. 1985. *Promoting health: a practical guide to health education*, John Wiley and Sons, Chichester, UK.

Feuerstein, M.-T. 1986. *Partners in evaluation: evaluating development and community programmes with participants*, Macmillan, London.

Gilmore, G.D., Campbell, M.D. and Becker, B. 1989. *Needs assessment strategies for health education and health promotion*, Benchmark Press, Indianapolis, Indiana.

Hawe, P., Degeling, D. and Hall, J. 1990. *Evaluating health promotion: a health workers' guide*, MacLennan and Petty, Sydney.

Henderson, P. and Thomas, D.N. 1987. *Skills in neighbourhood work*, Allen and Unwin, London.

Houston, S. and Legge, D. 1992. Aboriginal health research and the National Aboriginal Health Strategy, *Australian Journal of Public Health*, 16(2), 114–15.

Kane, P. 1991. *Researching women's health: an issues paper*, Australian Government Publishing Service, Canberra.

Kelly, J. G. 1988. *A guide to conducting prevention research in the community: first steps*, Haworth Press, New York.

King, L. 1990. Indicators of social participation, in *Healthy environments in the 90s: The community health approach, Papers from the 3rd National Conference of the Australian Community Health Association*, Australian Community Health Association, Sydney.

Lower, T. 1992. Town survey: horse falls top injury list, *Better Health Briefing*, January, 10.

Matrice, D. and Brown, V. 1990. *Widening the research focus: consumer roles in public health research*. Consumers' Health Forum, Curtin, ACT.

Mies, M. 1983. Towards a methodology for feminist research, in Bowles, G. and Duelli Klein, R. (eds), *Theories of women's studies*, Routledge and Kegan Paul, London.

Minkler, M. 1991. Improving health through community organisation, in Glanz, K., Lewis, F. M. and Rimer, B. K. (eds). *Health behaviour and health education: theory research and practice*, Jossey-Bass, San Francisco.

New South Wales Consultative Committee on Ageing. 1991. *Public policy and older people*, Office on Ageing, NSW Premier's Department, Sydney.

New South Wales Department of Health. 1990. *Directions on ageing in New South Wales*, Office on Ageing, NSW Premier's Department, Sydney.

New South Wales Department of Health. 1991a. *Dental health in NSW: A strategic plan (draft)*, Dental Health Unit, NSW Department of Health, Sydney.

New South Wales Department of Health. 1991b. *Health care at any cost?*, NSW Department of Health, Sydney.

New South Wales Department of Health. 1992. *Promoting health in the workplace*, NSW Department of Health, Sydney.

Oakley, A. 1990. Who's afraid of the randomized clinical trial? Some dilemmas of the scientific method and 'good' research practice, in Roberts, H. (ed.) *Women's Health Counts*, Routledge, London and New York.

Oakley, P. 1989. *Community involvement in health development*, World Health Organization, Geneva.

Patterson, A. F. 1990. Who caries? A report on the dental health status of children in the Moree district, New England, NSW, unpublished report.

Queensland Health. 1991. *Rural health policy*. Queensland Department of Health, Brisbane.

Queensland Health. 1992. *A Primary Health Care Implementation Plan*, Queensland Department of Health, Brisbane.

Queensland Health. 1992. *A Primary Health Care Policy*, Queensland Department of Health, Brisbane.

Queensland Health. 1992. *Corporate Plan 1992–97*, Queensland Department of Health, Brisbane.

Rissel, C. 1991. The tyranny of needs assessment in health promotion, *Evaluation Journal of Australia*, 3(1) 26–31.

Short, S. 1989. Community participation or community manipulation? A Case Study of the Illawarra Cancer Appeal-A-Thon, *Community Health Studies*, 13(1), 34–8.

South Australian Health Commission. 1988. *A social health strategy for South Australia*, South Australian Health Commission, Adelaide.

South Australian Health Commission. 1988. *Primary health care in South Australia: a discussion paper*. South Australian Health Commission, Adelaide.

South Australian Health Commission. 1990. *A child health policy for South Australia*, South Australian Health Commission, Adelaide.

South Australian Health Commission. 1991. *Youth for health for youth: South Australian Health Commission youth health policy*. South Australian Health Commission, Adelaide.

South Australian Health Commission. 1993. *Strategic directions for primary health care*, South Australian Health Commission, Adelaide.

Southern Community Health Research Unit. 1991. *Planning healthy communities: a guide to doing community needs assessment*, Southern Community Health Research Unit, Bedford Park, South Australia.

Tasmanian Department of Health. 1991. *Building better futures: the public's view*, Background Paper No.1, Health Policy Division, Department of Health, Hobart.

Tasmanian Department of Health. 1992. *Health goals and targets for Tasmania*, Health Policy Division, Department of Health. Hobart.

Tasmanian Department of Health. 1992. *Health promotion in Tasmania: what does it mean for health workers?*, Health Policy Division, Department of Health, Hobart.

Thomson, N. 1991. A review of Aboriginal health status, in Reid, J. and Trompf, P. (eds), *The Health Of Aboriginal Australia*, Harcourt Brace Jovanovich, Sydney.

Twelvetrees, A. 1987. *Community work*, Macmillan, London.

Waddell, V. P. and Lee, N. A. (eds). 1991. *Our state of health: an overview of the health of the Western Australian population*, Health Department of Western Australia.

Wadsworth, Y. 1982. The politics of social research: a social research strategy for the community health, education and welfare movement, *Australian Journal of Social Issues*, 17(3), 232–46.

Wadsworth, Y. 1984. *Do it yourself social research*, Victorian Council of Social Service in association with Allen and Unwin, Collingwood, Victoria.

Wadsworth, Y. 1992. *Hearing the voice of the consumer: an annotated bibliography of consumer research in public health*, Action Research Issues Association, Melbourne.

Walker, M. and Dixon, J. 1984. *Participation in change: Australian case studies*, Mitchell College Of Advanced Education, Bathurst, NSW.

Wass, A. 1990. The new legitimacy of women's health: In whose interests?, in Smith, A. (ed). *Women's health in Australia*, Angie Smith, Armidale, NSW.

CHAPTER 4

Evaluating health promotion

In the previous chapter we examined the role of the research process and looked in some detail at needs assessment in health promotion. In this chapter we will re-examine some of those issues as they relate to evaluation and describe some of the important elements of evaluation applied to your own practice and the activities with which you are involved.

As we described in the previous chapter, in an action research approach we are guided by a recurring process of planning, acting, observing and reflecting in a continuous cycle of reflection and action. In such an approach, the lines between assessment, planning, action and evaluation become thin. Moreover, as this process continues and then recurs, the line between evaluation and assessment becomes particularly unclear. As a result, many of the issues discussed in the previous chapter are extremely relevant to evaluation. You may therefore find it valuable to read chapters 3 and 4 together.

Evaluation in health promotion has so far been grounded in the traditional approach to research, with its focus on (largely quantitative) measurement of outcomes. This approach is clearly not appropriate for many health promotion activities, such as working for policy change or community action where longer-term outcomes may not be amenable to statistical analysis. Even in more traditional health promotion, such as health education, focus on quantitatively measured outcomes may not always be appropriate since they cannot answer all the questions we need to ask. There is growing recognition of the importance of both qualitative and quantitative approaches to evaluation, as well as recognition of the importance of a wide range of outcomes not directly related to disease processes.

The limitations of a quantitative approach to evaluation have been recognised for some time, although it seems that the primacy of the quantitative approach remains, particularly with many government decision makers. This is not to suggest that quantitative approaches to evaluation are not useful. Rather, they can contribute significantly to evaluation processes when they are used appropriately and in balance with other approaches. However, as discussed in the previous chapter, they do not embrace the Primary Health Care approach automatically, and care must be taken to ensure they are used appropriately.

We are still very much coming to terms with how to evaluate appropriately from a Primary Health Care perspective. One of the key features of working with a Primary Health Care approach is that the evaluation process actively involves the people for whom the project is running, building on their active involvement in the assessment, planning and implementation of health promoting activities. It is for this reason that participatory evaluation fits most comfortably with a Primary Health Care approach, because it is built on this active involvement of community members in the evaluation process (Feuerstein 1986 and Wadsworth 1991). Wadsworth points out that while non-participatory research may come up with useful outcomes, 'a non participatory, non democratic process of evaluation cannot ensure a user-appropriate outcome' (Wadsworth 1991: 10).

Much detailed evaluation of the effectiveness of different strategies is beyond the scope of health workers in their everyday practice and more in the realm of special evaluation projects, conducted by either health workers or skilled researchers or a team of both (Hawe et al. 1990: 10–11). This chapter will focus on evaluation which can be comfortably incorporated into a health worker's daily life and can realistically be expected of health workers as part of their evaluation of their practice. A number of books examine in detail how to plan and implement evaluation. Although this chapter will examine a number of the principles of evaluation, you are advised to read elsewhere for more in-depth examination of the issues and skills (see, in particular, Feuerstein 1986, Wadsworth 1991 and Hawe et al. 1990).

What is evaluation?

Evaluation has been described as 'the process by which we judge the value or worth of something' (Suchman 1967, cited by Hawe et al. 1990: 10). Despite the impression we are often given that evaluation is an objective process which will inform us of the 'best' way to proceed, it is clearly a process of judgment, and this judgment can never be value-free. On the contrary, evaluation is very much a value-driven process, and in a Primary Health Care approach it is the values of Primary Health Care that drive the evaluation. That is, the needs of the people for whom the activity is carried out are foremost, as are issues of community control, social justice and equity.

Why evaluate?

Evaluation of activities carried out to promote health makes good sense, as a way of ensuring that people's needs are being met through those activities and that each activity is the best it can be. However, some concern has been expressed recently that health promotion work is expected by funding bodies and the illness management system as a whole to be evaluated to a much greater extent than is expected of the rest of the health system. Many expensive medical technologies and treatments have not been evaluated for effectiveness. This is not to suggest that evaluation of health promotion is not a useful enterprise — clearly, it is very useful. However, those who express concern about evaluation at a greater level than that expected of the mainstream illness management system are concerned that health promotion is being set up to fail by being required to demonstrate its impact on people's health over a short period of time and after relatively minor activities. Furthermore, evaluating activities beyond a reasonable level acts as a drain on the very limited resources available for health promotion. For those reasons, evaluation activities need to be critically reviewed and carefully considered so that inappropriate evaluation does not become part of the problem.

There are a number of different reasons why you may be evaluating, and these are important because they will determine to a large extent just what you will examine in your evaluation. For example, you might want to find out if your activities are meeting the needs of members of the community for whom they were designed. Also, you might need to find out how your activity measured up against the criterion set by your funding body in order to justify continuation of your funding. Or you may want to evaluate the achievements of your agency or team in the process of working to promote health, in order to plan further staff development. The requirements of each of these types of evaluation are quite different, and may require you to evaluate the activity from a different perspective and to ask different questions. At any one time, you may be evaluating in order to address one or all of these issues. However, there may also be times when an evaluation is conducted to justify a decision already made, such as when an evaluation is used to justify closure of a service or a cutback of funds. Conversely, an evaluation may be conducted in order to justify the continued development of the service (Owen and Mohr 1986: 96).

One of the concerns of health workers is that the needs of these different evaluation perspectives often seem to conflict. Health workers may fear that if they evaluate their practice honestly and highlight areas for improvement, this information may be used to justify reduction of funding for their activities. This may realistically mean that evaluations should not be expected to be all things to all people, and evaluations conducted for different reasons can be conducted separately. The key here, of course, is to ensure that this does not result in too much repetition and excess energy being expended on evaluation. Another important point to be considered is that all these perspectives should share a concern for the needs of the people for whom the service or activity is performed. Evaluation from the point of view of whether the needs of the group for whom the service or activity is designed are being addressed should permit some common ground between evaluation from these various perspectives (Wadsworth 1991: 9–10).

Thinking through the implications of all these perspectives at the planning stage will mean that much of the information that is required by the different perspectives can be built into the implementation of the activity, making even formal evaluation for the managers or funders of a project more easy than it might be if evaluation is regarded as an 'add on' activity.

Evaluation to demonstrate program success or programs to demonstrate evaluation success?

Evaluating any activity needs to be built around evaluation methods which are appropriate to the program and enable it to maintain a level of flexibility in order to respond to the needs of the people for whom it is being implemented. Unfortunately, many of the research approaches used, particularly quantitative methods based on the principles of the scientific method, do not fit comfortably with all health promotion work, particularly that built on a Primary Health Care approach. There is a great deal of important work still to be done in this area, in order to develop useful evaluation methods for health promotion. Unfortunately, what is happening in some areas is that workers are so driven to evaluate that programs are developing to match the evaluation methods available, rather than the other way round. 'Too often the evaluation tail wags the program dog as practitioners choose objectives amenable to evaluation' (Freudenberg 1984: 46).

One of the real dangers of the current emphasis on evaluation in health promotion is that it may discourage health workers from taking up innovative health promotion work, because it is difficult to evaluate. It is not surprising that evaluation methods lag behind innovative strategies (Hawe et al. 1990: 9), but it is vital that this should not prevent innovation and experimentation.

What to evaluate?

There is real value in health workers evaluating every aspect of their work, using appropriate methods and approaches. The daily practice of an individual health worker, the overall work of the agency or team with whom you work, and the individual health promotion activities or projects which you develop will all benefit from regular evaluation, either formal or informal. Each health promotion activity, whether it is community development, lobbying for policy change or health education, will require some form of evaluation. The basic principles which apply to evaluation will all be relevant in varying degrees to each of these situations. It is up to you to apply these to your own evaluation requirements.

Planning to evaluate

Despite the impression that is often given, effective evaluation is not an activity that is added on to the work of an agency. Rather, evaluation strategies should be integrated into the activities they are designed to evaluate.

Before planning any evaluation, you will need to address the question of whether you should evaluate the program. There are three questions to be considered here (Northern Community Health Research Unit 1991: 7):

1. Why is the evaluation being done?

2. Is the program able to be evaluated? Are aims and objectives for it clearly set down?

3. Do you have the time and resources to evaluate appropriately?

The evaluation itself needs to be realistic and achievable, within the budget (in terms of time and other resources) which you can afford. This may mean that you will need to prioritise your evaluation questions and ask those that will give you the most useful information at the most reasonable cost (Rissel 1991: 30).

The importance of the evaluation process

In addition to what you do to promote health, how you do it is very important and can have a positive or negative impact on the people with whom you are working. This is just as true for evaluation as for any other aspect of health promotion — the process of the evaluation activity can itself be a positive or negative experience for both community members and health workers. It is recognition of this fact, along with recognition of the expertise which community members have on issues with which they are involved, which is behind support for participatory evaluation. Evaluation which makes conclusions about a health promotion activity but does so in a way which is disempowering will be of limited value.

Components of evaluation

There are three key components to evaluation — process evaluation, impact evaluation and outcome evaluation. Together, these components should paint a fairly comprehensive picture of your activity. Which elements fit into each of these categories will depend on just what your activity was aiming to do — something which forms the process of one activity may be part of the outcome of another.

Process evaluation

Process evaluation is about evaluating the way in which the health promotion activity was implemented. Because of the centrality of process in the Primary Health Care approach to health promotion, examination of the process of the activity is probably even more important than in more traditional evaluation.

For a comprehensive evaluation of the process of health promotion a number of issues will need to be examined (Hawe et al. 1990: 61):

- Is the program or activity reaching the people for whom it was designed?
- What do the participants think of the program or activity?
- Is the program or activity being implemented as planned?
- Are all aspects of the program of good quality?

In addition, the particular process elements important in a Primary Health Care approach will include such things as:

- How was power shared between health workers and participants? That is, what kind of participation occurred?

- To what extent was the direction of the project changed in response to the needs of the participants?

Impact and outcome evaluation

Impact and outcome evaluation consider what you have achieved through your action. Most commonly, impact and outcome evaluation occur when one is examining the extent to which the aims and objectives of the project have been met. In this case, impact evaluation measures the extent to which the objectives of the activity or project occurred, while outcome evaluation measures the extent to which the aim or aims of the project occurred (Hawe et al. 1990: 44). This form of evaluation is known as goal-based evaluation, since you are evaluating against goals set for the activity or project (McKenzie and Jurs 1993: 204).

Evaluation will therefore be a matter of examining the extent to which the aims and objectives of the program or activity have met. Objectives which are clearly stated will be relatively easy to evaluate. However, it will be difficult to evaluate objectives which are not clearly stated, because it may not be possible to work out just what was intended by the person or people who wrote the objectives. Of course, when people evaluate their own work and they were involved in setting the objectives, they may be able to compensate for poorly written objectives to some extent. The question remains, though, whether they were clear enough about what they wanted to achieve when they set their objectives.

However, it is recognised that evaluation carried out by comparing results with aims and objectives is not a complete evaluation of the outcome of a project, because it does not provide an opportunity to note any outcomes which do not relate directly to the aims and objectives. These outcomes may either add greater benefit to the activity or undermine some of its other benefits. In either case, these unpredicted consequences are an important part of the program, and reliance solely on evaluation against aims and objectives would have caused them to be missed. For these reasons, some evaluation not directly linked to the aims and objectives is useful. This is described by some as goal-free evaluation (McKenzie and Jurs 1993: 207).

Wadsworth describes this goal-free evaluation as open-ended inquiry (1991: 35). She highlights the importance of conducting it before starting any examination of whether specific aims and objectives have been met. This is because this process of measurement against objectives is itself a fairly narrow process which does not encourage creativity. Doing this evaluation first may mean that it is then very difficult for people to think broadly and creatively. Open-ended inquiry will not, however, make it difficult to examine later the extent to which aims and objectives have been met, and, indeed, may help you to evaluate your aims and objectives themselves.

Another limitation of evaluation against aims and objectives is that the value of the evaluation is dependent on the quality and appropriateness of the aims and objectives, and therefore the quality of the research on which they were based

(Wadsworth 1991: 25). Relying solely on aims and objectives, when they may not have been drawn up under optimum conditions, severely limits the potential value of any evaluation.

Wadsworth (1991: 25) suggests that the philosophical statements which guide the development of an organisation may provide better guidance for an evaluation than the specific aims and objectives. This is because aims and objectives may not reflect the value base of the organisation, and the extent to which this has been implemented may in fact be the most important thing for you to evaluate.

Evaluating your own practice

In discussing action research in chapter 3, we described its potential use as a process for health workers' critical reflection on their own practice. Evaluation of your own practice is something which can be a part of every working day. It can also be part of a more formal process in which health workers, either individually or as part of the team with which they are working, take time out every so often to formally review the activities with which they have been involved and the priorities to which they have been working. Building informal and formal evaluation into your own practice will add greatly to the relevance and the power of your health promotion work.

No amount of formal evaluation will be able to make up for the quality of evaluative work which is possible when informal evaluation is a part of your way of working or that of your team. That is, if you keep an 'ear to the ground' and are receptive to learning about what other people think of your work and that of your agency as a whole, and if you informally evaluate your own practice on a daily basis, the quality of your evaluation will be considerably higher than if you had considered your evaluation only at those times when a formal evaluation was being conducted. In addition, this ongoing evaluation will enable you to respond to problems which you see and needs which arise, and your resultant activity is likely to be so much more dynamic and in line with the needs you are attempting to address.

Wadsworth has described this process as developing a 'culture of evaluation', and it is an essential part of Primary Health Care practice. Questions such as 'What went well there?', 'What would I like to do differently next time?' and 'What else would I like to experiment with next time?' are ones which you can ask as a matter of course at the end of each activity. These are questions which can easily be asked by every health worker on a regular basis throughout his or her working day.

Evaluating the work of your agency

Whether you are working as a sole practitioner, in a team within a larger institution or as part of a small agency or centre, you will need to find out if your work overall addresses the needs of those to whom you are accountable. This firstly raises the issue of the dual accountabilities that health workers usually face. On the one hand, health workers have a responsibility to their employer to work in accordance with any 'reasonable' demands made of them, while on the other hand they have a responsibility to the individuals and communities they are meant to serve. Discussion of the ramifications of this dual responsibility is beyond the scope of this book. What is important to note here is that it has implications for each worker's practice, and the evaluation of the work of the agency.

In work done from a Primary Health Care approach, health workers' responsibility to the community they are meant to serve is taken very seriously. If health bureaucracies and employers uphold a Primary Health Care approach, they are supportive of this primary responsibility and help health workers to respond to the needs of their own communities. Unfortunately, the Australian health care system is not yet reoriented to a Primary Health Care approach, and health workers may often find themselves experiencing some difficulty as they attempt to grapple with their dual accountabilities to central planning agencies and their communities. There may be times when projects planned at regional or state level are implemented at the expense of projects planned at community level. Although the former can be extremely useful, if they replace community-based projects they will not promote the health of the community to the extent that we would hope to do, and the process of their imposition may be disempowering for the communities they are meant to assist. Hopefully, this will change as we come to grips more fully with the implications of Primary Health Care.

Evaluating the work of your agency or team is a vital process to prevent it wandering from its original goals or away from addressing the needs of the community you are working for. Informal evaluation can be incorporated into the normal work of the agency or team, for example, through discussion and reflection at weekly staff meetings. It will be necessary, however, for the agency or team to take time out to evaluate itself more formally, and to involve the community in this process. This can be done by setting time aside specifically for evaluation and strategic planning. Although much of this can occur as a regular internal process, such as yearly evaluation and planning days, it can also be done by involving the agency or team in formal evaluation processes which include external evaluators. In these situations, however, care must be taken to ensure that the process is a supportive and useful one for the health workers and community members concerned.

Community Health Accreditation and Standards Project (CHASP)

One formal evaluation process which has developed in recent years, which is built around the principles of Primary Health Care and offers an exciting model around which other evaluation processes can be built, is the Community Health Accreditation and Standards Project (CHASP). It began in New South Wales in 1982 under the auspices of the Australian Community Health Association, and has now been developed into an Australia-wide accreditation project (Fry 1992: 132). What is exciting about the CHASP accreditation process is that it draws on the principles of Primary Health Care and, although designed originally for community health centres, provides a model on which evaluation and accreditation processes for other types of teams and services can be built in order to enable them to be evaluated against the principles of Primary Health Care. Already the CHASP evaluation process is being developed to evaluate Aboriginal health services, women's health services, statewide health agencies (Sinclair 1993), one-person remote and rural health services (Rauch 1992), and Home and Community Care (HACC) services. Furthermore, CHASP workers are currently developing ideas to strengthen community involvement in the CHASP review process.

The CHASP process involves examination of an agency in ten key areas (Australian Community Health Association 1993):

- assessment and care;
- early identification and intervention;
- health promotion;
- community liaison and participation;
- rights of consumers;
- client health and program records;
- education, training and development;
- planning, quality improvement and evaluation;
- management;
- work and its environment.

Each of those areas is reflected by a principle which guides the evaluation (see p. 94). This principle is then examined by means of a number of standards, and each standard is then operationalised by a number of indicators against which an agency is evaluated. The CHASP review involves examination of a total of 404 indicators, which present quite a comprehensive examination of an agency's work and the philosophy which drives it.

One of the real values of CHASP is that it not only reflects Primary Health Care in the issues it addresses, but also incorporates Primary Health Care principles into the accreditation process. As a result, that process can be an important developmental one, both for the agency as a whole and for individual workers. Indeed, it may also be an important educational process for board or management committee members, for whom it may provide the first real opportunity to examine Primary Health Care principles and their implications for health care services.

The CHASP evaluation process typically follows a number of steps. Firstly, workers at a community health centre conduct an internal assessment of their practice comparing it to the CHASP standards and complete a preparatory questionnaire. The review team (which includes a member of staff from the centre being reviewed and two or three workers, managers or board members from other community health centres) conducts an on-site review, examining records, interviewing staff and inspecting the facilities. It also interviews those responsible for community health policy in the area. The team then prepares a report, which includes suggestions for improvement of the centre's operation. The report is discussed with staff at the centre. Recommendations for action may then be negotiated, and a framework for carrying out this action may be set. A further review can then be conducted 12 to 18 months later if the centre wishes to gain accreditation (Ryan 1992: vii–viii).

The CHASP review process has itself recently been evaluated to determine whether it is effective in improving community health services. CHASP has been

---

CHASP principles for effective services

Assessment and care — A community/primary health care service will provide services for people that address the physical, social, cultural, emotional and environmental aspects of their health. Multidisciplinary teamwork and the education and involvement of clients will be emphasised in providing assessment and care services.

Early identification and intervention — A community/primary health care service will identify potential and early stage health problems of individuals and communities to enable effective early intervention and better management of health problems.

Health promotion — The community/primary health care service will work with the community it serves to protect and promote its health, by addressing the physical, emotional, social, cultural and environmental aspects of health.

Community liaison and participation — The community/primary health care service will have a high level of mutual exchange and active involvement with the community it serves. The participation of community members and groups in debate and decision-making about health issues and their own health care will be actively developed.

Rights of consumers — A community/primary health care service will uphold the rights of the consumers to informed decision-making, freedom of expression and confidentiality.

Client health and program records — A community/primary health care service will systematically document its assessment and care, health promotion, early identification and intervention work to ensure accountability evaluation and effectiveness.

Education, training and development — A community/primary health care service will encourage all those involved in its operation to participate in continuing education activities that will increase their knowledge of community/primary health care concepts and practices.

Planning, quality improvement and evaluation — A community/primary health care service will assess the health needs of the community it serves, and will plan, evaluate and continuously improve services and other activities to ensure they are appropriate, of high quality and effective.

Management — A community/primary health care service will have accountable and effective methods of management which will facilitate the achievement of community/primary health goals.

Work and its environment — A community/primary health care service will protect the health, safety and well-being of staff and consumers by developing a supportive working environment.

For further information about CHASP, contact the CHASP National Director at PO Box 657, Bondi Junction 2022 tel: (02) 3891433.

positively evaluated by both the managers of services that have undergone a review and the internal reviewers from those services. Many unexpected benefits, 'such as better team cohesion and more critical reflection amongst community health workers', are becoming apparent in addition to the benefits derived from actual implementation of the CHASP recommendations (McDonald et al. 1993). Overall, CHASP provides an excellent framework against which health workers can evaluate their practice and set goals for future development.

Conclusion

From discussions in this chapter and the previous one, it is clear that evaluation is not something that occurs at the end of a health promotion activity, nor is it in any way an 'add on' activity. Rather, it is an integral component of good health promotion practice and therefore an integral component of the daily practice of health workers. Of course, evaluations should rarely, if ever, be an end in themselves. The ultimate value of any evaluation will be determined by what action resulted.

REFERENCES AND FURTHER READINGS

Australian Community Health Association. 1993. *Manual of standards for community health*, Australian Community Health Association, Sydney.

Baum, F. and Brown, V. 1989. Healthy Cities (Australia) project: issues of evaluation for the new public health, *Community Health Studies*, 13(2), 140–9.

Bichmann, W., Rifkin, S. B. and Shrestha, M. 1989. Towards the measurement of community participation, *World Health Forum*, 10, 467–72.

Birrell, C. 1993. *The health promotion evaluation kit for community health staff*, Inner South Community Health Centres Project Group, Melbourne.

Braw, J., Sheldon, J. and Gaffney, D. 1991. *Self evaluation kit: Drug and Alcohol Services, NSW*, Rozelle, NSW.

Community Development in Health Project. 1988. *Community development in health: a resources collection*, District Health Council, Preston/Northcote, Victoria.

Copeman, R. C. 1988. Assessment of Aboriginal health services, *Community Health Studies*, 12(3), 251–5.

Ewles, L. and Simnett, I. 1985. *Promoting health: a practical guide to health education*, John Wiley and Sons, Chichester, UK.

Feuerstein, M.-T. 1986. *Partners in evaluation: evaluating development and community programmes with participants*, Macmillan, London.

Freudenberg, N. 1984. Training health educators for social change, *International Quarterly of Community Health Education*, 5(1), 37–52.

Fry, D. 1992. Quality assurance and community health services, in Baum, F., Fry, D. and Lennie, I. (eds), *Community health: policy and practice in Australia*, Pluto Press in association with the Australian Community Health Association, Sydney.

Furler, E. 1979. Against hegemony in health care service evaluation, *Community Health Studies*, 3(1), 32–41.

Green, L. W. and Kreuter, M. W. 1991. *Health promotion planning: an educational and environmental approach*, Mayfield, Mountain View, California.

Hawe, P., Degeling, D. and Hall, J. 1990. *Evaluating health promotion: a health workers' guide*. MacLennan and Petty, Sydney.

McDonald, J., Michels, D. and Ryan, P. 1993. National evaluation of CHASP, in Clarke, B. and MacDougall, C. (eds), *The 1993 Community Health Conference*, vol.1, papers and workshops, Australian Community Health Association, Sydney.

McKenzie, J. F. and Jurs, J. L. 1993. *Planning, implementing, and evaluating health promotion programs: a primer*, Macmillan, New York.

Moodie, R. 1989. The politics of evaluating Aboriginal health services, *Community Health Studies*, 13(4), 503–9.

Northern Community Health Research Unit. 1991. *Research and evaluation in community health kit*, Northern Community Health Research Unit, Adelaide.

Owen, A. and Mohr, R. 1986. Commentary: politics and pitfalls in evaluation, *Community Health Studies*, 10(1), 95–9.

Rauch, A. 1992. The development of Community Health Accreditation and Standards Project (CHASP), in Courtney, M. (ed.), *Issues in rural nursing: proceedings of the 1st National Conference of the Association for Australian Rural Nurses*, University of New England, Armidale, NSW.

Rissel, C. 1991. The tyranny of needs assessment in health promotion, *Evaluation Journal of Australia*, 3(1), 26–31.

Rovers, R. 1986. The merging of participatory and analytical approaches to evaluation: implications for nurses in primary health care programs, *International Journal of Nursing Studies*, 23(3), 211–19.

Ryan, P. 1992. *Cases for change: CHASP in practice*, Australian Community Health Association, Sydney.

Sinclair, A. 1993. Reorienting to Primary Health Care: a case for national standards, in Clarke, B. and MacDougall, C. (eds), *The 1993 Community Health Conference*, Vol. 1, papers and workshops, Australian Community Health Association, Sydney.

Stewart-Brown, S. L. and Prothero, D. L. 1988. Evaluation in community development, *Health Education Journal*, 47(4), 156–61.

Wadsworth, Y. 1991. *Everyday evaluation on the run*, Action Research Issues Association, Melbourne.

CHAPTER 5

Using the mass media

The mass media have a powerful influence on people's lives and the manner in which they view the world. In this chapter we will review the ways in which the mass media can be used to lead or support health promotion work, and how we can develop our skills in this area. In doing so, we will examine both the ways in which the mass media can be used by health workers on a broad social level to present information about health issues, and how different forms of media can be used on a smaller scale in developing health education materials for use with individuals and groups.

When health messages are presented in the media, they may be used on a number of levels: they may be used alone, as the 'primary change agent'; they may be used to support other health promotion activity; they may be used to advertise services available; or they may be used to encourage the maintenance of healthy behaviours and to keep health issues on the agenda (Flora and Cassady 1990: 143–8). However, some authors have cautioned against expecting the use of the media by itself to be effective in all types of health education. Nutbeam and Blakey (1990: 237) suggest that while a well-developed media campaign may be useful in raising awareness or influencing public opinion, use of the mass media is not appropriate in helping people develop new skills and behaviours. It is extremely important to bear that in mind when considering use of the media.

There are two key approaches to the use of the mass media in health promotion, representing different philosophical approaches to health promotion generally. They are media advocacy, in which the media are used to lobby for particular health issues, so as to change the way in which the community, including decision makers, sees them; and social marketing, in which the media are used to 'sell' health through a particular health behaviour or health product. However, these two approaches are by no means mutually exclusive, and may both be valuable in health promotion work (Wallack 1990a: 143).

Media advocacy

Media advocacy is about using the media to change the public debate on various issues and the way in which they are seen. It is built very much on the principles of empowerment and participation (Wallack 1990b: 376), and on the recognition that health is a result of the social conditions in which people live. For these reasons it fits well into a Primary Health Care framework.

Media advocacy involves presenting a viewpoint about a particular issue that may not be commonly discussed, in order to raise public awareness and debate and put pressure on those who develop public policy, so that the direction of public policies changes (Wallack 1990a: 150). It is therefore used to influence the environment in which people live and make their choices, with the aim of increasing the opportunity to make healthy choices more easily.

An important part of media advocacy is the framing, or reframing, of an issue. That is, the issue being discussed is presented in a way which is different from the way it is normally presented in the mass media, and which creates a quite different view of the situation. Wallack describes the way in which anti-smoking media advocates began discussing tobacco companies' exploitation of women, children and minority groups to change the public image of tobacco companies (Wallack 1990a: 151–2). Greenpeace has used the same approach through its public events and media campaigns to draw attention to environmental pollution. By drawing attention to pollution caused by large chemical companies in Sydney, for example, Greenpeace works to break down the image of these companies as environmentally responsible and demonstrates their pollution of Sydney waterways. Using the media to reframe an issue, health workers can work to have public policy issues put on the government's policy agenda.

An important part of media advocacy is presenting issues so that they are seen as newsworthy items. That is, rather than focus on discussions in community noticeboard space, media advocacy involves presenting information in such a way that it will run as a news item (Wallack 1990a: 152). This may include contacting local newspapers and television stations and presenting an opinion on a national issue, discussing its local implications, or presenting a totally local issue in a newsworthy style.

Social marketing

Social marketing aims to influence people's behaviour by encouraging healthy choices in individual lives. It is built on the recognition of the powerful influence of the mass media on the choices that people make: not only do television shows provide the images and role models on which people may model themselves, but also advertising influences us to want what we see as being available and desirable. Social marketing aims to use the principles on which advertisers work, but to use them to 'sell' a healthy message and therefore undo some of the work of advertisers who sell products and lifestyles which create ill health.

Of course, this is a huge task. Millions of dollars are spent annually on advertising unhealthy, but profitable, products. Health promoters, even when they are supported by national media campaigns, are in no position to match the extent to which unhealthy products are marketed — they simply do not have the same financial resources at their disposal (Eisenberg 1987: 110).

One recent attempt to help balance the influence of unhealthy and healthy advertising in Australia has been the banning of some unhealthy advertising, most notably tobacco advertising. However, for an impact to be made on unhealthy advertising overall, there would need to be considerable legislative control of advertising. This would be likely to be vigorously opposed, because it would be regarded as seriously eroding people's expectations about freedom of speech and freedom of choice. It would also raise ethical questions about the right of the state to take over the life of the individual. This is by no means a simple issue; after all, it is argued that current media advertising manipulates people's free choice, often beyond recognition (Connell 1977: 195–6). Much of what we decide we want has been constructed by the mass media, but to turn the tables and limit private enterprise control over the media would, so it is argued, threaten the basis of our social existence.

Replacing unhealthy messages with healthy ones: the Victorian Health Promotion Foundation

The Victorian Health Promotion Foundation was established as a result of the *Tobacco Act 1987*. One of the key elements of its work is tobacco replacement in sport sponsorship and billboard advertising. Billboards previously used for advertising tobacco products are now being used to present healthy messages. Many of these are 'quit smoking' messages, while others are healthy messages supporting other health promotion programs (for example, the 'Active at any age' campaign).

This billboard advertising is financed by the 5 per cent levy imposed on tobacco products under the Tobacco Act. It is only because of this unique arrangement that a public health promotion foundation is able to afford the costs of billboard advertising and tobacco replacement messages.

(*Tobacco's out* Ⓢ *Vic Health is in for basketball sponsorship*)

It is to be expected, then, that advertising is here to stay, but within this framework social marketing may have some influence. Those who support social marketing in health promotion believe that it can contribute positively if it is part of an integrated health promotion program and if too much is not expected of it, given the context in which it is being used.

It is important to bear in mind that the advertising industry itself conducts considerable market research and targets its advertising very specifically to the groups it wishes to convince. Health workers simply do not have the resources or the skills to match these activities. This is an important point because it alerts health workers to the problems inherent in trying to emulate (and undo!) the larger campaigns run by the advertisers. Two issues arise here: the need to draw on the expertise of those in the field when planning major advertising campaigns, and the need to work very carefully when running small social marketing campaigns or using the social marketing approach to support other health promotion work.

A question of ethics in social marketing

The whole notion of social marketing does not sit comfortably with everyone. The tactics which advertising companies themselves use are often held to be unethical, since they are based on the idea of influencing people's choices, often without their knowing about it. Using the same tactics, and therefore trying to beat advertisers at their own game, does have some ideological problems.

Much media advertising is built on unhealthy stereotypes of people, and much social marketing seems to accept these unquestioningly, rather than challenge them. There is therefore much work to be done in challenging these stereotypes, which themselves can contribute to narrow views of health and normality and reduced feelings of self-worth in individuals. If social marketing builds on these stereotypes, rather than challenging them, the overall health benefit from any messages may be limited.

Proponents of social marketing argue that it can be used effectively in a way which supports Primary Health Care work and is empowering for those it is designed to assist. For example, it can be used as a reminder of healthy behaviours and therefore be supportive of other health promotion strategies. The principles of Primary Health Care, however, are not an inherent component of social marketing, and so it is up to each individual health promoter to ensure that he or she uses social marketing in a way which supports the principles of Primary Health Care. This may require considerable effort, for, as Joan Byrne's discussion of the use of media campaigns demonstrates (see pp. 112–13), a great many assumptions are made in media health messages.

Balancing the media's presentation of health

Over the last few years, there has been growing media interest in health issues, and this has been largely welcomed by health promoters. If the media themselves take an interest in health issues, health promoters may have to do less work to keep them on the public agenda. However, it may take some work to balance the media's coverage of health issues. Karpf (1988: 9–22) has categorised media coverage of health issues into four groups:

- the medical approach, in which the focus is on disease and the marvels of modern medicine in curing disease, with the doctor as the linchpin in this process;

- the consumer approach, in which problems in the doctor–patient relationship and unfair treatment of people in the health system are examined;

- the look-after-yourself approach, in which the focus is on the behaviour of individuals in preventing ill health (this could also be called the lifestyle approach);

- the environmental approach, in which the focus is on the social and environmental causes of ill health and the need to make changes at those levels if we are to create health in individuals and groups.

It seems that the greater proportion of media coverage of health issues fits into the first three groups, where the focus is on individuals and individual cure, prevention and responsibility for disease. The media play a substantial role in maintaining a focus on individual responsibility for and treatment of disease, which further supports a 'blame the victim' approach to health issues.

Health promoters have an important part to play in trying to reorient the mass media's coverage of health issues, so that due recognition is given to the environmental and social issues which impact on health. Otherwise, the media's growing interest in health issues will serve to further support public belief in high-technology curative medicine at the expense of health promotion. Furthermore, health workers using the mass media have a role to play in ensuring that they use them in a more balanced way, presenting the environmental and structural issues related to health as much as the individual issues. Otherwise, we may end up being part of the problem of unbalanced media presentation of health issues.

Skills in using the mass media

Preliminary work

An important first step in using the mass media is establishing contact with the people who make the decisions in local newspapers, radio stations and television stations, as well as the writers and production people there (Weiss and Kessel 1987: 40). Getting to know all these people may increase the chance of your articles or stories being accepted. Furthermore, speaking to them will enable you to find out more about how you need to present your stories so that they are more likely to be accepted. They may also be able to provide you with some valuable advice on how to improve your presentation skills.

Working with the local press

When I became a community mental health nurse at Kempsey Community Health Centre, I discovered that 10 per cent of my time was to be devoted to health promotion. I decided to offer articles for the 'Go Health' column in the local paper. The health promotion nurse had had a column running for several years and was delighted to acquire an extra writer. As she was so encouraging, I wrote more and more often, and eventually took over responsibility for the column, with her blessing. I wrote about many areas of health, both physical and mental, always in the form of a short story, simply written, with a lot of conversation, and always with some facts, or some information about where to get more facts or seek help. The editor of the paper was particularly helpful and supportive. He always used the stories, was adept at writing a good headline, and made sure they were set up so that they caught the reader's eye and read well. Our successful working relationship contributed much to the quality of the articles published. Unfortunately, good editors move on to better things, and in time he left. There was an interim period when a senior journalist functioned as editor. The stories continued to be used, but without such good headlines, and without so much care being given to presentation. Eventually, a new editor was appointed. It was not possible to develop a positive working relationship with this person, who was prepared to run my stories only if I provided him with 'inside information' about the hospital and photos of newborn babies. I wasn't prepared to do either, and said so politely but firmly. My next story appeared, but it was the last to do so!

Through these experiences, I really came to appreciate the value of a good editor, and if I'm ever in a similar situation, I will always put energy into developing a good working relationship with an editor or journalist.

Anna Treloar
Clinical Nurse Specialist (Mental Health)
Kempsey District Hospital

When you are in touch with any of these people, find out about the deadlines for copy. You will need this information if you are planning on having articles or stories support other work you are doing. It can be very frustrating if you miss the deadline and your story therefore runs too late.

Check the local paper and radio station to see if particular journalists or interviewers seem to have an interest in health issues, and then establish a working relationship with them. Working with those people will be much more useful, since they are the ones most likely to be interested in your stories. They may also be more inclined to call you for information about other issues should they need it. Establishing an ongoing relationship in this way can be useful for both health workers and media people.

A word of warning, however. You will need to check the protocol of the institution for which you are working. Many hospitals and health services require all contact with the mass media to be approved and overseen by the chief executive officer. If that is the case in your area, make sure you use the correct channels and prepare your material sufficiently in advance to enable it to be reviewed and passed on.

What makes an item newsworthy?

If you are hoping to present stories as news, it is worth checking that they are what stations and newspapers regard as newsworthy. Levey (1983, cited by Weiss and Kessel 1987: 40) makes a number of points about newsworthy items. They are as follows:

1. *Information*. The item will need to give information that is new to people or provides a new angle on what they know.

2. *Timeliness*. The item will need to be presented at a time which fits in with other local or national events. Indeed, part of the skill in producing newsworthy items is in taking advantage of other events which are already newsworthy by 'dovetailing' into them. If your item is to be timely, it will also need to be presented far enough ahead of any action in which you are encouraging people to become involved, so that they have the opportunity to become involved if they wish to.

3. *Significance and relevance*. The item will need to present material that is significant and relevant to the lives of the audience. If the relevance is not likely to be obvious to the whole of the audience, the item should outline the significance of the issues discussed.

4. *Scope*. The item will need to be relevant to many community members or a significant group in the community.

5. *Interest*. The item will need to be interesting to the audience. Weiss and Kessel (1987: 40) suggest that items can be made more newsworthy by involving a famous person, linking the story to a national or historical issue, or presenting the story with interesting photographs or cartoons. It is important to note, however, that these things need to be done with some sensitivity or they may backfire. Joan Byrne's discussion of the use of famous sportspeople (usually men) in media campaigns directed at people with arthritis (see pp. 112–13) is a good illustration of this point.

6. *Human interest*. The item is more likely to be newsworthy if it is made directly relevant to the lives of ordinary people or the life of the community.

7. *Uniqueness*. The item is more likely to be newsworthy if it presents an element not found in other stories about the issue.

The more of the above points you can act on, the more likely it is that your item will be accepted for publication. Remember, however, that these are a guide only, and an item which really stands out on one or two of these points may be more newsworthy than an item which just satisfies each point. Since decisions about newsworthiness are made more on the 'feel' of the editor than the application of any equation, the way in which your story is presented and how it appeals to the editor will be a key factor.

Another key factor will be when your story is submitted and what other stories have come in that day. An excellent story may be rejected if it arrives on the editor's desk at the same time as stories about a forthcoming political battle, a bus crash and a rags-to-riches lottery win! In such a case, you may need to wait a few days and resubmit your story. Furthermore, some days are easier for having stories accepted because they are less likely to be days when the media have many stories to deal with. Beauchamp (1986: 76) suggests that Fridays are invariably bad days to submit items, and so should be avoided unless you think you have something that will stop the presses!

Health activities may be better assured of media coverage if the events connected with them are sponsored by the local media. The Taree Community Health Centre in New South Wales, for example, had its 'Walk Oz' program well publicised because the local television station was a sponsor of the program (Sunderland 1993, personal communication).

Do media campaigns motivate people or put additional pressure on them?

The practice of using famous people as role models in media campaigns on arthritis is generally accepted, but does their use motivate those of us who have arthritis, or does it just put unnecessary pressure on us? I think the latter is the case, and as an arthritis activist, researcher and lobbyist with a long personal experience of rheumatoid arthritis, I believe the practice needs to be questioned.

There is a lack of awareness of the impact on people with arthritis, when the achievements of television personalities or sportsmen are continually emphasised during fundraising campaigns. Their achievements certainly help to raise funds, but with the reports of these 'Super Cripps' doing remarkable things despite their arthritis, comes the implication that we should be emulating them, and that is impossible for many of us. Getting out of bed in the morning is a major achievement for some people with arthritis, and these people in particular can do without the 'buck up and go out' treatment presented by current media campaigns.

Our society's obsession with competition and achievement is inappropriate when people are sick. It is also inappropriate to use male role models, when arthritis predominantly affects women. In the Arthritic Women's Task Force's video 'Women with rheumatoid arthri-

tis: don't take us at face value', one of the women talks about the arthritis posters, which depict the achievements of a famous AFL footballer, and the resulting pressures on her also to be an achiever. Those pressures are usually exerted by well-meaning relatives, friends and neighbours, who are impressed by the media campaigns. They do not understand the difference between rheumatoid arthritis and the milder forms of arthritis, and fail to realise the seriousness of her illness. They just look at her face and do not see the rest.

This is probably an even greater problem for those women whose arthritis has not yet reached the obvious stage. They do not look sick, and if their husbands do not understand what rheumatoid arthritis is like, or if their husbands have deserted them, the pressures to achieve, according to male perceptions of achievement, are especially distressing. These women are already aware that they are considered to be inadequate underachievers, and having media pressure put on them, particularly when they are trying to cope with a major flare-up of their arthritis and care for their homes and children at the same time, only increases their problems.

There is another aspect of the practice of using famous people in media campaigns which should be questioned.

That is the failure of the media and the fundraising organisations to recognise the fact that some of these people are doing irreparable harm to their bodies in their determination to achieve stardom, and that they are not, in fact, good role models for people with arthritis to emulate. The pressures on television personalities and sportspeople to perform to a very high standard are just as destructive as the pressures on us to emulate them, and it is distressing to see how soon famous people are forgotten when they are no longer able to perform.

It is extremely difficult for people with arthritis to object to or challenge the way media campaigns are carried out, because the famous people, the fundraisers, the media and the community at large all believe that they are helping us. The concept of charity is deeply rooted in our culture, and we are seen as ungrateful when we question the way it is dispensed. The fact that no one asked us whether we wanted that sort of media campaign, or whether we want to be treated as objects of charity, is overlooked in a sea of hurt feelings.

The needs of a great many people are met when they participate in a media fundraising campaign. It makes them feel good, and until they question the real impact of their actions on us, or until we, the people with arthritis, become politically active consumers, I think the failure of media campaign organisers to recognise the difference between motivation and pressure (the latter exemplified by the threatening slogan 'Move it or Lose it') will persist.

Joan Byrne
Consumer and arthritis activist

Writing to persuade: writing letters and media releases

Rather than merely letting a journalist know that an important event is soon to occur or that a particular issue warrants discussion, and hoping that he or she will write an article about it, you can submit a media release. This increases the chance that the story will run, because most of the work has already been done for the journalist. Moreover, the media release itself may provide the information that convinces the journalist that the issue is a valuable one and a newsworthy item. There may have been many times when journalists have rejected potential news items simply because they did not have enough information at their fingertips.

Similarly, you may want to present your views on an issue to members of a community. Writing a letter to the editor of a local or major newspaper may be a useful way to get your message across. If you can present a good argument, and present it in a way that is interesting, you are more likely to have your letter published.

Whether you are writing a media release, a letter to the editor of a newspaper or a letter to a member of parliament, the key to success is to write persuasively. This takes some practice, but there are a few simple steps to follow to increase the chance that your written material will present a persuasive argument. Keep in mind, also, the elements of a newsworthy item. Firstly, you will need to write clearly and simply, so that your message is understood. Robert Gunning (cited in Anderson and Itule 1988: 39) has suggested 'ten principles of clear writing', which provide a useful guide to help you express yourself. These are:

1. Keep sentences short, on the average.
2. Prefer the simple to the complex.
3. Prefer the familiar word.
4. Avoid unnecessary words.
5. Put action into your verbs.
6. Write the way you talk.
7. Use terms your reader can picture.
8. Tie in with your reader's experience.
9. Make full use of variety.
10. Write to express not impress.

As well as being clearly written, your media release or letter will need to be well structured. Wrigley and McLean (1981: 264) suggest four steps in the development of persuasive writing. They are:

1. Get the reader's attention.
2. Arouse the reader's interest.
3. Motivate the reader to take action.
4. Tell the reader what action to take.

Hints for media releases

- Present the release in typewritten form on A4 paper, double spaced, typed on one side only and with a wide margin.

- Use letterhead paper, so that the organisation presenting the release is clearly identifiable.

- Ensure that the release is clearly dated, or that the date for publication of the material is given.

- Clearly mark the document with the heading 'News Release'.

- Use plain language, and short, sharp sentences.

- Put the most important information first.

- Keep the release short — no more than two pages.

- Suggest an attractive title.

- Include quotations from relevant people.

- Include a contact name and phone number (and be prepared to be contacted).

(Based on Flood and Lawrence [1987: 84–5] and Beauchamp [1986: 71–2])

Hints for writing letters to the editor

- Check the newspaper to which you are writing for any guidelines on presentation of letters.

- Type or write clearly, using double spacing and leaving a wide margin.

- Be as brief as possible. Examining the length of letters previously published may be a useful guide.

- Keep your sentences short and sharp.

- Present constructive criticism, rather than simply being critical.

- Avoid using too much emotional language.

- If you wish to have your letter published anonymously, you can request this, but you will still need to supply your name and address, explaining why you want your name withheld.

- If your letter does not appear, you can contact the Letters Editor to find out why. It is not unusual for letters to take a number of weeks to be published.

(Based on Beauchamp [1986: 64–7])

Get the reader's attention

Wrigley and McLean (1981: 250) suggest two ways in which you can get the reader's attention: using an attractive layout, and making the content relevant to the reader. The layout of the document will give the reader an idea of whether he or she wants to read it, and this is therefore very important. It includes a title which grabs the reader's attention, together with the use of headings and white space to help break up the document. These will be discussed in more detail below. Making the content relevant to the reader will need to start with your being clear about whom you intend the article for and writing with that audience in mind. Writing to the reader (by saying 'you' and 'your'), focusing on people, using graphics where appropriate and keeping your message simple and clear will all help.

Arouse the reader's interest

You will need to arouse the reader's interest through your title and the first paragraph of your document, which, like any good introduction, should summarise what the document will tell the reader.

Motivate the reader to take action

You will need to present a succinct summary of the issues in a way which helps the reader to work through the facts and come to an opinion. You can do this by arranging information in a logical order, explaining where necessary and documenting any new or contentious information you present.

Tell the reader what action to take

Although putting all the above into practice may have convinced the reader that your message is valid, your aim is often to do more than that. If the aim is to encourage people to act on an issue, you need to tell them what action they can take. If you do not do so, they may feel more informed when they have finished reading, but no more sure of what to do. It is important, then, that you tell them clearly what they can do to make a difference.

Martin Street story in the news

When the residents of the Martin Street subdivision in Armidale, New South Wales, began dealing with environmental pollution in the land on which their homes were built, they made sure that the local media knew about all the important things as they happened. They presented their perspective, being careful not to overstate the facts so that people were not turned against the issue, and worked for three and a half years to keep the story in the media. Many of their actions were newsworthy because of the way in which they presented the story. For example, a year after the environmental pollution was discovered, they constructed a large cross inscribed 'Martin St subdivision died 15.1.90. R.I.P.'. This had great visual and emotional impact, and a photo of it appeared on the front page of the local newspaper as the lead story. Throughout their fight for environmental health, many such stories have appeared in the local paper. Residents are aware of the value of visual impact, and make sure that they inform the local media whenever an opportunity to take a good photo arises.

Martin St residents mourn the anniversary of the creosote discovery in their subdivisions.

Martin St residents' unhappy anniversary

It is 12 months today since creosote contamination was discovered on a block of land fronting Martin St.

One year after this discovery residents of the contaminated subdivision are bewildered, angry and concerned that they appear to be no closer to a solution than they were in January 1990.

Spokeswoman for the residents Mrs Irene Thompson said that there was general concern that they were awaiting results of a second report on the subdivision.

Mrs Thompson said: "It is time that something positive was done to resolve the problems facing residents.

"Over the past 12 months we have heard a great many words but witnessed very little action.

"Why is it that our children are still forced to play on land contaminated by copper chrome arsenate and creosote

"All available information indicates that the components of creosote are all either known or highly suspected of being carcinogenic."

Mrs Thompson said that many people were now questioning why the present consultants AGC Woodward-Clyde had not carried out further tests.

She said that the 25 metre grid used by Sinclair Kinight and Partners was always intended as a base for further testing.

"Every report we have seen indicates there was a strong possibility of further hot spots"

"Residents have faced 12 months of worry and concern about our health and financial future.

"One resident has recently been retrenched but cannot accept an offered transfer because of the impossibility of selling the family home in Martin Street."

● Support for residents, Page 2

Using photographs

Whether you are submitting a press release to a journalist or simply asking him or her to cover a particular issue, providing a photo, or advising of a photo opportunity so that the journalist can take a photo, will help your story in two ways. Firstly, it will increase the chance that your story will be published, because it will be a more interesting piece for the newspaper to print with a photo nearby. Secondly, because your story has visual appeal, more people are likely to read it when it appears in the paper. Photos, then, can attract a reader and persuade just as successfully as words, and sometimes even more so. If you are providing a photo, it will need to be of a high quality and preferably black-and-white, although a sharply contrasted colour photo may be acceptable.

Advertising a program

When you are advertising a health promotion activity or event, many of the principles of persuasive writing are relevant. In particular, you need to attract people's attention and motivate them to act, and provide information about how they can obtain further information.

Advertising a new group

When I was planning to run a new self-esteem group for women, I needed to advertise the program in a way which was lively, non-threatening, fun and different enough to catch the reader's attention. The advertisement, which was placed in the community health centre, the TAFE, and some doctors' waiting rooms, and sent out to some women in the community (as part of a personal letter), read as follows.

Announcing: the PYF group for women

What's PYF? You pronounce it 'Piff' and it stands for 'Put Yourself First'. How much chance do you have to do that in your everyday life? Do you think you deserve to put yourself first sometimes? Would you be game to have a try?

We will be a small group (about six) and will meet once a week for one and a half hours for six weeks at 10.30 am, on Wednesdays at the Community Health Centre. We won't be discussing our problems (except incidentally) or sitting around feeling depressed. I hope we'll have fun together and be able to put a higher price on ourselves at the end of the meetings. Curious? Why not give it a go? It's free!

Anna Treloar
Clinical Nurse Specialist (Mental Health)
Kempsey District Hospital

Preparing for a radio or television interview

Radio and television interviews are useful means of getting across a message to a wide audience. However, since the pace is usually fast, complex issues are often not given the depth they may require. Because of the fast pace, preparation for such an interview is important.

Wherever possible, present your interviewer with a list of the questions you believe should be asked in order to cover the topic. You may need to explain to this person why the questions you have chosen are important, but it is well worth the effort. There is nothing worse than a two-minute interview disappearing without having got your message across because the interviewer did not understand a basic point, which you could have clarified beforehand, and subsequently asked an irrelevant question.

Using television to discuss health and illness issues

My first television interview! Yes, I was nervous, but I was also looking forward to it. I was to talk on the local television station about the need for a hostel for the frail aged in Hervey Bay, Queensland, and to encourage the community to support it financially. It was a subject I knew well, so it held no fears for me. After the first session I spoke with the show's compere (Melissa Davies) and we found that we shared a concern about the community's lack of access to information on health issues. We decided to start a regular health issues segment. We agreed that the range of topics was probably infinite, and so we decided to start on a small scale. I was to do a four-minute segment once a month.

It sounded so simple. I would send the compere a topic and the sort of information that I wanted to cover, and she would do the rest. But I started to feel frustration! Four minutes went so quickly and I found that I was not covering all of my subject. We discussed the problem and I offered to write my own questions, with brief notes on the answers I would give. That proved much more successful, although I was still surprised at how quickly four minutes went by.

In 1991, with the restructuring of television services, Melissa was given a daily show and I was given the opportunity to have a four-minute segment every week. We tried to tie these in with nominated health weeks, such as National Heart Week or Diabetes Awareness Week. We covered many topics, but the ones that created most public response were a series of three on continence. In the first segment I discussed continence promotion and then followed up with two segments which examined the impact of continence education and the aids which are available to people who are incontinent. The response was heart-warming — many people (mainly women) had just not known that there was an alternative to incontinence and being confined to the house.

During 1992 we covered many subjects, from childhood immunisations to Alzheimer's disease, from asthma and its treatment to caring for someone who has suffered a stroke, from healthy eating to HIV infection, from breast self-examination to management of diabetes. We also had sessions on relaxation, medication and women's issues.

Putting subjects into plain language that people would listen to and understand was an exciting challenge. The informal feedback we received from the general public indicated that having a nurse talking about health issues was well received. Presenting health discussions to local people, using a local television station and local health staff, provides an excellent opportunity to give people access to the information they need if they are to make the most of their lives and make informed decisions.

Judyth Collard
Director of Nursing
Blue Nursing Service
Tablelands, Queensland

In addition to presenting your interviewer with questions, prepare your answers, even if you will be talking on a topic that you feel you know like the back of your hand. It is very easy to become nervous and forget what you wanted to say. Also, because you will not have very long to answer the interviewer's questions, you need to make sure you say the most important things first. Preparing answers in advance will help you to do that. There is no shame in not doing totally off-the-cuff interviews; indeed, only very experienced interviewees can usually get away with them.

If you are not able to provide your interviewer with a list of questions, you should be able to discuss with that person beforehand the questions he or she plans on asking you. Use this discussion as an opportunity to suggest other questions if you feel they are appropriate. Remember, you are likely to know more about the topic than the interviewer, and he or she will usually appreciate any suggestions which will improve the quality of the interview. Once again, take the time to plan your answers, making sure that you give your most important information first.

Find out if the interview is going to be pretaped or live. If it is pretaped, there will be an opportunity for it to be edited if necessary. You may be able to request that your interview be pretaped if you are nervous and being interviewed for the first time; many interviewers will be happy to oblige if it is possible.

One valuable hint when being interviewed, even on radio, is to ensure that you make eye contact with the interviewer. Maintaining eye contact with the interviewer, rather than reading your notes, is enough to help keep your voice sounding conversational. If you read from something, your voice can very often become a monotone. However, talking directly to the interviewer as much as possible will help keep your voice interesting.

Controversial topics and radio/TV interviews

You may find yourself being interviewed on a controversial topic. If so, you may find an interviewer who asks you a question for which you are unprepared. This may be part of a deliberate strategy by the journalist to create some controversy. The important thing to remember in these situations is to stay focused on the issue and not get caught up in the controversy that is being created. This takes some self-discipline but is well worth it if you do not want to cloud the issues. Since health issues can so often involve differences of opinion, it is a good idea to go into every interview expecting the unexpected!

Preparing health education materials

Using media to support or strengthen a personal health message is increasingly part of health promotion work. It is vital, therefore, that you understand enough about their use so that you can critically review any materials you are considering using, in order to determine whether they are appropriate to the needs of the people you are hoping to use them with. With some skills in this area, you will also be able to develop your own material if nothing suitable is available. Below are some general principles which guide the way in which these materials are produced for maximum effect.

Written materials

Written materials, such as brochures, posters and booklets, can provide useful reinforcement for other health education materials and enable people to take information home with them. With any written materials, a few key elements can make the difference between a readable, appealing document and one which does not invite the potential reader to go beyond a casual glance. These are the use of white space, a variety of print sizes, readable language, and drawings and photographs to help any words used come alive.

White space

White space is simply the amount of empty space left in the document. It is very important, because without adequate white space, a document can seem crowded and difficult to read. Space between words and paragraphs helps potential readers to see that the document is unlikely to swamp them, and will help them to stay clear as they work their way through it.

Variety of print sizes

Varying the print size, through the use of headings and different type fonts, makes the words on the page interesting and again helps to break it up. Headings which stand out also act as a summary of the document for people flipping through it, and so enable them to see if they would like to continue reading.

Readable language

Of course, no amount of variety in print size will counteract words which are difficult to understand or unreadable by the people your materials are supposedly designed for. So many written materials produced for health education contain language which makes the information in them inaccessible to many people. A number of formulas to assess the readability of education materials have been suggested (see, for example, Hawe et al. 1990: 70–2). Involving some of the people you are designing the materials for in the development process will ensure that they are readable. It will also ensure that they are appropriate and acknowledge the expertise of these people in issues related to their own lives. (Schwab et al. 1992 provide an example of how this process was implemented in the preparation of a Wellness Guide. It is apparent that the developers of this guide gained a great deal more than a 'readability test' from involving people in the development process.)

Drawings and photographs

Drawings and photographs are key ingredients in written health education materials. Indeed, there are times when they may appropriately represent all the 'writing' in the document. The old saying 'A picture is worth a thousand words' is relevant here. Drawings and photos may well tell the reader a great deal more than words alone could do, and this is the case not only for people who have difficulty in reading, but for all readers. Drawings and photos help to make sense of

Check for hidden meanings in drawings!

Some time ago two student nurses, gaining experience in health education and promotion as part of their studies, were asked to talk to a group of older people on arthritis and self-help strategies. They worked hard preparing their materials, which included a number of posters to use as teaching aids. One of these posters showed a knee joint, to help demonstrate the physical impact of arthritis. One student was explaining the process of arthritis, using the poster of a knee joint to assist her. After approximately five minutes, a member of the group inquired, 'That's a stomach, isn't it?'

Although any student of human bioscience has been trained to recognise a synovial joint at fifty paces, laypeople clearly do not have the same mind-set! Pictures of the human body, particularly its internal functions, need to be put in context if they are to help, rather than confuse, people trying to learn a little more about how their bodies work.

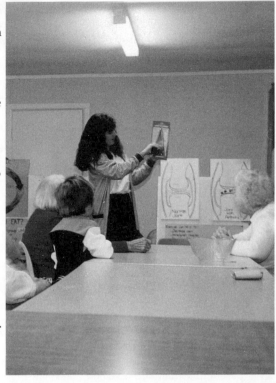

any words, and may clarify things which are expressed with difficulty in words. They also give the document appeal and break up any writing in much the same way as white space does.

A word of caution about drawings, however. Ensure that they make sense to the people you are presenting the material for. Drawings, like words, have readability levels. Health workers have a range of knowledge about matters of health and illness, and it is easy to forget how much of this is not shared by members of the community. This point is demonstrated very well by the example above.

Audiovisual materials

Videos and audiotapes can provide useful health education in a form that is often more interesting than written materials and accessible to people who do not have good literacy skills. They may also be preferred by many people, those who learn more readily through listening and watching than through reading.

If you wish to make a video, it is well worth having the expertise of an experienced producer; otherwise, you may waste valuable resources, including time. Producing a video is expensive, but it is possible to keep the costs down by engaging a producer to take on the role of consultant.

The process of making a video can itself be a valuable educational experience if you involve community members in developing it. In addition, materials produced by community members themselves are more likely to address a group's needs and be acceptable to it. In fact, amateur videos may be quite successful if made by members of the group whose needs you are addressing, and can be very useful teaching tools.

'Koorie Booris Need Ears That Hear' — using video as part of a Primary Health Care project

The Aboriginal Hearing Program is a program which was designed after a needs assessment in the local community. It focuses on a single problem and utilises resources in the local community to help develop awareness of the problem of hearing loss in its children, and then address it.

The needs assessment took the form of a mass audiometry and questionnaire screening of Aboriginal children at a local public school. It showed that 20 per cent of the children tested had a significant hearing problem. Evaluation of the parent questionnaire revealed that while parents recognised that their children had signs of ear problems and hearing loss, they did not realise that these could be significant or have serious sequelae.

Before it was attempted to design a program to address this problem, the Koorie community and Koorie health education officers were consulted to enable a culturally acceptable and accessible program to be designed. What resulted was a three-pronged program, covering screening, follow-up services and awareness and education.

It was decided that a video should form the basis of the awareness and education program. The visual media, it was felt, would be more appropriate than written media, as storytelling is still an important method of relaying information in Koorie communities.

On the basis of the needs assessment, which indicated that parents could identify signs of hearing loss, but did not always seek intervention, the video was targeted at Koorie families and focused on the importance of intervention rather than actual detection. One of the goals of the video was to increase community development within the Koorie community, and to encourage families to own the issue and seek help rather than be told what to do by a health worker.

The first step was planning the video. Its length had to be decided in advance, as this determined how much information was to be included, how it would be presented and, of course, how much the video would cost to make.

Before the script was written, a rough plan of who could or should be involved in the video was drawn up. At this stage, the Aboriginal health education officer gauged community support and asked many members of the community to take part. Everyone was eager to have their children involved and the local Aboriginal preschool was chosen as the most appropriate location for shooting. Getting adults actually to appear on the video was much more difficult. Most were too shy to appear but came along on shooting day to lend support. The Aboriginal health education officer acted as presenter. He introduced the topic, interviewed parents and provided the voice-over for visual shots. All his lines were carefully scripted to ensure that accurate information was conveyed in an appropriate manner that would be easily understood. All the Koorie parents and children spoke spontaneously, as it was felt that they would feel more comfortable this way and their own words would mean more to those watching the video than any script could.

Members of the Koorie community also arranged and played culturally acceptable music to open and close the video. The video has many shots of children laughing, playing and singing. On the day of shooting all the parents were eager that Koorie people be portrayed in a very positive manner, and were also a little apprehensive that this would not happen.

From the earliest planning stages, it had been our aim to produce a video that would be positive, enthusiastic and informative. The result was a seven-minute video which has been accepted very well by the Koorie community and also by non-Koorie workers.

The Aboriginal Hearing Program is now entering its fifth year and is still growing. Thanks to adequate planning, implementation, evaluation and modification, it has become increasingly accepted and used. The video, 'Koorie booris need ears that hear', still forms the cornerstone of our awareness and education program, but it is important to see it as the beginning of a complete program and not just an end in itself. The program as a whole is a good example of Primary Health Care, one in which workers work with the community to achieve a goal.

Karen Williams
Paediatric Clinical Nurse Specialist
Griffith Community Health Centre

Adapting material from state or national campaigns to your local area

There may be times when your agency is implementing a campaign developed at a level somewhat removed from that of your workplace. For example, the region's Public Health Unit or the state's Health Promotion Unit may plan a health promotion program to be implemented in a number of areas. You may be provided with health education materials as part of the program. Once you are satisfied that the need addressed is relevant to your local area, you will have to assess the materials to decide whether they are relevant to your community or group. If they are not, you may be able to adapt them to suit the specific needs of your group, or you may need to put them aside and develop your own materials.

Conclusion

This chapter has reviewed the various ways in which the mass media can be used to promote health; most notably, media advocacy and social marketing. Whether you are working in collaboration with media specialists on a major program or working with colleagues to use the media in local health promotion activity, the principles outlined in this chapter provide a framework for working with the mass media.

REFERENCES AND FURTHER READINGS

Anderson, D. A. and Itule, B. D. 1988. *Writing the news*, Random House, New York.

Beauchamp, K. 1986. *Fixing the government: everyone's guide to lobbying in Australia*, Penguin, Ringwood, Victoria.

Chesterfield-Evans, A. 1988. Why the media makes you sick: aspects of the relationship between the media and public health, *Australian Journal of Communication*, 14, 34–47.

Connell, R. 1977. *Ruling class, ruling culture*, Cambridge University Press, Cambridge.

Eisenberg, L. 1987. Value conflicts in social policies for promoting health, in Doxiadis, S. (ed.), *Ethical dilemmas in health promotion*, John Wiley and Sons, Chichester, UK.

Flay, B. R. 1987. Mass media and smoking cessation: a critical review, *American Journal of Public Health*, 77, 153–60.

Flood, M. and Lawrence, A. 1987. *The Community Action Book*, NSW Council of Social Services, Sydney.

Flora, J. A. and Cassady, D. 1990. Roles of media in community-based health promotion, in Bracht, N. (ed.), *Health promotion at the community level*, Sage Publications, Newbury Park, USA.

Hastings, G. and Haywood, A. 1991. Social marketing and communication in health promotion, *Health Promotion International*, 6(2), 135–45.

Hawe, P., Degeling, D. and Hall, J. 1990. *Evaluating health promotion: a health workers' guide*, McLennan and Petty, Sydney.

Hevey, D. 1992. Fear for sale, *New Internationalist*, July, 20–2.

Karpf, A. 1988. *Doctoring the media*, Routledge, London.

Novelli, W. D. 1990. Applying social marketing to health promotion and disease prevention, in Glanz, K., Lewis, F. M. and Rimer, B. K. (eds), *Health behavior and health education: theory research and practice*, Jossey Bass, San Francisco.

Nutbeam, D. and Blakey, V. 1990. The concept of health promotion and AIDS prevention: a comprehensive and integrated basis for action in the 1990s, *Health Promotion International*, 5(3), 233–42.

Palmer, D. 1992. Mass media for health promotion: health Leninists or change agents?, *Australian Journal of Public Health*, 16(2), 206–7.

Research Unit in Health and Behavioural Change. 1989. *Changing the public health*, John Wiley and Sons, Chichester, UK.

Schwab, M., Neuhauser, L., Margen, S., Syme, S. L., Ogar, D., Roppel, C. and Elite, A. 1992. The Wellness Guide: towards a new model for community participation in health promotion, *Health Promotion International*, 7(1), 27–36.

Spark, R. and Mills, P. 1988. Promoting Aboriginal health on television in the Northern Territory: a bicultural approach, *Drug Education Journal of Australia*, 2(3), 191–8.

Tones, K., Tilford, S. and Robinson, Y. 1990. *Health education: effectiveness and efficiency*, Chapman and Hall, London.

Wallack, L. 1990a. Two approaches to health promotion in the mass media, *World Health Forum*, 11, 143–64.

Wallack, L. 1990b. Media advocacy: promoting health through mass communication, in Glanz, K., Lewis, F. M. and Rimer, B. K. (eds), *Health behavior and health education: theory research and practice*, Jossey Bass, San Francisco.

Weiss, E. H. and Kessel, G. 1987. Practical skills for health educators on using mass media, *Health Education*, June/July, 39–41.

Windschuttle, K. 1984. *The media*, Penguin, Ringwood, Victoria.

Wodak, A. 1991. I feel like an alcohol advertisement, *Australian Journal of Public Health*, 15(3), 170–1.

Wrigley, J. and McLean, P. 1981. *Australian Business Communication*, Longman Cheshire, Melbourne.

CHAPTER 6

Community development

Working at the level of the community, and community development in particular, has become very popular in the health field since the Declaration of Alma-Ata highlighted community development and community participation as important strategies for health promotion. Before that, many health workers were unfamiliar with the concept of community development, although it had been used in other fields and by health workers in developing countries for some time.

An essential component of the Primary Health Care approach to health promotion is the recognition that it is necessary to change the structures that influence people's lives in order to improve their health. There is also recognition that people themselves have a right to work for changes to those structures. A key challenge in health promotion work is to put these ideas into practice by encouraging and supporting community-led and community-controlled activities, rather than only those activities that are led and controlled by health workers or the health system.

In community-level work, the environment, rather than the individual, is defined as the target for change (Labonté 1986: 347). As a result, community-level work is appealing because it has the potential to address some of the structural issues which lead to poor health. In addressing those issues, community-level work is more obviously political than other health work, since it means working for change to create social justice. While any form of health work is political in nature (since it involves either acting for social change or as social control — see Connell 1977: 219), in community-level work the political nature of the health worker's action is usually more explicit.

In this chapter we will examine ways of working *with* communities, through community development, and in the following chapter we will examine ways of working *for* communities to help create healthy public policy and supportive environments.

What is a community?

In chapter 2, we briefly examined the question of what a community is and reviewed some of the key issues in considering community and community health. Important points discussed include the multiple ways in which the term has been defined and the value-laden nature of the term, which is often used in an 'add-on' way to help create a positive bias for government programs or to help disguise the exploitative nature of such things as community care. We also examined definitions of 'community', which are often geographically based, and 'community of interest', which recognises that communities may be built around a common interest or concern. We noted further that, importantly, communities often include groups with conflicting interests, and that this fact is often hidden behind the romantic connotations of the term 'community' (see pp. 36–8).

These issues are of particular importance in considering community development, since it is not immune to these issues. Indeed, workers using the community development process may have to consider the implications of these issues for their work on a regular basis.

A sense of community

A number of writers describe what they call a 'sense of community'. This is an ideal state in which everyone affected by the life of the community participates in that life, the community as a whole takes responsibility for its members and respect for the individuality of the members is maintained (Daly and Cobb 1989: 172). It is described by Clark (1973: 409) as a 'sense of solidarity and a sense of significance'. Two points are worth making here. Firstly, this description of an ideal sense of community is reminiscent of romantic descriptions of community life, and we need to take care not to oversimplify the consequences of human beings living in communities. Secondly, we must be careful not to assume that this sense of community is an ideal state for everyone, because some people may not choose living in community as their ideal.

However, this sense of community can be an important component of people feeling as though they belong to a community, and it also has implications for the process of community development.

What is community development?

Community development is increasingly recognised as the process by which health workers are most able to work *with* communities. It is quite a complex concept, and one not easily captured in a simple definition. It is also fraught with ambiguities and is often described in a simplistic manner and applied uncritically. Some of the particular issues surrounding it will be discussed in the following pages. The more general issues of the uncritical use of community development parallel those discussed previously about participation (see pp. 43–9).

Community development has been defined as a process of moving towards the state of 'community' described above (Dixon 1992: 2). That is, community development aims to increase people's participation in the life of their community and the interdependence of community members. It has also been defined as a process of 'working with people as they define their own goals, mobilize resources, and develop action plans for addressing problems they collectively have identified' (Minkler 1991: 261).

While the latter definition was coined to refer to community organisation, it describes community development. The terms community development and community organisation are both defined variously, and often overlap in their definition. Rothman (1987) describes community development as one form of community organisation. Egger et al. (1990: 87) have described the difference between the two terms as one of directiveness, because they regard community organisation as being a process more directed by workers, while community development is more directed by members of the community.

Sanders' four views of community development

Sanders (1958, cited by Dixon, 1989: 86–7) argued that community development may be seen as a process, a method, a program and a movement. You will notice the similarity here to the different ways in which Primary Health Care is conceptualised. You will also notice the way in which these four aspects are inextricably linked.

The community development process

The community development process is the series of steps that an outsider would normally take in establishing community development. These steps have been listed as 'establish felt needs, use local leadership, foster self-help and follow up with an institution to carry forward the gains' (Walker 1982, cited by Dixon 1989: 87).

The community development method

The community development method is described as community development as 'a means to an end' (Dixon 1989: 86). As a method, community development is used to increase the autonomy and competence of the community, through its involvement in decision-making and problem-solving processes (1989: 87).

Community development programs

Community development programs are those programs which use the community development method and process in their implementation.

The community development movement

The themes of collectivity and empowerment which run through community development represent a particular philosophical approach which sits comfortably within Primary Health Care. This community development philosophy can guide the way in which people work, even when they are not working on community development programs, and is likely to sensitise them to times when community development is appropriate. Sanders (1958) argues that widespread support for this philosophy represents a community development movement.

Concepts in community development

At this point, it will be valuable to examine in more detail the key concepts in community development. Together, these help construct a picture of what community development practice is about. Perhaps the two most important ones are the community's identification of its own needs and the importance of the *process* as well as the *outcome* of the participation of community members in the community development process. Other important concepts, identified by Minkler (1991: 267–74), are empowerment, creating critical consciousness, the development of community competence and the careful selection of issues to be dealt with.

Need

In working with need in the community, community developers are particularly concerned with the needs of those who have little power, since it is these people who are most likely to be suffering ill health as a result of their lack of access to, and influence over, the structural things which are impacting negatively on their health. If these people are not skilled in articulating their needs or do not believe they are likely to have them met and so do not express them, finding out what they believe they need may be a slow (but important) part of the community development process.

You will recall that in chapter 3 we examined Bradshaw's typology of needs, which emphasised that needs may be identified either by people themselves or by 'experts'. This is a particularly useful framework in community development, because unless we start from where people are at we are unlikely to succeed, since they will not be committed to act on issues which they do not see as relevant to them. Therefore, the people must identify the needs being addressed (that is, felt or expressed needs must be present); for otherwise they will be unlikely to involve themselves in working for change or to support it in any other way.

Although the presence of felt need is a prerequisite for community development, relying on its presence alone may mean that communities will act on problems they see without fully understanding the issues. The presence also of comparative need or normative need will increase the likelihood that the work will be successful. For example, if a community is working for increased public housing in its area, evidence of a low rate of public housing or a high rate of people on low incomes (comparative need) will provide valuable support for increased housing, and will be a stronger argument than if residents' demand for more housing was the only rationale.

Participation — process and outcome

In chapter 2, we discussed the range of approaches to participation (see pp. 43–9). In examining the importance of participation by community members in community development, it is apparent that those aspects of participation appropriate in Primary Health Care generally are also the approaches to participation necessary in community development. In other words, for the process of participation to be empowering, it must be one of true participation rather than manipulation. Control over decision making by community members is encouraged and supported by health workers with a community development philosophy. A fundamental part of community development is participation which fits into the upper rungs of Arnstein's Ladder of Citizen Participation (see p. 136). This is where power is shared between workers and community members, or may even be completely handed over to community members.

As mentioned before, the process of participation in change is often considered to be just as important as the outcome. By participating in community development, people gain skills in such things as negotiation, submission writing, organisation, working with the media and working as part of a group. These skills, the networks people establish with others in the community and their sense of being able to negotiate the system and achieve something are regarded as valuable, and sometimes as more valuable than any outcome of the group's activity.

However, although the process elements of community development are extremely important, giving more importance to them than to the outcome elements has some limitations. There is a real danger that this is paternalistic towards community members, for it effectively says that even though they worked long and hard and lost, it was good for them. Community members themselves may not define this as success, but rather may be quite horrified by the suggestion (though if they learnt from the process, they may acknowledge this some time later). Certainly the process of involvement may be very important for community members, but they may regard it as such only if they are successful in achieving what they set out to achieve.

The particular process and outcome elements of community development have been described by Butler and Cass (1993: 10) as follows:

Process elements

Control of decision-making — community members participate to control the project and particularly to control the identification and definition of the issue.

Involvement in action — the project involves the people concerned with the issue in action for change.

Development of community culture — the project contributes to a culture of groups of individuals taking responsibility for improving and protecting their area and services.

Organisational development — the project builds a new organisation or improves an existing one.

Learning — the participants are acquiring new skills, information and/or new perspectives on themselves, their community and their concerns.

Objective elements

Concrete benefit — the project sees the achievement of some new or improved service or facility, or the protection of something valued by the community.

New power relationships — the project changes the social landscape of the community so that new and more equitable power relations are formed (this is also a process aspect).

Empowerment and the creation of critical consciousness

Central to community development is the importance of empowerment of those people for whom the activity is occurring. Empowerment within the community development context has been defined as:

> a social action process that promotes participation of people, organizations, and communities in gaining control over their lives in their community and larger society. With this perspective, empowerment is not characterized as achieving power to dominate others, but rather power to act with others to effect change. (Wallerstein and Bernstein 1988: 380)

Two important points about empowerment are worth noting. Firstly, empowerment is a term which is currently popular and tends to be used quite frequently, often in a band-aid fashion without consideration of the real implications of the term. Secondly, empowerment is not something which can be 'done to' someone. Rather, people can only empower themselves (Labonté 1989: 87), and, indeed, if empowerment is forced upon people, can it rightly be called empowerment?

If people are to gain greater power over their lives, they need greater access to information, supportive relationships, decision making and resources (Benn 1981: 82), and health workers can play an important role in creating a climate for empowerment by enabling access to these things. Empowerment is not about people simply feeling better about themselves, but rather about people improving their control over issues impacting on them (Hawe et al. 1990: 115).

Workers using the community development process focus on those people who have the least power, and endeavour to improve their level of control over the situations impacting on their lives. Often the first step in this process of empowerment is critical consciousness raising (Friere 1973). In other words, people need to see the causes of their problems as they are rooted in the social, political and economic structures which constrain their lives before they can be ready to work to change those structures.

This empowerment needs to occur at the level of the outcome of the community development activity and at the level of the process of action and communication. That is, it is not acceptable to take over from community members in order to achieve a positive outcome for them, when in the process they are left feeling no more capable, or even less capable, of acting more independently next time. While there may be times when quick action on issues by workers is warranted, this action cannot be described as community development.

Minkler (1991: 267) suggests that empowerment needs to occur on two levels: individuals need to be empowered by the process and the community as a whole also needs to be empowered. If empowerment occurs at the individual level only, we would have to question whether *community* development has been occurring (Dixon 1992).

One last point is worth emphasising: empowerment is about increasing people's power over things influencing their lives, but power is rarely a neutral concept. An increase in the power that one person or group has over something in their lives will often result in someone else losing that power. This fact is extremely important because it reminds us that while ever community development concerns itself with the empowerment of people, those involved in the process risk experiencing conflict. Although consensus building is an important part of community development, conflict may be an inherent part of it as well.

Community competence

Very much linked to community empowerment is the concept of community competence (Minkler 1991: 268). A competent community is one which is able to recognise and address its problems. If a community learns to better solve its own problems, then it is being empowered and becoming a more competent community.

Hawe et al. (1990: 114) suggest that an increase in a community's competence can be examined by considering 'changes in the community itself, its networks, its structures, the way in which people perceive the community, ownership of community issues, [and] perceived and actual "empowerment" in health and social issues'.

Careful selection of issues

A number of writers suggest that the choice of issues used in community development is important. Minkler (1991: 272) suggests that if an issue is to be a good one for community development, the community must feel strongly about it, and it must be 'winnable, simple and specific'. She argues that this is particularly the case early in the community development process. Once people have started to develop a sense of their ability to effect change, they may be less easily swamped by resistance from others, or by lack of success on a particular issue. In the early stages, however, failure or resistance may lead the group to give up, and so starting with winnable issues while people develop some skills can be useful. Other, more difficult issues can then be tackled, with people building on the skills that they have already developed through these experiences.

In practice, however, this idea of starting with winnable issues may not be realistic, since it may well be a difficult, even almost unwinnable, issue which brings a community to the point of wanting to act. In that case, the idea of starting with winnable issues goes out the door! This is more likely to be so where the community development process begins spontaneously, as a result of people responding to an issue crucial to their lives.

The role of the health worker in community development

> *Go to the people*
> *Live among them*
> *Love them*
> *Start with what they know*
> *Build on what they have*
> *But of the best leaders*
> *When their task is accomplished*

> *Their work is done*
> *The people all remark*
> *We have done it ourselves*

(Chabot 1976, cited by Ashton 1990: 8)

The approach described by the poem above is the approach taken by a health worker using a community development approach. However, the community development process may also begin without the assistance of employed health workers. Local people and community leaders are often committed to using that process and may work away quietly in their own areas or groups, attempting to build consensus and initiate collective action to address people's needs. (See Henderson and Thomas 1987 and Twelvetrees 1987 for a more detailed examination of the approach to take when 'entering the community').

Health workers have an important role to play in supporting the people involved in community development, whether the community development process began through the efforts of strong local leaders or was instigated by health workers themselves. There are a number of reasons for this. Firstly, it is quite clear that the Ottawa Charter for Health Promotion urges health workers to take up community development strategies if they are to promote the health of the people they are working for. This may mean that their work becomes uncomfortable because it has political implications, but it is not sufficient reason for us to ignore this way of working. Secondly, health workers are well placed to work for community development, because they come into contact with members of marginalised groups as part of their everyday work. Indeed, because of the special relationship that develops between many health workers and their clients, the context in which they work and the 'crisis' situations in which they often meet their clients, health workers are often already in a position of trust with regard to these community members. In addition, their close involvement with people in crisis situations means that they see quite clearly the health implications of poverty and disempowerment. On the other hand, however, health workers may still need to break free from some community perceptions that they should be dealing directly with illness through clinical services only.

A health worker working with people in a community development mode places particular emphasis on the roles of enabler, catalyst, coordinator, teacher of problem-solving skills, small-group facilitator and advocate (Rothman 1987: 17). You can see once again how well this fits in with the particular roles of advocate, enabler and mediator which the Ottawa Charter for Health Promotion highlighted as important roles for health workers in health promotion action.

How might these roles be translated into everyday practice?

There are a number of things that health workers or health centres can do to effectively resource and support a community if they are to take up their responsibility for community development and health promotion. These can be valuable whether the community development activity in progress began spontaneously or as a result of worker 'encouragement' (although greater support may be needed if the activity did not begin spontaneously, as it is likely that the community involved did not have many skills to begin with). Some of the political nature of community development work may become apparent as you consider the health worker activities described below.

Providing resources

Workers can support the community by providing necessary resources in their campaign. These might include access to photocopying and typing facilities and the use of meeting rooms if this is necessary. (The group may want to meet in its own environment, as many community health centres have not sufficiently broken down the barriers between themselves and the community, so that groups would choose the centre as their preferred meeting place. Furthermore, the fact that many community health centres are not centrally located may be inconvenient.)

Assisting with skills development

Community members may need assistance with developing skills in such things as communicating with the media, writing press releases and writing letters to members of parliament, the public service or local companies involved in a particular issue. Health workers can be active in teaching people how to carry out these tasks effectively in order to get the message across.

Assisting with research

Health workers may have better skills than community members in researching information, and better access to databases holding useful information. They can therefore assist communities in developing their research skills where appropriate and can themselves conduct research through information systems to which members of the public may not have easy access.

Planning action

If health workers have a better knowledge than community members of the bureaucratic process and other useful channels to follow and approaches to take, they can provide valuable information which will help the community group to plan an effective campaign. This can save it much worry and uncertainty, as well as a great deal of valuable energy that might have been wasted if the group had acted inappropriately owing to lack of knowledge.

Supporting localism

While not all communities are locality-based, many of them are. Health workers can support opportunities for community development through actions which support the local community. For example, ecouraging the establishment of local credit cooperatives will help keep local money in the local area and will make more money available for financial support of local endeavours (Williams 1986). Endeavours such as local food cooperatives will also help strengthen the resources available to people in the local community. For example, staff at the Fitzroy Community Health Centre in Victoria organised a regular fresh food market to increase the availability of cheap, fresh food in the local area. Local employment initiatives, too, present valuable opportunities to support local economic development (see Sindal and Dixon 1990: 246).

Supporting community members

Community development is hard work and can be exhausting, physically and emotionally, for those involved. Unless support is provided when necessary, community members involved in the process can end up burnt out, unable to continue and feeling disempowered. Health workers therefore have a key role to play in supporting community members involved in community development. (Community development work can also be a very tiring process for health workers, and so it is vital that you develop support systems which enable you to remain active in this work.)

Encouraging community development: in whose interests?

'Pure' community development can be described as a process by which members of a community are enabled to work together to solve a problem which they face; and through their involvement they may develop skills and greater power over some of the issues which impact on their lives. However, community development is not always used to empower communities and increase their access to a range of choices. In many instances, some of its principles may be used to increase the compliance of community members with a program being imposed on the community, as a means of increasing the success of that program. Indeed, Tones et al. (1990: 251) suggest that there is a continuum of approaches to the use of community development strategies, ranging from community development as empowerment at one end through to the use of community development strategies to impose the beliefs of professional groups or politicians at the other end (see figure 6.1). In between these extremes lie a number of variations. As can be seen from figure 6.1, this continuum of approaches parallels the range of approaches to participation in Arnstein's Ladder of Citizen Participation (discussed on pp. 44–5).

Community health projects (Tones et al., 1990: 251)

Type 1	Innovators' goal for the community are primarily self-empowerment and improvement in socioeconomic status. Self-empowerment = health.
Type 2	As above but during the process of developing a community profile and identifying felt needs, the community itself acknowledges needs which are consistent with standard preventive medical/health education goals — e.g. need for better primary care services, accident prevention, dealing with child health problems.
Type 3	Characterized by 'community health projects'. Innovators' goals are to enhance health and prevent disease. They aim to do this by raising the profile of health but are prepared to help the community work through other more pressing 'felt needs' prior to their acknowledging a need to improve cardiovascular health, for example.
Type 4	Innovators' goals are primarily those of preventive medicine. This type is epitomized by the various CHD–prevention programs. It is more 'top-down' than Types 1–3 but it understands the importance of taking the community with it and utilizing existing leadership patterns, etc.
Type 5	More limited 'out-reach' programs; limited community participation but uses mix of agencies, e.g. media plus schools, plus drop-in centres and delivery of services to housing estate or workplace.

Figure 6.1 A continuum of approaches to community health projects.
Note how the continuum of approaches to community work mirrors the approaches to participation demonstrated by Arnstein's Ladder of Citizen Participation

Werner (1981: 47) describes the two extremes of this continuum as the difference between community-supportive programs and community-oppressive programs.

> *Community-supportive* programmes or functions are those that favourably influence the long-range welfare of the community, that help it stand on its own feet, that genuinely encourage responsibility, initiative, decision-making and self-reliance at the community level, that build upon human dignity.

> *Community-oppressive* programmes or functions are those which, while invariably giving lip-service to the above aspects of community input, are fundamentally authoritarian, paternalistic or are structured and carried out in such a way that they effectively encourage greater dependency, servility and unquestioning acceptance of outside regulations and decisions, and in the long run cripple the dynamics of the community.

In terms of community development, this difference can be described as the difference between community development *as* health promotion and the use (or abuse!) of community development *in* health promotion.

When a more limited form of community development is used, it is worth asking whose interests are being served. To what extent is this type of community development likely to serve the needs of the disempowered in the community? As Werner's definition of community-oppressive programs suggests, some uses of community development may serve more the needs of the workers or bureaucracies whose decisions are being imposed than the needs of the people they are meant to assist. There may be times when the community may benefit from the imposition of good ideas, but this may be the case only in the short term. In the

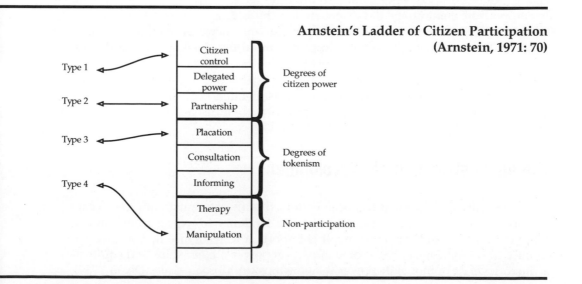

Arnstein's Ladder of Citizen Participation
(Arnstein, 1971: 70)

Type 1

Citizen control

Delegated power

Degrees of citizen power

Type 2

Partnership

Type 3

Placation

Consultation

Degrees of tokenism

Type 4

Informing

Therapy

Manipulation

Non-participation

longer term, the community may have become more, rather than less, dependent on the health workers, and so the principles of Primary Health Care may not be operating. It is only when 'pure' community development is being used that community development can live up to its reputation for addressing the structural causes of ill health. While it may be argued that some of the projects which utilise the more limited form of community development are useful, they will not result in structural change or change in the power relationships between health workers and community members.

Mal Walker (1986) has described the aim of community development as being to 'establish a dialogue between people and the system, so that people can demand things from the system, and the system can be responsive to their needs'. If community development activities result in people being more obedient to health workers, rather than making the system more aware of and responsive to the needs of the community, then we have a fair indication that the aims of community development and the principles of Primary Health Care are not being addressed.

Critical evaluation of your own practice is therefore a vital component of community development practice. It often needs to include critical evaluation of the way in which the employing agency or funding body sees community development being applied. If they have unrealistic or manipulative uses of community development in mind, you may need to provide some clarification, because administrators and bureaucrats, like others, are still coming to terms with community development.

With the endorsement of community development in health work in recent years, and its enthusiastic adoption in many policy documents, a critical review of its support by governments is in order. Community development places emphasis on people working together as a group to achieve things for themselves, and changing the structures that influence their lives at the local level. Governments might therefore support community development because it takes the focus of responsibility away from government, public policy and broad social change. Community development also provides a cheap option for government. In supporting community development for those reasons, governments may have little regard for its goals of empowerment and increased community competence. This may mean that they support community development in theory, but in practice support only those limited forms described by Tones et al. (1990). Indeed, this is reflected in recent government expectations that community development will be used to meet specific disease-related goals and targets — for example, to improve nutrition or reduce cardiovascular disease.

The limits of community development

As community development has been endorsed with great gusto in recent years by those working in health, there has been a tendency to expect from it much more than it is capable of achieving. It is important to recognise that while community development can have some impact on power relationships and equity at a micro level, it cannot shift power relationships on a broad scale (Dixon 1989).

That is, even with the best intentions in the world, it cannot by itself change widespread social, economic and political conditions that are creating inequality and ill health.

Conclusion

With the recent endorsement of community development as a health promotion strategy, and recognition that it reflects the Primary Health Care approach due to its focus on working *with* people and enabling them to take a leadership role, health workers need to develop their skills in community development. However, if we are to work with community development realistically and optimistically, we need to recognise its limits. We also need to develop skills in those forms of action that may help bring about social change on a broader level. The next chapter will address these issues.

REFERENCES AND FURTHER READINGS

Arnstein, S. 1971. Eight rungs on the ladder of citizen participation, in Cahn, E. S. and Passett, B. A. (eds), *Citizen participation: effecting community changes*, Praeger Publishers, New York.

Ashton, J. 1990. Healthy Cities: an overview of the international movement, in Australian Community Health Association (eds), *Making the connections: people, communities and the environment, Papers from the First National Conference of Healthy Cities Australia*, Australian Community Health Association, Sydney.

Benn, C. 1981. *Attacking poverty through participation: a community approach*, PIT Publishing, Bundoora, Victoria.

Blakely, E. J. and Bowman, K. 1986. *Taking local development initiatives: a guide to economic and employment development for local government authorities*, Australian Institute of Urban Studies, Canberra.

Bryson, L. and Mowbray, M. 1981. Community: the spray-on solution, *Australian Journal of Social Issues*, November, 255-67.

Butler, P. and Cass, S. (eds). 1993. *Case studies of community development in health*, Centre for Development and Innovation in Health, Northcote, Victoria.

Clark, D. B. 1973. The concept of community: a re-examination, *Sociological Review*, 21(3), 397–415.

Community Development in Health Project. 1988. *Community development in health: a resources collection*, District Health Council, Preston/Northcote, Victoria.

Community Development in Health Project (eds), 1989. *Community development in Health for All: Proceedings of a national workshop*, 12–14 July, Melbourne University, Community Development in Health Project, Northcote.

Connell, R. 1977. *Ruling class, ruling culture*, Cambridge University Press, Cambridge.

Copeman, R. C. 1988. Assessment of Aboriginal health services, *Community Health Studies*, 13(3), 251–5.

Daly, H. E. and Cobb, J. B. 1989. *For the common good: redirecting the economy toward community, the environment and a sustainable future*, Beacon Press, Boston.

Dixon, J. 1989. The limits and potential of community development for personal and social change, *Community Health Studies*, 13(1), 82–92.

Dixon, J. 1992. The logics inherent in evaluating CD: evaluating community development programs, the community development approach and community interventions, paper presented at the Fourth Annual Health Promotion Workshop, Adelaide, 16–18 February.

Dwyer, J. 1989. The politics of participation, *Community Health Studies*, 13(1), 59–65.

Egger, G., Spark, R. and Lawson, J. 1990. *Health promotion strategies and methods*, McGraw-Hill, Sydney.

Hawe, P., Degeling, D. and Hall, J. 1990. *Evaluating health promotion: a health workers' guide*, MacLennan and Petty, Sydney.

Henderson, P. and Thomas, D. N. 1987. *Skills in neighbourhood work*, Allen and Unwin, Sydney.

Hunt, S. 1990. Building alliances: professional and political issues in community participation. Examples from a health and community development project, *Health Promotion International*, 5(3), 179–85.

Labonté, R. 1986. Social inequality and healthy public policy, *Health Promotion* 1(3), 341–51.

Labonté, R. 1989. Community and professional empowerment, *Canadian Nurse*, March, 23–8.

Labonté, R. 1989. Community empowerment: the need for political analysis, *Canadian Journal of Public Health*, 80, March/April, 87–8.

Minkler, M. 1991. Improving health through community organization, in Glanz, K., Lewis, F. M. and Rimer, B. K. (eds.), *Health behavior and health education: theory, research and practice*, Jossey Bass, San Francisco.

Mowbray, M. 1992. The medicinal properties of localism: a historical perspective, in Thorpe, R. and Petruchenia, J. with Hughes, L. (eds), *Community work or social change? — an Australian perspective*, Hale and Iremonger, Sydney.

Rothman, J. with Tropman, J. E. 1987. Models of community organization and macro practice perspectives: their mixing and phasing, in Cox, F. M., Erlich, J. L., Rothman, J. and Tropman J. E., *Strategies of community organization*, F. E. Peacock. Itasca, Illinois.

Rifkin, S. 1985. *Health planning and community participation: Case studies in South-East Asia*, Croom Helm, London.

Sanders, I. T. 1958. Theories of community development, *Rural Sociology*, 23, 1–12.

Scott, D. 1981. *Don't mourn for me — organise*, Allen and Unwin, Sydney.

Short, S. 1989. Community participation or community manipulation? A case study of the Illawarra Cancer Appeal-A-Thon, *Community Health Studies*, 13(1), 34–8.

Sindal, C. and Dixon, J. 1990. Creating supportive economic environments for health, in Australian Community Health Association (eds), *Healthy environment on the '90s: the community health approach; papers from the 3rd national conference of the Australian Community Health Association*, Australian Community Health Association, Sydney.

Thorpe, R. 1992. Community work and ideology: an Australian perspective in Thorpe, R. and Petruchenia, J. with Hughes, L. (eds), *Community work or social change? — an Australian perspective*, Hale and Iremonger, Sydney.

Tones, K., Tilford, S. and Robinson, Y. 1990. *Health education: effectiveness and efficiency*, Chapman and Hall, London.

Twelvetrees, A. 1987. *Community work*, Macmillan, London.

Walker, M. 1986. Community development lecture, Mitchell College of Advanced Education, Bathurst, 12 August.

Wallerstein, N. and Bernstein, E. 1988. Empowerment education: Freire's ideas adapted to health education, *Health Education Quarterly*, 15 (4), 379–94.

Werner, D. 1981. The village health worker: lackey or liberator?, *World Health Forum*, 2(1), 46–68.

Willams, S. 1986. Community based finance, *Community Quarterly*, 8, 4–10.

CHAPTER 7

Working for communities

Although community development is an important means of working with communities to deal with issues which impact on their lives, it is not the only form of community-level work. As we discussed in chapter 6, not all work that attempts to address needs at a community level can be correctly labelled 'community development'. After reviewing the previous chapter, you should have a reasonable idea of what community development is about. In this chapter we briefly review a number of ways in which you can work for communities while maintaining, as much as possible, the spirit of Primary Health Care.

The distinction between working *with*, working *for* and working *on* communities is a useful one, because it provides a framework in which we can critically examine the perspective of community-level work. *Working with communities* is reflected in 'pure' community development, where the focus is on the developmental process and on the partnership between health workers and community members as they work for change. *Working for communities* describes those instances where health workers are more directive in planning action and implementing it, but where they continue to act with the philosophy of Primary Health Care to involve community members as much as possible and to work for changes which increase people's control over their health. *Working on communities* describes those activities where health workers impose on communities interventions which they believe are important, but do this with little reference to the way in which communities define their needs.

The distinction between these three sets of activities is by no means clear: there may be overlap between these areas and a fine line often separates them. Nevertheless, the distinction can be a useful framework for assessing community-level work and evaluating the approach that is driving it. If working *for* communities is to be successful, the principles of Primary Health Care need to guide any action that occurs. That is, even when health workers are working *for* communities, it is vital that the people themselves be involved as much as possible so that working *for* communities does not become working *on* communities.

It is not appropriate to expect community development to be the answer to every problem which a community faces. There may be times, for example, when this would be unethical because there is a risk to people's health or because people do not feel empowered enough to act. Conversely, people may not be interested in actively participating in an issue and may believe that their taxes provide the wages of health workers so that others do not have to become involved in every health issue which arises. Expecting members of a community to deal with all the things which challenge their health may amount to a form of victim blaming, and be based on an expectation that people — often those with the least resources — should take responsibility for issues over which they have little or no control. At these times, it may be more appropriate to work on behalf of the people concerned in order to help make the health and social systems more responsive to the needs of the community; that is, health workers themselves can work, particularly to build healthy public policy and therefore create supportive environments, through the processes of advocacy and mediation, as recommended by the Ottawa Charter for Health Promotion.

Finding the balance between working *with* communities through community development and working *for* communities is an ongoing process for health promotion workers. Finding the appropriate point of balance between these two requires critical reflection by health workers to ensure that the work that is done reflects the principles of Primary Health Care.

Working for healthy public policy

The Ottawa Charter for Health Promotion, with its emphasis on building healthy public policy as an integral component of health promotion action, marked the formal recognition of the role that all public policy plays in influencing health and the role of the environment in shaping choices for health. This acknowledgment of the importance of healthy public policy was reflected in the fact that the Second International Conference on Health Promotion, held in Adelaide in 1988, focused on healthy public policy. This acknowledgment is vital, because it recognises that people's social and physical environments impact strongly on their health and the health choices they can make, and that all public policies, not just those labelled as health policies, have health consequences.

Healthy public policy is central to the promotion of health, because without the support of healthy public policy other health promotion actions are likely to be of limited value. As Milio (1990: 295) has expressed it:

> *by definition, even the most effective projects have limits, in time and/or the people who benefit. Projects can demonstrate, but only policies can perpetuate the effects. Projects can create oases of health, but only policies can redistribute and equalize their benefits.*

Of course, policies can equalise benefits only if they are appropriately implemented. This is discussed later, but that is another matter.

Any examination of healthy public policy and action to build healthy public policy must start with a consideration of what policy is, and how it can be influenced.

What is policy?

Defining 'policy' is not easy, because the term is used in a number of ways. In some instances it is a formal process, in others an informal one. Graycar (1979: 135–6) describes three common ways in which the term 'policy' is used: it may be used to refer to 'some sort of basic goal' and may resemble a promise; it may refer to a course of action; or it may refer to a set of rules and regulations. In many instances, too, policies may be reflected more by what is not said than what is said.

Public policies are defined as those policies which affect the public interest. Many of them are largely the responsibility of governments (Palmer and Short 1989: 22). However, they are not determined solely by public interest, since a great many private interests have power in determining the direction of public policy (Gardner and Barraclough 1992: 10). For example, the medical profession, guided largely by its interests in private practice and entrepreneurial activity, has a very powerful influence over public policy related to health. Medical insurance companies are in a similar position with regard to health financing.

Until relatively recently, health workers have been concerned only with health policy, because it was assumed that only this policy impacted on health. It is now recogni ed, however, that health policy may have very little impact on health by comparison with the impact of social policy and economic policy, since it focuses largely on the structure of health care delivery. Social policy, for example, deals with such issues as income distribution, housing and transport provision, while economic policy affects such things as employment rates, inflation and standard of living. Policies which impact on the physical environment include policies on land use, mining and farming. It will be obvious to you that all these things do a great deal to structure the environments in which people live. The notion, then, of public policies having a substantial impact on health makes good sense, and the need for economic, social and health policies to be responsive to the requirements of the community is quite apparent. One recent result of the growing recognition of this fact is the increasing concern for the health of the environment.

The process of public policy making

Policy making has been described as a dynamic social and political process (Milio 1988: 3). It is also a competitive process, with the competing interests of different groups involved in trying to shape the direction that public policies take (Gardner and Barraclough 1992: 11). Brown (1992: 104) suggests that public policies result from 'a synthesis of power relationships, demographic trends, institutional agendas, community ideologies [and] economic resources'.

Milio (1988: 3–4) divides those involved in the policy-making process into three groups — the public (including formal interest groups), political and bureaucratic policy makers, and the mass media. However, this does not reflect the fact that some interest groups involving themselves in the policy-making process have a great deal more power than others because of their political position and play a large part in developing the views represented in the mass media. For example, medical interest groups are usually listened to by members of parliament and shape the public agenda more strongly than many other groups, and their opinions are reported more often by the mass media.

Until relatively recently, the opinion of ordinary community members was rarely asked for. These days, however, with the growing recognition of the importance of community participation, public comment is being requested on new and developing policies. Nevertheless, it is the politicians, bureaucrats and professional groups who set the agenda and decide the framework and philosophy of a policy. Members of the public commenting on a document are therefore in the position of trying to change the policy by tampering with the edges. It is to be hoped that this will change if Australia takes seriously its commitment to the Health for All movement, with its emphasis on increasing true community participation.

A number of authors have described the policy-making process using a variety of relatively similar models. Palmer and Short (1989: 30–2) describe it as a five-stage model. It is important to note, however, that this model accounts only for those policies which are formally developed, not those which never reach the public agenda but develop incrementally.

1. *Problem identification and agenda setting.* A public problem is recognised as a political issue, and is placed on the political agenda.

2. *Policy formation.* New policies are developed or existing policies are redeveloped.

3. *Adoption.* A new policy is formally accepted, through either legal enactment in parliament or approval of the appropriate minister.

4. *Policy implementation.* A policy is actually put into practice, and the 'product' seen at this point may be quite different from what was imagined when the policy was first formulated. For example, its power may be eroded by the way in which it is implemented, or it may have unforeseen consequences when it is put into practice. The outcome of policies which are implemented with an inadequate budget may be quite different from that envisaged when they were originally formulated.

5. *Policy evaluation.* Policies are evaluated for their impact. Clearly, if policy evaluation is to be meaningful, it needs to be an ongoing process. Policy making is a cyclical process, and evaluation of a policy in action may lead to the policy issue being put back on the policy agenda, and thus to the cycle beginning again.

Community members and groups affected by the policy concerned may be able to influence the policy-making process at any stage in its life, but this is more likely to happen during policy formation and policy evaluation. In addition, because of the cyclical nature of the stages in the policy-making process, community members and interested groups can be part of the process that puts issues back onto the policy agenda. With regard to those issues which have never been formally discussed as policy issues but have developed incrementally, community members may be involved in the important process of getting them onto the public agenda and reviewed critically, perhaps for the first time.

Public policies can be influenced through social advocacy and lobbying. These are discussed in more detail later. It is important to note, however, that affecting public policy in this way is often a slow process, and it may take a number

The Victorian Health Promotion Foundation

The Victorian Health Promotion Foundation was established in 1987 following the proclamation of the Tobacco Act, which was supported by all three political parties in Victoria. The Act introduced a 5 per cent levy on all wholesale tobacco sales. It was estimated that this would raise $23 million each year. This money was to be distributed by the Victorian Health Promotion Foundation (also known as Vic Health) to projects which aim to promote health or prevent disease or disability.

Vic Health funds programs in five areas — tobacco replacement, sport sponsorship, arts and culture sponsorship, health promotion programs, and research.

1. *Tobacco replacement.* Money is used to sponsor events and teams previously sponsored by tobacco companies (for example, the Socceroos). It used to be very difficult for sporting clubs which would not accept funds from tobacco companies to find sponsorship. Now, through its 'tobacco buyout', Vic Health is actively seeking to replace tobacco sponsorship totally by 1993. In addition, it has replaced tobacco advertising on billboards with healthy messages. The Tobacco Act provided for the termination of billboard advertising of tobacco by the end of 1991.

2. *Sport sponsorship.* Funds are available for previously unsponsored sports, both competitive and non-competitive. Sporting activities which target groups of people who have little access to sport or have been susceptible to unhealthy lifestyle messages are particularly welcome. Examples of projects funded in this category are the Vic Health Masters Games for mature age competitors, table tennis for people over 40 years of age, especially those with arthritis, the Vic Health Sun Tour bicycle race and a program to help disabled people involve themselves in sport.

3. *Arts and Culture sponsorship.* Arts and cultural projects which provide an opportunity to communicate a health message can obtain funding, particularly if they reach a wide audience and increase community involvement in the arts. Projects funded in this category include the Melbourne Comedy Festival's comic writers' performance, the 'Festival of Bands' in the 1989 Spoleto Festival, the Bendigo 'Youth on Fire' Festival and 'Danz in the Streetz' during the Moomba festival.

4. *Health promotion programs.* Specific health promotion programs run by either health promotion organisations or community groups are also eligible for funding. Successful applications include those by the Well Women's Project, a program based on cervical cancer screening by nurses of women previously underscreened; Health In Primary Schools; Feeling Great, a program aimed at discouraging risky behaviours amongst teenagers; and Active At Any Age, a program designed to improve the lifestyles of older people.

5. *Research.* Funding is also available for research which improves our knowledge of what promotes health. This is important because most money currently spent on research goes to research which examines disease treatment rather than health promotion. Through the research being funded, we may find more non-medical solutions to common health problems. Examples of research funded in this category include examination of domestic violence, hypertension in the elderly, diabetes prevention, satisfaction with maternity care, and the effects on foetal outcome of exercise during pregnancy.

Vic Health is one example which raises many of the political implications of attempting to make structural changes in order to impact on health (see Barraclough 1992 for a critique of the Victorian Tobacco Act and its consequences).

of years of concerted effort by a number of people to change the major direction of a policy process. Working with people and keeping your sights set on your goal are important. Hancock (1990: 29) describes this process of changing public policy as one of 'goal directed muddling through'.

Working for healthy public policy at the local level

Although state policy and national policy have a great influence on the way our daily lives are structured, a remarkably large number of policy decisions which shape our environment are taken at the local level, particularly through local government. Responsibility for such issues as land use, placement of industry, housing standards, availability of recreational areas and location of shopping areas is all exercised at the local level. Local government, therefore, is quite a powerful influence on our environments, and the impact of public policy at the local level can be profound. In recognition of this, the 1992 National Review of the Role of Primary Health Care in Health Promotion recommended strengthening the role of local government in health promotion.

However, developing healthy public policy at the local level may be quite difficult. Zabolai-Csekme (1983: 3) points out that Primary Health Care may challenge the concept of development quite fundamentally because its focus is on the health of people and the environment. Most local councils operate from a philosophy of development, which usually means expansion of industry and population. These are not necessarily conducive to health, yet they are assumed to be good for the community. Recent acknowledgment of the concept of sustainable development may help to break down this assumption. However, it is unlikely that local councils will embrace the principles of Primary Health Care without considerable 'assistance', both from community demand and from legislation at state and federal government levels, because the expansion of industry and population is highly regarded by society generally. Until it is quite clear that other approaches are acceptable, councils may feel compelled to remain with this approach. This may mean that community members have considerable work to do in lobbying local councils to take their concerns about healthy public policy seriously.

Some local councils, however, are working for healthier communities. One notable recent attempt to encourage local councils to become involved in health promotion has been the Healthy Localities Project, funded by the Victorian Health Promotion Foundation and under the auspices of the Municipal Association of Victoria. A total of 134 local councils received development grants to enable them to assess the needs of their area and apply for project funding, provided in the form of an award. Most of the winning projects developed one-off projects rather than working for healthy public policy, but the Healthy Localities Project may have an important role in increasing awareness of health promotion in local government, and we may see more work for healthy public policy at the local level in the future.

The principles of working to influence local government are much the same as those (described later) of working to influence public policy at state and federal levels. How they are put into practice varies slightly, though, and because local

Healthy Cities

The Healthy Cities project is an attempt to establish healthier living conditions in cities through the development of widespread healthy public policy, supported by a broad range of private and public sectors. Developed originally for European cities by the World Health Organization, it has been adapted to suit Australian conditions. Following a yearlong pilot project in three areas (Illawarra in New South Wales, Canberra in the Australian Capital Territory and Noarlunga in South Australia), it was evaluated quite positively. Other cities or local council areas were then invited to join the Healthy Cities Australia network.

The Healthy Cities project focuses on intersectoral action and espouses the value of the community development process. Many examples of action under the Healthy Cities project are available (see, for example, Rees 1992, Clarke and MacDougall 1993, Australian Community Health Association 1990 and Healthy Cities Australia 1990). However, the extent to which different cities are using a 'working with communities' approach varies greatly. Some are working to develop a strong community participation base with a focus on community decision-making, while others are more directive and have major decisions made by professionals. For example, Short (1990) has described the

way in which professionals are more 'on top' than 'on tap' in the Illawarra Healthy Cities project.

Regrettably, the federal government decided against refunding the Healthy Cities project at a national level when funding for the project ran dry in June 1992. This decision was taken before the evaluation of Healthy Cities was completed. It decided instead to 'target fewer and more specific areas of strategic importance' (Department of Health, Housing and Community Services, cited by Lennie 1992). Unfortunately, this hardly explains the removal of funding from the program. Loss of national funding for Healthy Cities is a great shame, since it is one of the few health promotion activities which could have been funded to enable Australia to take a broad structural approach to health. The National Review of the Role of Primary Health Care in Health Promotion has recommended the continued funding of the Healthy Cities project in Australia (National Centre for Epidemiology and Population Health 1992). In the meantime, many of the cities and localities already involved in the Healthy Cities movement will continue with the processes set in train. However, without ongoing support and network building, and if new cities do not join the project, its future impact is unclear.

councils are one step closer to the ground, people often find it easier to involve themselves in working at the local level for change. The issues at stake here arise more often just down the street or in their own backyard, and the decisions are taken in a building with which most people are familiar. Because of this, local government does not have quite the same mystique as politics at the state and federal levels, and people may more readily act for change.

As in the case of work for public policy change at state and federal levels, people can work through the media, writing letters to the editor and bringing issues to the attention of local television, radio and newspaper reporters. You can also lobby local councillors, who may feel very committed to representing local people on issues of public concern. Once you have discovered which local councillors seem most open to hearing your views and most concerned about the issues you raise, develop a relationship with them and keep them up to date on the issues you are concerned about to enable them to make more informed decisions when issues come up without notice. They may contact you for information if they recognise you as a trustworthy source of information on issues which impact on health.

Local government is usually dominated by people representative of business and professional groups in an area. Many community groups have put forward candidates to represent the community perspective in local government. You might work to support one of these candidates, or you might consider standing for the local council yourself and working for change from the inside.

One excellent example of a community health centre working for healthy public policy at the local level is provided by the 'Vote For Health' campaign conducted by the Parks Community Health Service in South Australia. The campaign encouraged people to vote in the local government elections by providing information about how to vote and discussing the central role of local government decisions in promoting the health of the community. The campaign also elicited information from all local government candidates about their attitudes to health issues, and this information was published to provide a basis on which people could make their voting decisions. This information also provided a basis against which local government councillors could be accountable (Phillips-Rees et al. 1992: 54–5).

Working for healthy institutional policy

In addition to public policy developed at government levels, policies operating at the institutional level can have a big impact on people's lives. The policies of institutions, such as workplaces, schools and hospitals, influence people's lives as they come in contact with these institutions, and often influence the lives of community members even when they are not in direct contact with the institution. For example, work-related exposure to hazardous substances results in a great many workers becoming sick or dying (Tesh 1981: 382). Moreover, workers who take toxic substances home on their work clothes affect not only their own lives beyond the workplace, but also those of their partners and children, since they too are exposed to the chemicals. It is vital, therefore, to work for healthy institutional policy, in addition to healthy public policy.

Workplaces illustrate extremely well the importance of establishing healthy institutional policy as the basis of institutional health promotion. In recent years, despite the framework for action provided by the Ottawa Charter for Health Promotion, a great deal of the focus of workplace health promotion has remained on individual behaviour change for healthy lifestyles. Workplace health promotion must accord priority to the issues which arise in the workplace, particularly those which require changes to policy. Within workplaces, this may need to be done in close partnership with occupational health and safety workers and with unions.

Some useful examples of work to develop healthy institutional policy are health promoting hospitals and health promoting schools (both developed

Working for healthy institutions — the problem of asbestos

It could be thought that knowing about an environmental health hazard and taking appropriate action to minimise the hazard would go hand in hand. Not so — at least not in the case of one higher education institution.

When the presence of very substantial amounts of friable and powdery asbestos lagging around heating pipes was raised in the institution, there was general nonchalance by the management. Finally, under sustained pressure from a small group of employees, aided by the Workcover Authority, removal of the asbestos was initiated. Then the problems really began.

The initial problem was to get the contractors to carry out the removal in accordance with the Asbestos Removal Code of Practice, and to get the institution's management to enforce the contractor's compliance.

Subsequent problems arose in the institution's own maintenance staff, who, although some of the supervisors had been trained in asbestos work, had what could only be described as a cavalier attitude to asbestos. This attitude was demonstrated by repeated breaches of the Code of Practice for working with asbestos. Many of the maintenance staff seemed to treat the issue of asbestos exposure as insignificant and amusing, despite the wealth of evidence to the contrary. Again the institution's management seemed either unwilling or unable to deal with the situation. Every attempt was made to stifle discussion of the issue and suppress knowledge of the problems.

Change in the institution's attitude to asbestos did not come easily. It took concentrated and sustained action to reach even a minimal level of acceptance of the need for safe work practice in relation to asbestos. The change was brought about by appropriate use of union industrial muscle, in conjunction with the provisions of the NSW Occupational Health and Safety Act (1983), though this alone would not have achieved the desired result.

It was necessary for unions to work closely with the site Occupational Health and Safety Committee and the Workcover Authority. It was also necessary to make full and judicious use of the media, both print and electronic. The media made the real difference to the initial campaign. Before media involvement the institution was loathe to take any rectifying action. When the media became involved and the general public became aware of the situation, it was suddenly an acute embarrassment for an institution of higher learning to be shown to have serious defects in environmental safety.

The results of this intensive and multifront campaign were heightened awareness of asbestos hazards in some of the staff and a change in management attitude. The most senior managers began to take the issue of asbestos seriously and this filtered down to most of the supervisors. However, in the end it took a Workcover prosecution to really force the issue.

It would be nice to be able to end this story on a positive note, but it's the old story: winning the battle doesn't necessarily mean winning the war. Breaches of the Asbestos Code of Practice still occur. The institution has to be closely scrutinised and constant vigilance is essential to ensure that safe work practices are maintained.

The important role of unions in working within institutions and with statutory authorities in promoting health on difficult issues such as that described above cannot be overestimated.

Jenny McParlane
Senior Lecturer, School of Health,
University of New England — Armidale.

originally as WHO intitatives, and now adapted for Australian conditions). Recent work to develop more environmentally responsible hospitals, led by members of the Australian Nursing Federation's 'Nursing the Environment' group, provides another useful example.

A word of warning, however. Working for healthy institutional policy, while valuable, cannot replace work for healthy public policy. In the light of recent attempts by some Australian state health departments to limit the work done in an 'Ottawa Charter' approach to health promotion to work traditionally carried out by health workers, there is a tendency to try to limit public policy work to work for policy change within organisations, rather than addressing broad public policy issues. Health workers need to ensure that they work for public policy change on issues which impact on health at the same time as they work for institutional policy change. Otherwise, we may end up with a sanitised version of health promotion, which may ignore the hard issues which have the biggest impact on people's health and address issues only at the level of the individual or institution.

The ways in which you can work for healthy institutional policy will vary depending on the institution, the ways in which it relates to the public and your relationship with it. Working for change within an organisation for which you work will require you to follow the organisation's normal lines of communication. However, working to change an organisation which sees itself as responsible to the public may require you to follow lines of communication similar to those for working towards change to healthy public policy; that is, in dealing with such an organisation, you can write to its Chief Executive or any people in key positions relevant to the particular issue. Remember that you may need to keep at it, and that if requests for change come from more than one person, they are more likely to be successful. In the case of public services, if you do not have any success you can take your suggestions to others who have influence over the organisation, such as a government minister.

Developing networks for intersectoral health action

If health workers are to influence the direction of policy and action in a way which makes environments healthier, then clearly they need to influence policy and action in a number of sectors. They cannot do this alone, but must work with a range of other people who recognise the health impacts of actions in what are traditionally regarded as non-health areas. These people include workers in industry, transport, agriculture and education, in addition to members of the community.

It is vital, then, that you plan to make and maintain valuable working relationships with people in other disciplines, other agencies and other sectors in order to maximise the joint actions which you can take to promote health. These working relationships can be very powerful, even though there may be times when conflict may arise. More often than not, though, when a working relationship exists between people, it seems much easier to deal with any conflict than when there is no previous working relationship.

Health Action, New Zealand

Health Action is a community-based health project which aims 'to create a social and political environment that supports actions leading to good health' (Langford 1990: 14). It has chosen to focus on those aspects of health promotion because it is the 'hard edge' of health promotion which tends to be neglected by health workers, who tend to focus on health education (Langford 1990: 18). It has done this by working with community groups acting on issues of health concern, supporting them in their endeavours and bringing groups with shared or related concerns together for joint action.

The way in which Health Action addressed the problem of high skin cancer rates gives us some valuable insights into how the Ottawa Charter can be implemented. Rather than focus on sun sense education, Health Action aimed to reduce the emission of ozone-depleting substances in the Nelson region of New Zealand and reduce demand for these products. It formed a coalition of a number of local groups—the Environment Centre, the Forest and Bird Society, the Cancer Society and a conservation group — and some local health administrators, and worked together to deal with the issue. It informed consumers of the ozone-friendly choices they could make, lobbied the city council to develop a policy on ozone-depleting substances (which has resulted in the local council recycling chlorofluorocarbons [CFCs] and a total of three councils committing themselves to an ozone-friendly policy), contributed at a national level to the development of an Ozone Layer Protection Bill and worked successfully to encourage shop managers to stock only ozone-friendly products. This activity has been very successful and a number of other New Zealand communities have taken similar initiatives.

This is just one example of the work of Health Action. The principles behind its other work are the same, and by working with community groups it is achieving healthy change which will be supportive of the community and provide opportunities for health and healthy choices (Langford 1990).

Creating supportive environments

The World Health Organization is encouraging the building of healthy public policy because it creates supportive environments in which it is easier for people to make healthy choices. While, as Milio (1990: 295) notes, one-off projects do not have the impact that healthy public policy does, one-off projects which impact in a positive way on the environment can support people's healthy choices, and either encourage the establishment of healthy public policy or promote individual behaviour change. The previous example of 'Health Action', and the following 'Tobacco sponsorship replacement at the local level' example, demonstrate ways in which this can be done.

Tobacco sponsorship replacement at the local level—a success story

In November 1991 the New South Wales State Parliament enacted the Tobacco Prohibition Act, which prohibited community groups from obtaining sponsorship from tobacco companies without specific government approval.

In January 1992 the Mid North Coast Art Society suffered what it saw as a grave financial blow when the Rothmans Foundation withdrew its sponsorship of the society's annual art show. Extensive media coverage, both electronic and print, carried numerous stories of the adverse effects of the Tobacco Prohibition Act on such community events as this. This publicity, we observed, created a backlash against the legislation, and with the loss of their long-term sponsor, small community organisations were left feeling helpless and unsure of which direction to take in fundraising.

In 1990 the Manning Great Lakes Health Service, in rural New South Wales, had in place a five-year plan for health promotion in their Health For All program. This plan evolved from the Health for All initiatives of the World Health Organization and the consequential Australian and New South Wales programs. Two major components of this program are the Country Heart-Throb program and the Smoke Free program. The community health centre staff acting as their facilitators proposed to the health service management that, as a one-off demonstration, staff would work to raise money to replace the tobacco sponsorship. The intention of this was to demonstrate to the community that community activities and events could survive and prosper with the new legislation.

Reorienting the health system

As this was a new approach to health promotion, in that fundraising is not a normal health promotion activity, a proposal was presented to the health service management. It responded enthusiastically and with full support, and a number of guidelines were set:

1. All monies raised would be collected by the health service. Donations would be receipted to it and amounts over $2 would be tax-deductible.

2. The final aggregated donation would be paid to the Mid North Coast Art Society with the following requests:

(a) that the Country Heart-Throb and Smoke Free programs be presented on a health promotion display at the art show;

(b) that a sponsor board be provided for those donors who wished to be recognised;

(c) that publicity by the art society acknowledge the health service, in particular its Country Heart-Throb and Smoke Free programs.

When contacted, the president of the art society was sceptical about the ability of the health service to raise sufficient funds to replace tobacco sponsorship.

The announcement that the health service was to take up this challenge received wide media coverage. To facilitate media interest, a direct approach was made to the editor of the local newspaper and to journalists on commercial and ABC radio stations. The local television station was also contacted. As a result, all activities and events received wide media coverage and support, which ensured that the whole issue remained firmly in the community's awareness.

Community involvement

As a result of the media interest, a number of direct donations were quickly made to the fund by members of the public and health service personnel who felt strongly about this issue. These included a donation by a 74-year-old pensioner who had recently stopped smoking after 50 years (this was used to good effect in a press release). It soon became apparent, however, that a more aggressive approach to fund-raising was needed.

Since the purpose of the project was to demonstrate to the community that events could be funded by sources other than tobacco sponsorship, it was decided to organise events that involved participation by a wide cross-section of the community. This provided opportunities for health education. The events included:

- a healthy barbecue for health service staff;

- raffling of a T-shirt donated by renowned Australian artist Ken Done;

- a poster design competition in schools;

- a healthy fund-raising breakfast;

- raffling of an original Australian landscape by a local artist.

It is important to emphasise that these activities had more benefits than just fundraising. Although we maintained the principle of replacement of tobacco sponsorship in fundraising, a health promotion theme was emphasised during all activities.

The first activity was a healthy barbecue for health service staff during their lunch period. Since there are a large number of smokers among the staff, the opportunity was taken to highlight the benefits of going smoke-free. The barbecue was well attended by both smokers and non-smokers. The Ken Done T-shirt raffle proved popular.

The Manning Base Hospital had already developed its canteen into a public restaurant, called Stitches, which is oriented towards healthy food. A healthy breakfast was offered at Stitches and the general community was invited. To maintain the relationship between fundraising and art, a local artist and art

teacher, Ron Hindmarsh, was the guest speaker. During his talk he began work on an Australian landscape, which was then available for us to raffle.

Raising health awareness

Continuing with the art theme, a poster design competition was held throughout the local schools. Children from kindergarten to Year 6 were invited to paint or draw their views on tobacco use and smoking. Teachers were encouraged to include a session on smoking in their health studies. Prizes, in the form of Hot Tuna surfwear and K Mart educational material, made competition keen. The best posters were displayed in the local shopping mall during World No Tobacco Day. This attracted much attention from both school children and adults. Prizes were presented to the winners during school assemblies, which again reinforced the non-smoking message to school-age children. Every entrant in the competition received a certificate of merit.

Each fundraising event received broad media coverage in which the reason for the fundraising was emphasised. As a direct result of its involvement with us, the art society has now lobbied the local council to make the hall they meet in smoke-free.

Conclusions

The tobacco sponsorship replacement program was an example of how an adverse event can be turned to advantage and used to create a series of opportunities for health promotion. They have also opened the way for further health promotion activities. Despite criticism by some health professionals that fundraising is not an accepted health activity, we believe that the principle and the activities clearly demonstrated to previous recipients of tobacco sponsorship that they were not reliant on tobacco sponsorship, and achieved wide-reaching positive results.

The school poster design competition opened up the subject of smoking in the schools and provided a forum for education on tobacco use. Presenting the popular prizes at the school assemblies had beneficial effects. Children whose teachers had not involved them in the competition demanded to know why, and most schools requested that we run the competition annually.

Since we raised $380 more than our target figure of $1000, the excess funds were given to the Great Lakes Art Society, which had also lost its tobacco sponsorship. This generated further publicity and extended the benefits of the program to another community.

The extensive media coverage throughout the fundraising ensured that the community was kept constantly aware of the fact that there is art, and sport, and life after tobacco sponsorship.

The art show, which was on for a week, attracted 3000 people. A non-smoking health promotion display and material featured prominently. There was only one thing missing on the opening night—the tobacco company's logo!

Trish Abbott
Generalist community nurse and facilitator,
Country Heart-Throb program,
Taree Community Health Centre

Bob Berry
Clinical Nurse Consultant,
Alcohol and Other Drugs Service,
and facilitator,
Smoke Free program,
Taree Community Health Centre

Social advocacy and lobbying

Social advocacy and lobbying are very much recognised as part of the health worker's role, particularly since the Ottawa Charter for Health Promotion acknowledged their importance. They constitute a key strategy with which to work for healthy public policy. Health workers have two key roles to play in social (or health) advocacy: acting as advocates and lobbyists themselves, and encouraging and supporting other community members to take up advocacy and lobbying. In chapter 2, discussing participation, we examined the fact that on the whole individuals are poorly prepared for participating in the political process and are not encouraged to do so. Developing skills in this area, as well as assisting others to do so, is therefore a vital part of health promotion work if we are to take up our advocacy role effectively.

Joining advocacy groups

People can do advocacy work as individuals, and they can do it as part of an organisation which includes advocacy and lobbying work in its activities. There are a number of key organisations which currently act to advocate for community members and consumers in the health system. Some of them are specifically designed for community and consumer advocacy work, for example the Consumers Health Forum and the Health Issues Centre; others are professional organisations which include community and consumer advocacy as part of their role, for example the Australian Community Health Association and the Public Health Association. All these organisations are among those you can involve yourself in. In addition to adding your weight to the voices behind their advocacy work, you will learn a great deal about effective advocacy work and about work being conducted by others.

The Health Issues Centre

The Health Issues Centre is an independent, non-government organisation which conducts health policy analysis and social advocacy. It aims to create a more equitable health care system which is more responsive to the needs of its community. It argues for a more balanced system of illness treatment and health promotion, and for more equitable allocation of the health dollar.

As well as lobbying for change to the health system, the Health Issues Centre produces a quarterly journal and regular issues papers. Papers published to date include *What's wrong with the health system?*, *Getting off the sickness-go-round: are we on the right track?*, *Where the health dollar goes*, *Organ transplants: the need for community debate* and *Our better health: getting it together*.

Membership of the Health Issues Centre and copies of its papers are available by contacting:

*Health Issues Centre
1st Floor,
257 Collins Street,
Melbourne VIC 3000.
Tel: (03) 650 7511
Fax: (03) 654 6108*

Writing to members of parliament

Lobbying members of parliament to act on issues which impact on the health of the community can be a useful way of having your views represented, and (hopefully) taken account of when decisions are being made at the political level.

There are a number of possibilities. Firstly, you can approach your own state and federal representatives. It is worthwhile when communicating with them to emphasise the impact of your concern on the local people, since parliamentarians are elected by local people in the expectation that they will represent those people's interests. Secondly, members of parliament responsible for particular portfolios relevant to the issue are useful people to lobby. For example, the state and federal ministers of health may be approached regarding your concerns about a health issue. Ministers responsible for other relevant portfolios can also be approached. The transport, agriculture, sport, education and environment ministers are just some of the ministers whom it may be appropriate to approach regarding different health promotion issues. Thirdly, the prime minister and the premier of the state in question can be approached if you believe the issue has more serious or urgent consequences.

Lobbying members of parliament is more likely to be successful if done by a number of people, and much of this approach therefore involves working with other people, and educating them about the ways in which lobbying skills can be used to affect the public agenda. Encouraging other people to lobby members of parliament, and to keep at it by regularly contacting them until you get the response you want, will increase your chances of success. They are best reached via their electoral offices, as their offices at Parliament House are often unattended (Beauchamp 1986: 122). Beauchamp (1986: 124) recommends approaching a member of parliament by letter rather than by telephone, since a written request is more difficult to ignore.

Responding to calls for public comment

The Commonwealth Department of Human Services and Health (and other government departments) places advertisements in all the major metropolitan newspapers, usually on a Saturday, when it wishes to advise of the availability of a new report for public discussion, canvass public opinion on an issue, invite public involvement in an activity or advertise the availability of funding for health promotion activities or research. Other bodies, for example the National Health and Medical Research Council, do the same. It is therefore extremely valuable to read the major paper in your state every Saturday as a way of finding information and influencing government policy on issues affecting health. More often than not, calls for public discussion are responded to by more skilled and articulate members of the community, and many other people do not feel confident about writing to government departments with their opinion. Regrettably, this may mean that the final reports of government do not accurately reflect a broad range of public opinion, and so it is vital that as many people as possible put forward their views. It is most worthwhile to respond to these calls for submissions, and to encourage as many people as possible around you to do so.

Unfortunately, many health workers themselves miss out on opportunities to respond to these calls because they assume that they will gain access to the discussion papers through their workplace. In fact, in many instances these discussion papers do not trickle down through the bureaucracy to ground-level health workers. Unless you search for them yourself, in the same way as other members of the public do, you may have no opportunity to influence the direction of public policy and health in your state or region, or Australia-wide.

It may be a good idea to arrange for a group of people to get together to discuss these draft documents, and perhaps to put together a group response. This can be very useful if you think the people who may be affected by the proposal are unlikely to respond individually because they do not have enough time, confidence or skills.

Major Australian newspapers

The *Sydney Morning Herald*
The *Courier Mail*
The *Age*
The *West Australian*
The *Advertiser*

The *Hobart Mercury*
The *NT News*
The *Canberra Times*
The *Australian*
The *Land* (rural issues)

Attending public hearings

Also advertised in the major metropolitan newspapers are public hearings or forums, which a government department or parliamentary committee may organise in order to hear the views of the public on particular issues.

Some examples of calls for public comment

National Approaches to Ecologically Sustainable Development and the Greenhouse Effect

The Prime Minister, Premiers and Chief Ministers have requested the Ecologically Sustainable Development Steering Committee and the National Greenhouse Steering Committee to prepare and release as officials' discussion papers the:

- **Draft National Strategy for Ecologically Sustainable Development**
  and the
- **Draft National Greenhouse Response Strategy**

The draft strategies draw together current government policies, and propose a range of new measures and approaches. The issues dealt with are complex and have an impact on all Australians.

Your views will be valuable in assisting governments to finalise the strategies by the end of the year.

If you are interested in commenting on the strategies, or just wish to keep in touch with developments, you can obtain a copy of either of the documents by writing to:

ESD/Greenhouse Discussion Papers
Natural Resources Branch
The Cabinet Office
GPO Box 5341
SYDNEY NSW 2001

The closing date for comments on the draft strategies is 21 August 1992.

THE PARLIAMENT OF THE COMMONWEALTH OF AUSTRALIA
HOUSE OF REPRESENTATIVES STANDING COMMITTEE ON ABORIGINAL AND TORRES STRAIT ISLANDER AFFAIRS

Inquiry into the Implementation of the Recommendations of the Royal Commission into Aboriginal Deaths in Custody

The Committee has been asked to inquire into and report on the *Report of the Recommendations of the Royal Commission into Aboriginal Deaths in Custody*. The Committee will also take into account the implementation reports of the states and territories in regard to those recommendations where there are joint Commonwealth/State responsibilities.

The Committee invites written submissions to the inquiry and is particularly keen to receive submissions from Aboriginal and Torres Strait Islander people and organisations. Public hearings will be held in a number of centres around Australia at which some of those who have made submissions may be asked to give supporting evidence.

The Committee asks that submissions be received by 29 April 1994. Submissions and requests for further information regarding the inquiry should be made to:

Mr Allan Kelly, Secretary
House of Representatives
Standing Committee on Aboriginal and Torres Strait Islander Affairs,
Parliament House
CANBERRA ACT 2600

Telephone: (06) 277 4559
Fax: (06) 277 2219

PARLIAMENT OF NEW SOUTH WALES
LEGISLATIVE COUNCIL

Standing Committee on Social Issues

Inquiry into Suicide in Rural New South Wales

The Standing Committee on Social Issues is undertaking an inquiry into suicide in rural NSW. The terms of reference are as follows:

That the Standing Committee on Social Issues inquire into and report on:
- *the extent and nature of suicide in rural NSW;*
- *possible causes for the increase in suicide in rural NSW;*
- *the provision of relevant services; and*
- *strategies fo the prevention of such suicides.*

The Chairman invites comment, by way of written submissions, on issues relevant to the terms of reference.

Given the sensitive nature of the Inquiry, any contact made by individuals with the Committee will be treated as confidential.

SUBMISSIONS MUST BE LODGED BY 31 MARCH 1994

Inquiries can be directed to the Committee Secretariat on telephone (02) 230 3074 or facsimile (02) 230 2981.

The Hon. Dr. M. H. Goldsmith, MLC
Committee Chairman

Using the media

As a key influence in placing issues on the policy agenda, the mass media are powerful tools to use in working for healthy public policy. Using the media in this way is known as media advocacy, which we discussed in chapter 5. Letters to the editor and news releases can put forward an alternative view and help to reshape the public perception of an issue. In addition, they can widen discussion on draft documents open for public discussion by making other people aware of the documents and their implications.

Ensuring community representation on committees

If public committees are to conduct work which reflects a broad view of community opinions, community members or consumers need to be adequately represented on them and have adequate decision-making power. Health workers have an important role to play in lobbying for community representation on, and effective participation in, committees whose work impacts on the life of the community. Working to achieve those two goals is an important way in which you can ensure that the work of these committees is more working for the community than working on it.

As well as securing community representation on committees, health workers on committees can present the perspective of consumers. To do this successfully, you may need to maximise your effectiveness in working in a committee. Some people may wonder why community representatives are necessary if health workers are able to present a community perspective. However, as the Consumers' Health Forum points out, there will be times when the perspective of community members may clash with that of health workers, and health workers should not assume that they are always able to represent the community perspective in an unbiased way (Consumers' Health Forum 1990: 2–3). Furthermore, accepting community members as partners with health workers means according them partnership status, not simply speaking on their behalf.

Representing consumer interests, whether as the community representative or as a health worker concerned to represent the consumer perspective, is not always a comfortable position to be in. The perspective of community members can be threatening to many professionals if they believe that it is their job to make decisions on behalf of the community and that they know what is best. This is especially so if the consumers or community members do not agree with these professionals' opinions. Recognising that the community perspective may challenge professionals on the committees may help those representing it to deal with any negative feedback they receive from committee members. Supporting members of the community in this position, or finding support for yourself if you are in this position, is vital if the community perspective is to be maintained on the committee for a length of time that enables things to be achieved.

The Consumers' Health Forum (1990) has produced a very useful booklet which addresses many issues relevant to community members becoming involved with committees. It is worthwhile ensuring that agencies you work with keep a copy of this booklet and make it available to any community members or budding community representatives, so as to help them increase their effectiveness on committees.

Consumers' Health Forum of Australia

Strategic Plan

Principles underpinning the Plan

Basic principles underlie CHF's policies and practice:

- To reduce inequalities in the health status of Australians.

- To promote universal access to health services for all Australians.

- To protect and enhance the rights of health consumers.

- To promote the inclusion of consumers in the planning, conduct and monitoring of health related services in the public, private and community sectors.

- To present consumer views and experiences as a legitimate balance to the views of other stakeholders in the health field.

- To consult with members about all facets of the CHF's work.

About the Forum

The Consumers' Health Forum of Australia Inc. formed in 1987, is a national consumer organisation which represents consumers on health care issues. It provides a balance to the views of government, manufacturers, service providers and other health professionals.

CHF establishes policy in consultation with its membership and other consumers. Over the last six years, CHF has been active in developing consumer orientated policy in many areas including health financing, chronic pain management, mental health policy, rational prescribing of medicines and consumer rights.

In addition to its policy work, CHF provides an effective mechanism for disseminating information to the community by publishing a quarterly journal, *Health Forum*.

CHF nominates and supports consumer representatives on national government, industry and provider group committees. These representatives put the consumers' perspective and report back to the community through *Health Forum*.

CHF activities and policy are co-ordinated by the general Committee, which is CHF's governing body. It is elected every two years.

The information and resources of the Forum are available directly to consumer groups and individual consumers who wish to avail themselves of this service.

CHF has a secretariat based in Canberra and receives funding for its core activities from the Commonwealth Department of Health, Housing, Local Government and Community Services under the Community Organisation Support Program. It has also been successful in attracting funds for specific projects.

For further information on any of the Forum's activities, please contact:

Consumers' Health Forum
of Australia Inc.
PO Box 52
Lyons ACT 2606
Tel: (06) 281 0811
Fax: (06) 281 0959

Conclusion

This chapter has reviewed some of the ways in which we can work for healthier communities. It is in this area more than in any other area of health promotion that change and development are occurring, as practitioners develop more innovative ways in which to work for communities. It is in working for communities that we are most working to change the environment, rather than the individual. Doing this in a manner which enhances, rather than constrains, people's choices is perhaps the biggest challenge facing health workers in this area of health promotion. You are encouraged to keep developing your skills in that area, and to keep critically evaluating your practice, so that your ability to work for communities continues to be enhanced.

REFERENCES AND FURTHER READINGS

Australian Community Health Association (eds). 1990. *Healthy environments in the 90's: the community health approach: papers from the 3rd National Conference of the Australian Community Health Association*, Australian community Health Association, Sydney.

Baldry, E. and Vinson, T. (eds). 1991. *Actions speak: strategies and lessons from Australian social and community action*, Longman Cheshire, Melbourne.

Barraclough, S. 1992. Policy through legislation: Victoria's Tobacco Act, in Gardner, H. (ed). *Health policy: development, implementation, and evaluation in Australia*, Churchill Livingstone, Melbourne.

Beauchamp, K. 1986. *Fixing the government: everyone's guide to lobbying in Australia*, Penguin, Ringwood, Victoria.

Brown, V. 1992. Health care policies, health policies, or policies for health?, in Gardner, H. (ed.), *Health policy: development, implementation, and evaluation in Australia*, Churchill Livingstone, Melbourne.

Catford, J. 1991. Primary environmental care: an ecological strategy for health, *Health Promotion International*, 6(4), 239–40.

Clark, B. and MacDougall, C. (eds). 1993. *The 1993 community health conference: Vol 1: papers and workshops*, Australian Community Health Association, Sydney.

Consumers' Health Forum. 1990. *Guide-lines for consumer representatives: suggestions for consumer or community representatives working on public committees*, Consumers' Health Forum of Australia, Curtin, ACT.

Elder, J. and McBride, T. 1989. Local government embraces health promotion, *Health Issues*, 19, 6–8.

Everingham, R. and Woodward, S. 1991. *Tobacco litigation: the case against passive smoking: AFCO v TIA*, Legal Books, Sydney.

Evers, A., Farrant, W. and Trojan, A. (eds). 1990. *Healthy public policy at the local level*, Campus Verlag, Frankfurt am Main, Germany.

Gardner, H. (ed). 1989. *The politics of health: the Australian experience*, Churchill Livingstone, Melbourne.

Gardner, H. (ed) 1992. *Health policy: development, implementation, and evaluation in Australia*, Churchill Livingstone, Melbourne.

Gardner, H. and Barraclough, S. 1992. The policy process, in Gardner, H. (ed.) *Health policy: development, implementation, and evaluation in Australia*, Churchill Livingstone, Melbourne.

Graycar, A. 1979. *Welfare politics in Australia: a study in policy analysis*, Macmillan, Melbourne.

Hancock, T. 1985. Beyond health care: from public health policy to healthy public policy, *Canadian Journal of Public Health*, supplement to vol. 76, May/June, 9–11.

Hancock, T. 1990. From 'Public Health in the 1980s' to 'Healthy Toronto 2000': the evolution of healthy public policy in Toronto, in Evers, A., Farrant, W. and Trojan, A. (eds), *Healthy public policy at the local level*, Campus Verlag, Frankfurt am Main, Germany.

Health Promotion Unit. 1991. *Health promotion in the workplace*, NSW Department of Health, Health Promotion Unit, Sydney.

Healthy Cities Australia. 1990. *Making the connections: people, communities and the environment: Papers from the First National Conference of Healthy Cities Australia*, Sydney.

Howat, P., O'Connor, J. and Slinger, S. 1992. Community action groups and health policy, *Health Promotion Journal of Australia*, 2(3), 16–22.

Labonté, R. 1993. A holosphere of healthy and sustainable communities, *Australian Journal of Public Health*, 17(1), 4–12.

Langford, B. 1990. Community action in health promotion, in *Healthy environments in the 90's: the community health approach: papers from the 3rd National Conference of the Australian Community Health Association*, Australian Community Health Association, Sydney.

Legge, D. and Sylvan, L. 1990. Community participation in health: the Consumers' Health Forum and the Victorian District Health Council Programme, in Evers, A., Farrant, W. and Trojan, A. (eds), *Healthy public policy at the local level*, Campus Verlag, Frankfurt am Main, Germany.

Lennie, I. (Executive Officer, Healthy Cities Australia). 1992. Letter to Healthy Cities supporters, 26 August, Australian Community Health Association, Sydney.

Mason, C. 1990. Healthy public policy for women and workers: an Australian case study of employment discrimination, occupational health and safety legislation, in Evers, A., Farrant, W. and Trojan, A. (eds). 1990. *Healthy public policy at the local level*, Campus Verlag, Frankfurt am Main, Germany.

Mason, C. 1992. *Opportunities for an ecological strategy for health in NSW: possibilities for the health sector: an issues paper*, Health Promotion Unit, NSW Health Department.

McMichael, A. J. 1993. *Planetary overload: global environmental change and the health of the human species*, Cambridge University Press, Oakleigh, Victoria.

Milio, N. 1988. *Making policy: a mosaic of community health policy development*, Department of Community Services and Health, Canberra.

Milio, N. 1990. Healthy Cities: the new public health and supportive research, *Health Promotion International*, 5(3), 291–7.

Municipal Association of Victoria and Victorian Health Promotion Foundation. 1990. *Healthy Localities Project: Second Progress Report, October 1989–June 1990*, Melbourne.

National Centre for Epidemiology and Population Health. 1992. *Improving Australia's health: the role of primary health care: final report of the review of the role of primary health care in health promotion in Australia*, The Australian National University, Canberra.

National Health and Medical Research Council. 1989. *Health effects of ozone layer depletion,* Australian Government Publishing Service, Canberra.

Palmer, G. and Short, S. 1989. *Health care and public policy,* Macmillan, Melbourne.

Phillips-Rees, S., Sanderson, C., Herriot, M., and May, A. 1992. *The changing face of health: a primary health care casebook,* South Australian Health Commission and South Australian Community Health Association, Adelaide.

Pratt, R. 1992. The health of Planet Earth: the greening of nurses, in Gray, G. and Pratt, R. (eds), *Issues in Australian Nursing 3.* Churchill Livingstone, Melbourne.

Rees, A. (ed). 1992. *Healthy cities: reshaping the urban environment: Proceedings of the Second National Conference of Healthy Cities Australia: 13–15 May,* Australian Community Health Association, Sydney.

Shields, K. 1991. *In the Tiger's Mouth: An empowerment guide for social action,* Millenium, Sydney.

Short, S. 1990. Professionals on tap or on top in the Illawarra Healthy Cities project? in Australian community Health Association (ed), *Healthy environments in the 90's: the community health approach: papers from the 3rd National Conference of the Australian Community Health Association,* Sydney.

Tassie, J. 1992. *Protecting the environment and health: working together for clean air on the Le Fevre Peninsula,* Le Fevre Peninsula Health Management Plan Steering Committee, Port Adelaide.

Tesh, S. 1981. Disease causality and politics, *Journal of Health Politics: Policy and Law,* 6(3), 369–90.

Whelan, A., Mohr, R. and Short, S. 1992. *Waving or drowning? Evaluation of the National Secretariat: Healthy Cities Australia final report,* Australian Community Health Association, Sydney.

Zabolai-Csekme. 1983. Adult education: an agent of primary health care, *Adult Education and Development,* 20 March, 1–10.

CHAPTER  8

Working with groups

Much health promotion, whether it is lobbying for political change, community development work or more formal health education, involves working with groups of people, both community members and work colleagues. As you know from your own experience, groups often have dynamics which are so much more than the sum of the individuals in them. It is possible to develop an understanding of group dynamics and skills in working with a group, so that the group works effectively for what it is trying to achieve, rather than allowing its dynamics to work against what it is trying to achieve. In this chapter we will examine some of the important components of the group process and some practical strategies for working with groups.

Groupwork theory has been developing since the turn of the century, with a number of social psychologists researching the dynamics of group behaviour. After the Second World War, as concern for the future of democracy grew, there was a further increase in interest in group dynamics and the ways in which groups could be encouraged to operate democratically and collaboratively (Johnson and Johnson 1987: 12–13). It is from this base that groupwork theory has developed, and belief in the principles of democracy and collaboration underpins groupwork theory and its application. This focus means that the principles of groupwork are compatible with the Primary Health Care philosophy, and have much to contribute to the practice of health promotion.

Groupwork theory has not developed for use with any collection of individuals. Rather, in discussing groupwork theory, a particular vision of groups is used. Johnson and Johnson (1987: 8) define a group as 'two or more individuals in face-to-face interaction, each aware of his or her membership in the group, each aware of the others who belong to the group, and each aware of their positive interdependence as they strive to achieve mutual goals'. Clearly many groups which meet do not fit this definition. However, by recognising and working with the principles of group dynamics, health workers can help people to gain as much as possible from group membership.

The typical life of a group

A number of theorists have proposed that groups typically go through a series of stages as they establish themselves, develop and wind down. Probably the most commonly used model is Tuckman's model of group development. It has been further developed by others, and is known now as a five-stage model, suggesting that a group typically goes through five stages in its life — forming, storming, norming, performing and ending (or mourning). These stages describe the way in which the group goes about its activities (that is, the process of its behaviour). Groups will be attempting to get on with the business which brought them together at the same time as these processes are developing. The latter may, however, structure the way in which a group tries to do its business, and the effectiveness of the group may depend to a large extent on how it develops through the five stages. It is worthwhile, therefore, examining Tuckman's model, as it provides a useful framework for understanding behaviours which can commonly occur at different times in a group's life.

It is important to recognise that, despite the impression that Tuckman's model may give, the stages of a group's life do not necessarily occur in a neat straight line. Moreover, groups may not go through all these stages; for example, some groups may get stuck in the storming process, not resolve the power and control issues, and so not perform effectively. On another level, however, this series of stages may be experienced to some extent every time a group gets together (Brown 1986: 82–3). Tuckman's model provides a useful guide to what we might normally expect in the life of a group. However, it is not definitive, for other models also have merit and are worthy of examination (see, for example, Sampson and Marthas 1990 or Bundey et al. 1989 for discussions of other models of group development). Also, as you examine groups with which you are involved, you will see the extent to which the life of individual groups varies in relation to those models, and you may like to add important points of your own. The following explanation of Tuckman's model is based on the summary given by Brown (1986: 74–82).

Forming

When the group first comes together, and for some time afterwards, it may be little more than a collection of individuals, rather than a group with its own identity. People may be feeling apprehensive about joining it, and anxious about their role in the group and how they should perform. At this point, if the group has a designated leader, that person usually plays a significant role, the members of the group being reluctant to take responsibility for decision making. Members rely on the leader to make decisions and control the direction of the activity in hand. At this time, they may be 'sussing out' the group and their role in it to decide if it has something to offer them. Formal group leaders therefore have an important role to play in making clear what the aims of the group are, and in negotiating with the group regarding what it will set out to do and how it will do it. In those cases where there is no designated leader, the group may be tentative at this stage as a leader begins to emerge or a number of people take up leadership positions.

Storming

In the storming stage of the group's life, people look for the role or roles they can play. Issues of power and control are often most prominent at this stage as group members jockey for position. At the same time, people may be afraid of losing their individuality and being absorbed into the group. As a result of both these factors, the group may at this stage be quite fragile. The leader may need to ensure that dominant people are not permitted to take over and all members have an opportunity to establish an equal role. This may take some skill, and this stage may be the most difficult for the leader to deal with.

Norming

Once most of the issues of power and control have been sorted out, the group is in a position to develop a sense of cohesion and trust between members. Norms of appropriate behaviour are set, and so people have a sense of where they stand and what is acceptable behaviour. As a result, group members may start to settle into the group. At this point its leader may need to harness the cohesion developed and use it to get the group working effectively on its tasks.

Performing

When members start taking responsibility for the group and its tasks, they are in the performing stage of its life. At this stage, there is a high level of cohesion and trust between members and the group is largely self-sufficient in relation to the leader. In many respects this stage is similar to the previous one: they differ only in the degree to which the group is performing its tasks and the level of self-sufficiency with which it is doing this.

Mourning

When the time comes for a group to come to an end, this will have an impact on it, even if it was convened to work for change and the end of the group signifies success (as, for example, in the case of a community action group working to resist the development of a highway through their town). In this final stage of the group, it is important for it to evaluate its achievements and deal with any unfinished business. Some members may want to postpone the end of the group because they may have benefited a great deal from being a group member and may want to continue enjoying the company of other members and the sense of achievement which the group may have been experiencing. Having some form of ritual ending, such as having a meal together or carrying out a 'group closure' activity (see Pfeiffer and Jones, 1974-1985) may help the group to finalise its activities and members to acknowledge its ending.

Elements of successful group work

Johnson and Johnson (1987: 8) suggest that a successful group is one which accomplishes its goals, maintains itself internally and develops to improve its effectiveness. For group effectiveness to be optimum, the following elements must be present (Johnson and Johnson 1987: 9–10).

- Goals must be clear and relevant.
- Communication must be accurate and clear, and two-way.
- Participation and leadership must be shared among members.
- Decision-making procedures must suit the issue being dealt with.
- Power and influence must be shared.
- Conflict and controversy must be encouraged.
- Group cohesion must be high.
- Problem-solving ability must be high.
- Interpersonal effectiveness must be high.

In observing a group, therefore, and deciding what aspects of its operations are effective and what may need improvement, there are a number of issues worth examining.

The task, maintenance and individual activities of the group

The activities that a group performs can be roughly divided into three types: those that get the group's task done, those that maintain the life of the group and therefore may help it to get its tasks done, and those that individuals perform to look after their own needs. It is important that groups address these sets of activities. If members try to push through to accomplish their tasks while ignoring the needs of individuals, the group may soon become ineffective. If, on the other hand, a group concentrates on maintaining itself, people may communicate effectively and enjoy meetings for a while, but may leave the group without having addressed the issue which brought them to it in the first place. They may leave feeling frustrated at the group's lack of achievement.

Of course, not all activities fit neatly into task functions or maintenance functions. Some activities may have components of both, and whether an activity is a task or maintenance function of a group may vary depending on the context and the particular group. For example, a support group's task activities may be the development of friendship and support networks, an activity which may be regarded in another type of group as having a maintenance function. All groups need to address both their task functions and their maintenance functions in order to succeed, although there is no set proportion of activities which need to fit into either category. What is important is that each group has a balance between the two types of activities. This balance will depend on the reason each group is meeting, and to some extent on the individual needs of people in each group.

You could ask yourself the following questions when observing task, maintenance and individual activities in a group:

- Who keeps the group from getting too far away from its task?

- Who asks the group for suggestions about how to deal with a problem?

- Does anyone summarise group discussion?

- Does anyone try to involve people who do not seem to be participating (Bundey et al. 1989: E101–2)?

- Does the group take time out to talk socially and find out how everyone's doing?

- Do the needs of any individuals in the group dominate?

Leadership

The pattern of leadership within a group is well worth examining, as it will tell us a great deal about how the group operates and how involved members are. Many people assume that the originator of the group is the only person who should exhibit leadership behaviours, but this is not so. Even in a group where a worker has some responsibility for it, if the group is to be effective, its leadership should be shared.

You could ask yourself the following questions when observing the leadership patterns in a group:

- Is leadership shared by members of the group, or does one person maintain control?

- Who exhibits leadership behaviours and who does not?

Power and influence

Power and influence are very much linked to leadership in a group. Indeed, if the people with the power and influence in a group are not its leaders, conflict may result. However, people with power and influence may not be those who talk the most or are the most active in the group. Bundey et al. (1989: E100) point out that some people may have a great deal of influence, but say little; however, when they do speak, others take notice.

You could ask yourself the following questions when observing power and influence in a group:

- Are there any people in the group whose opinions are listened to very carefully?

- Are there any people whose opinions are ignored?

- Are people with influence helping the group to achieve its goals?

- Are there conflicts between people with influence?

Decision making

Bundey et al. (1989: B40) explain that there are several aspects of decision making that need to be considered when observing group process. They are:

- **when** decisions are made (timing);
- **how** decisions are reached (process);
- **who** is responsible (who monitors the decision making process);
- **what** issues are to be decided.

When decisions are made reflects a number of important elements of the group process. In a formal health education group, for example, this might include examination of what decisions the group leader makes before the group actually starts, thus preventing the whole group from being involved in those decisions. In community action groups it might include consideration of whether important decisions are left until the end of long and arduous meetings, when people may not be as fresh and capable of good decision making as they could be, or when people with other commitments have had to leave.

You could ask yourself the following questions when observing decision making in a group:

- How are decisions made in this group:
  — by one person?
  — by a small dominant group?
  — by simple majority?
  — by consensus?

- Who controls the decision-making procedures in a group?

Group goals

A key issue in determining whether people are involved in a group is the extent to which they share the group's goals. If the goals of an individual do not match the goals of the group, it is unlikely that he or she will be committed to it. Once again, this is just as relevant for community groups as for groups participating in health education activities. In either case, if someone or a small group of people dominate the goal-setting process, other people can be left out of the group or drop out because of lack of commitment. In formal health education groups, this can happen when the group leader alone establishes the goals of the group without involving members in the process. The goals of the group might then suit no one in the group, and might reflect only the group leader's ideas of what people want. What a waste of energy when simply determining group goals together could prevent this!

You could ask yourself the following questions when observing goal setting in a group:

- Does the group have clear goals?

- Who was involved in establishing them?

- Who 'owns' goals set?

- Are there members of the group who do not seem to share the group goals?

Communication

Patterns of communication in a group are extremely important. Distribution of leadership, participation, power and control, and conflicts of interest, will all be reflected in observable patterns of communication. Communication is both verbal and non-verbal, and occurs between individuals and between an individual and the group. It has a key role in facilitating the group's achievement of its tasks and group members' comfort and sense of belonging.

You could ask yourself the following questions when observing communication in a group:

- Who talks and to whom?

- Who keeps the interaction going in the group?

- Are people silent, and if so, how does the group respond (Bundey et al. 1989: B46)?

- Do people address the whole group when they talk or just some people? (Is this a function of anxiety in some group members or the dynamics of the group?)

- What non-verbal communication is happening?

- How powerful are the non-verbal messages?

- Is anyone giving mixed messages?

- Is more being not said than said?

Rules and norms

Many groups will establish appropriate rules of behaviour or ground rules to guide their activities. For example, it might be decided that only one person will speak at any one time, that only the spokesperson will speak publicly for the group or that discussions at group meetings are confidential. In addition to the rules themselves, what is important is how they were developed. Did the group as a whole decide on them and agree with them, or were they imposed on the group by a leader?

As well as these explicit rules by which the group operates, there may be a number of norms guiding the group, of which group members may or may not be aware (Bundey et al. 1989: E103). Norms are implicit rules which guide the activities of the group, often more strongly than the explicit rules. They influence the group powerfully, and can either support its activities or hinder its progress, depending on the norms themselves and what the group is trying to achieve. Some examples of group norms are that it is okay to turn up to group meetings 15 minutes late because they won't start until then; that it is okay to talk about each other when no one else is around; that it is okay to interrupt each other during discussions and dominate discussion; and that it is not okay to disagree with someone else in the group.

In deciding whether a norm is unhelpful, it is important to look carefully at what is happening and what role it plays in the group's behaviour overall. For example, what may at first glance seem like an unhelpful norm may actually act as a valuable means of releasing tension. Laughter and games interrupting meeting procedure may be one example of this. It is vital that cultural norms also be considered. For instance, what may seem like an unhelpful norm of people consistently being late for group meetings may stem from particular cultural views of time in which being ruled by the clock is not as strong as it is in Anglo culture. In these cases, it is more likely to be the group leader, not the group, that will need to do the adapting.

However, in those instances where unhelpful norms are minimising the group's ability to function, it will be necessary for the group leader to deal with the issue. This will mean making the group aware of what is happening, since it may not be conscious of the norm operating. Sometimes this will be enough: individuals will recognise how they are contributing to the norm and will agree to change their behaviour. If this does not happen, the group as a whole will need to decide how best to deal with it. Perhaps they will decide to leave things as they are and wear the consequences, or they may establish new ground rules and agree to stick to them. Alternatively, the norm may have arisen because a particular aspect of the group did not suit some group members, and the group may therefore decide to make the appropriate changes. For example, if people are consistently arriving late, it may be that the starting time for meetings needs to be altered to fit in with other commitments which people have.

You could ask yourself the following questions when observing rules and norms in a group:

- What are the rules guiding behaviour in the group?
- Which of these are 'written' (i.e. rules) and which are 'unwritten' (i.e. norms)?
- Which seem to be supporting the group's activities and which seem to be hindering its progress?
- Are there any which are hindering the group's progress which group members do not seem to be aware of?

Controversy and creativity

Controversy can be extremely important to the life of a group. From it come new ideas and challenges to people's thinking. Unfortunately, people sometimes think that controversy is bad and to be avoided at all costs, and so do not allow it to be explored. Not only does this deprive the group of the opportunity to develop new and innovative solutions to the problems they are addressing, it can also run the risk of damaging the group. Irving Janis has highlighted the great danger posed by 'groupthink' if controversy is not allowed to exist in a group.

Groupthink is described as a process which can occur when disagreement and creativity are stifled, and it results in extremely poor decisions, often out of touch with reality. It has been highlighted as the cause of some of the disastrous decisions made in political history. It typically occurs when the group has a strong directive leader, when criticism within the group is stifled and when opportunities for criticism from outside the group are removed. As a result, uncritical acceptance of the leader's opinions leads to extremely poor, even dangerous, decisions.

Janis (1982, cited by Johnson and Johnson 1987: 119–20) has outlined eight symptoms of groupthink. These are:

1. *Self-censorship*. Group members censor themselves by not voicing any concerns about the issue being discussed.

2. *Illusion of unanimity*. Because of the lack of discussion, group members assume that everyone else is in agreement about the issue.

3. *Direct pressure on dissenters*. If anyone does speak out, pressure is brought to bear on that person to conform.

4. *'Mind guards'*. Some particular group members take on the role of discouraging objections.

5. *Illusion of invulnerability*. Members assume that the group is in a powerful position and cannot be criticised by outsiders. This results in very risky decisions.

6. *Rationalisation*. Group members rationalise the decision taken, in order to justify to themselves the position adopted by the group.

7. *Illusion of morality*. The group does not consider the ethical issues involved, and assumes that it is morally above reproach.

8. *Stereotyping*. Group members stereotype critics or competitors ('they are all stupid') in order to rationalise any outside opposition.

Groupthink provides an extreme example of what can happen to a group and its decision making when creativity and controversy are discouraged. I am sure that many people have experienced at least mild forms of groupthink and been concerned about its impact.

You could ask yourself the following questions when observing controversy and creativity in a group:

- How do the others respond when a group member makes an unusual suggestion?

- Does the group use processes to encourage creative thinking amongst its members (for example, brainstorming)?

Rules for fighting fair

Do I want to resolve the conflict?
- BE WILLING TO FIX THE PROBLEM.

Can I see the whole picture, not just my point of view?
- BROADEN YOUR OUTLOOK.

What are the needs and anxieties of everyone involved?
- WRITE THEM DOWN.

How can we make this fair?
- NEGOTIATE.

What are the possibilities?
- THINK UP AS MANY SOLUTIONS AS YOU CAN. PICK THE ONE THAT GIVES EVERYONE MORE OF WHAT THEY WANT.

Can we work it out together?
- TREAT EACH OTHER AS EQUALS.

What am I feeling?
- AM I TOO EMOTIONAL NOW? COULD I GET MORE FACTS? TELL THEM HOW I FEEL?

What do I want to change?
- BE CLEAR. ATTACK THE PROBLEM, NOT THE PERSON.

What opportunity can this bring?
- WORK ON THE POSITIVES, NOT THE NEGATIVES.

What is it like to be in their shoes?
- DO THEY KNOW I UNDERSTAND THEM?

Do we need a neutral third person?
- COULD THIS HELP US TO UNDERSTAND EACH OTHER AND CREATE OUR OWN SOLUTIONS?

How can we both win?
- WORK TOWARDS SOLUTIONS WHERE EVERYONE'S NEEDS ARE RESPECTED.

Copyright The Conflict Resolution Network
PO Box 1016 Chatswood NSW 2057
Australia

Conflicts of interest

If controversy in a group is extreme, it may be that real conflicts of interest are present. Perhaps members of a community action group are there for very different reasons, and so the group cannot decide on an action plan. Perhaps a worker acting as group leader is in a group because of his or her agency's statutory responsibilities, and not because of a personal commitment to helping people facing the particular issue being addressed. In any case, when conflicts of interest are not handled well, they can damage a group and hurt individuals involved in it. It is therefore vital that group leaders be able to recognise conflicts of interest, and where possible structure activities to minimise the damage caused by those conflicts. The possibility of conflicts of interest is one reason why clarifying the group's goals and involving everybody in their establishment are so important. These may not be enough to prevent conflicts of interest, but they are an important start.

You could ask yourself the following questions when observing conflict in a group:

- Are there issues which always bring out anger?

- Is the group working through conflicts which arise or are these a barrier to action?

- Are there any people who seem to be always disagreeing and unable to allow others' viewpoints?

- How does the rest of the group respond to this?

This brief overview of the various elements of group dynamics should provide you with a standpoint from which to observe these elements at work. As you become more sensitive to group dynamics, you will learn to use these dynamics to enable the group to work together more effectively.

Working with experiential groups

Experiential groups are groups run with the emphasis on the process of group involvement and what people can learn about themselves and relating to others through the experiences of the group. They can play an important role in mental health promotion. However, working effectively with them requires skills which cannot be developed through reading alone. If you wish to work effectively in this manner, I recommend that you complete a training course in group leadership. For more information about such courses, contact the Institute of Group Leaders at 65 Cambridge St, Paddington, NSW 2021.

Some hints for working with groups

These hints for working with groups have been developed from Ewles and Simnett (1985: 122–6).

Numbers

In considering the optimal size of a group, the first consideration will be the purpose for which the group is meeting. If it is a public meeting designed to canvass opinion on an issue, the actual size of the group may not influence effectiveness. If it is a structured meeting where members of a number of interested parties need representation, the size of the group may be determined by the number of such parties.

If, on the other hand, the group is a health education group built on the principle of maximum participation by its members, it will be important to keep it to a manageable size. In such cases, the optimal size of a group is regarded as being between 8 and 12 people. If there are fewer than 8 people in a group, people may feel exposed and be unwilling to participate. Moreover, an insufficient number of ideas may be generated in a problem-solving group. However, if there are more than 12 people in a group, it is difficult for everyone to get involved, and often the louder members will dominate.

If you need to have more than 12 people in a group, consider whether you can split it up into smaller groups for discussion and activities. Alternatively, it may be worthwhile running two separate groups alongside each other. Which solution to choose will depend on the reason the group is meeting (can the topic 'cope' with a large group?) and the amount of resources you have (can you afford to run the same group twice?). If, however, you are dealing with a sensitive topic, it may be appropriate to have a group of fewer than eight people in order to enable people to speak comfortably about the topic. In these cases, you may also consider whether it is more appropriate to discuss the topic on a one-to-one basis.

Timing

The length of time that a group meets for is very important in determining whether members feel it is valuable or not. Groups need to be together long enough to break the ice, settle down and achieve something, but not so long that people begin to get bored or feel they are wasting their time. Generally, between an hour and an hour and a half is a reasonable amount of time. Breaks or changes in the group's activity will enable it to stay fresh for that length of time, or even longer if necessary. However, meetings lasting more than one and a half hours would need to be well planned, and you would need a good reason to justify them. Planning the length of meetings with the participants will increase the likelihood that the duration planned is realistic and fits in with the other needs of group members.

The day and time that the group meets will have a considerable bearing on who will attend. There are some commonsense rules you can follow to ensure that the timing does not prevent people from attending. For example, after school in the afternoon may not be a good time to run a single parents' support group unless child care is available. Meetings between 5.30 pm and 7 pm may be unpopular, since this is when many people have their dinner.

All the planning in the world, however, will not enable you to prevent clashes with the other commitments which members of each particular group may have. It therefore makes good sense to check at the group's first meeting whether the day and time suit members, and if they do not, to negotiate a day and time that suit most of them. Not only does this increase the likelihood that people can attend the group, it also makes it quite clear that the group belongs to everyone, not just the group leader. Furthermore, you may want to experiment with different meeting times in order to maximise attendance and ensure that people who want to attend the groups are not consistently missing out because of poor timing.

Location

Location can also be negotiated. It is important that group members feel comfortable in the venue. Obviously, if people feel threatened, they are unlikely to continue going to the group. For example, many Aboriginal people have had negative experiences in hospitals, and may not feel comfortable in a hospital or community health centre. If there is no local Aboriginal Health Centre, the local Aboriginal Land Council offices may be a comfortable place to meet.

Remember that hospitals, and to a lesser extent community health centres, have a history of being authoritarian and of being places where people lose control over themselves. It may be difficult for these associations to be broken, and so in the meantime if there is any doubt, find a more neutral place. Church halls, Country Women's Association halls, Youth clubs, Senior Citizens centres, Aboriginal Land Council offices and people's homes are just some examples of possible meeting places. Which venue is most appropriate will depend very much on the members of the group.

Another important point about location is that it needs to be accessible to group members. Organising a group to meet in a venue that is not accessible by public transport is likely to prevent some people from being able to attend.

Seating

If a group is to work successfully, all members need to feel that they have an equal right to participate. Obviously, seating such as that in a typical classroom is not likely to make people feel equal members of the group. For this reason, seating arranged in a circle is the most effective arrangement. If people have comfortable lounge chairs rather than school seating, they are more likely to feel comfortable. Ewles and Simnett suggest that removing desks and other furniture that is likely to create a barrier between people is important. However, until group members get to know one another, such barriers are sometimes useful because they stop people feeling exposed or threatened.

Green and Kreuter (1991: 77) point out, however, that even when seated in a circle people may not have equal opportunity to participate, because sitting directly in front of the facilitator makes it easier to speak owing to the additional eye contact likely to be received. The facilitator might therefore sit opposite shy people in order to encourage them to speak, or next to someone who is talkative in order to minimise eye contact with that person.

Self-help groups

Self-help groups have been growing in popularity over the last few years, and can offer a great deal to people who join them. They may work for social change or for personal change in their members, or a combination of both. The challenge for such groups is to find the appropriate balance between these two approaches (Biklen 1983: 206–7). 'Self-help refers to groups developed and controlled by affected people themselves, by consumers and by victims. They are, by their nature, committed to self-determination' (Biklen 1983: 185). Their roles include 'mutual support . . . education, advocacy, lobbying, research and information and service provision to both their members and other consumers of the health system' (Markos 1991: 4).

Self-help groups often develop as a challenge to the mainstream health system, or find themselves challenging the system once they are established. This is because they often form in response to inadequate services for their needs. Whether they actively challenge the system or not, professionals can feel threatened by people addressing their own needs because they are unhappy with the way in which the system addresses them. Self-help groups demand information from professionals when many are still unwilling to share it, and in so doing challenge the status and power differences between professional and client. They may even question the limits of professional knowledge and the basis on which it is developed (Biklen 1983: 201–4). There have been instances where health workers have been unhappy with consumers having control over their own health care and have felt threatened by consumers suggesting that they have knowledge and competence not possessed by the health worker (see, for example, Hunt 1990: 181).

Consciousness raising plays an important role in the development of many self-help groups. Through talking together and sharing their experiences, members of these groups discover their shared ground and the common sources of oppression or indifference (Biklen 1983: 193–4). Self-help groups may work to create their own alternative services or to change those already in operation (Biklen 1983: 195). In either case, they often demand greater control over services in order that they may better meet their needs.

Unless they are appropriately funded, self-help groups may be encouraged by government in a way which exploits the community members who join them, and particularly those who put considerable energy into organising and running them on a day-to-day basis. That is, governments may support self-help groups because they are a cheap option, and because they assume the burden of responsibility for action in what are often difficult or previously ignored areas. Health workers need to reflect critically on suggestions to encourage the development of self-help groups, so as to ensure that these groups do not develop more for the benefit of the health system than the community itself.

In deciding whether a self-help group should be established, health workers must consider whether the people concerned actually want such a group — that is, whether felt need is present. As obvious as this may sound, on many occasions health workers establish self-help groups and then wonder why people do not participate. Clearly, community members will not participate in a group if they do not feel they need to do so. Attempts to impose self-help groups are likely to be unsuccessful, and may well set similar groups up to fail, once a community perception of a self-help group as failing has been established.

Another problem with some health workers' approaches to self-help groups is that these people may support the idea of these groups being support groups, but are less supportive of, and even discourage, self-help groups which take on action group activities. However, supporting these groups for their support work only, and discouraging social action, amounts to a form of social control, where group members are expected to put all their energy into achieving tasks which could perhaps be achieved legitimately by the health system, and not supported to work for the necessary changes.

Health workers have an important role to play with self-help groups in supporting them and acting as consultants, when groups request this. They should act as resources, and not take over the decision-making process (Kearney 1991: 31). Developing a partnership between self-help groups and health workers may enable the former to continue their work effectively. Like any good partnership, the relationship between health workers and self-help groups should be one of mutual respect.

Self-help groups contribute a great deal to the health of members of the community. The examples of the 'Northcote Hydrotherapy and Massage Group' and 'Club 2430' provide some insight into the development and activities of two locality-based self-help groups which have developed with the support of health workers and gone on to be largely self-sufficient.

Northcote Hydrotherapy and Massage Group

We are a group of older women who had been attending hydrotherapy classes organised by the Northcote Community Health Centre's physiotherapist. We had a range of physical problems, with many of us experiencing great difficulty in getting about.

Because of increasing demands on her work, the physiotherapist suggested that we organise ourselves. One member with swimming qualifications became the group leader for the exercises, following advice from the physiotherapist. The group members work their own way through the hydrotherapy exercises now if the leader is not there, and we all contribute new exercises as we hear of useful ones. The group lobbied for two years to have the Melbourne City Council adjust the water temperature, and were successful. But because the button is not pushed early enough every day, we are still working on this.

Seven years ago massage was introduced into the group. We applied to the Women's Trust Fund and received funds for a masseur to teach us how to massage each other and to assist when specialist treatment was required. Everyone who is massaged has to massage one of the others. The health centre made a room available. Five men joined the group for massage, but left when their health improved.

We began more formal meetings when we had to put together a submission to apply for funding for the masseur. We recognised that the company and support we provided one another was a big plus, and so we decided to organise some bus trips we could go on together. We applied for more funds, this time to the Department of Sport and Recreation, for a bus driver (we were able to borrow the council bus). The physiotherapist helped with the submission writing and the health centre assisted by offering its treasury and auditing services. Much to our delight we received $4000 of the $5000 we had applied for. Since then we have organised a number of outings, which have been wonderful events for all.

The group holds a committee meeting once a month. Decisions are made democratically and a number of people have taken on specific roles as a result of their expertise. We have recently had some frail older people referred to us, as professionals have heard about the value of the group's activities. We also have been involved in writing a book, entitled *Put your whole self in* (McDonald 1992). Stories about the exercises we do in the water are included in it.

We think that our success is due much to the support and positive attitude of the Northcote Community Health Centre staff, who have given assistance when necessary, without taking over. We are encouraged to make our own decisions, and enjoy the independence. Remaining independent is very important to us.

Many of our lives have changed as a result of the group. As we have said before, 'Our group will continue going probably until we drop dead, or as long as we can get onto a bus or tram. Our ambition is to spread this message of self-help, dignity and independence to senior citizens groups, health centres and such places around the country. Our work should help do that' (Community Development in Health Project 1988: 42).

Members of the Northcote Hydrotherapy and Massage Group

The development of Club 2430

In 1982 the first case of the human immunodeficiency virus (HIV) was diagnosed in Australia. Most Australians took very little notice. A decade later, and with increased awareness and knowledge, Australia is beginning to sit up and take notice. We now know that approximately 16 500 individuals (as of August 1992) in Australia — male, female, old, young, black, white, heterosexual, bisexual, homosexual—have been infected with the HIV virus. This virus does not discriminate.

Conservative rural communities of Australia continue to see HIV/AIDS as a metropolitan disease and to believe they are not at risk. The challenge of addressing the needs of those who are at risk in a rural area is a difficult one. Accessing those at risk seemed to me, a high-profile middle-aged female community health worker, an impossible task. Could someone in my position contact those at risk and, more important, would I be accepted and trusted? Had I adequately addressed and dealt with my own prejudices?

The AIDS Council of New South Wales (ACON) in Sydney had appointed a rural outreach worker and he was touring rural New South Wales trying to contact those men who have sex with men, so as to provide peer support programs. His visit inspired me to make a concerted effort to address the needs of gay men and women. An advertisement was placed in the local newspapers (four in all) asking anyone interested in forming a gay support group to meet at the local community health centre on the third Tuesday in November 1991. A total of 19 people, both male and female, came along.

At this inaugural meeting a steering committee was formed. Members came and went, and within two months membership remained steady at five. In 1992, the group decided to call itself Club 2430.

To stimulate public interest, to present a positive image of the gay community and to show that HIV/AIDS was indeed a virus to be reckoned with, the club's first venture was to host a visit of the AIDS Memorial Quilt. Over 1400 people viewed the display, and three new quilts were handed over to join the existing 400. The success of this promotion prompted the quilt project representatives to ask the club to write a booklet on how to host a rural quilt display.

Twelve months passed and the first annual general meeting was held on 3 November 1992. Chairperson, secretary, treasurer and social secretary were the elected positions. Meetings are now held on the first Tuesday in the month. Membership is $20 a year. In December 1992 there were 19 financial members.

The first twelve months of the group have not been all plain sailing. Personalities, financial conflicts and differences of opinion have caused concern both for me and for members of the group. However, the group's achievements far outweigh any difficulties:

- Six club members have attended ACON's peer support workshop.

- One member voluntarily accesses the local beats offering support, HIV/AIDS and safer sex information, condoms and lubricant.

- Contact has been made with the local police to provide support services for gay members of the community who have been assaulted or bashed, and to provide positive gay/police networking.

- Members have represented the club at national and state HIV/AIDS conferences, with some presenting papers and workshops.

- Support, counselling and respite services are available to HIV-positive persons and their families.

Two gay and lesbian fundraising dances have been held, with new members making contact on both these occasions.

- A monthly newsletter, which is now distributed to over 40 contacts, is published. It contains updated information on HIV/AIDS, treatments, future social activities, workshops, conferences and contacts from other gay groups.

- A brochure, providing contact numbers and listing the aims and objectives of the club, has been distributed to health and support services in the local area.

Club 2430 has provided an identity for an otherwise unidentified group within our small rural community. It has provided educative and supportive services, networked with government departments and allowed members to socialise and interact with their community at large. Members report that their self-esteem, confidence and pride in their sexuality have all increased since joining the club. Comments from members include the following:

- 'I now feel that I belong.'

- 'For the first time in over 50 years I now feel that I am part of a group that truly understands me and where I can be myself.'

- 'I am no longer afraid to go to clubs. We have strength in numbers.'

- 'My self esteem has greatly increased and I now feel I can talk openly about the death of my lover.'

As the community health worker faced with the daunting task of accessing those at risk, I feel that Club 2430 members have enriched my life by:

- allowing me to truly analyse my prejudices;

- offering support and care at difficult times during my life as an HIV worker;

- challenging me to come up with new and innovative ideas to prevent the spread of HIV/AIDS;

- encouraging me to stay on track and continue against certain discriminatory forces;

- providing an opportunity for me to examine the 'need to be needed' concept, as a result of which I was able to let go and thus enable the group to control itself (I now act as a support person).

Club 2430 members' positive focus on support, socialisation and education, not homosexuality, has enabled them to be accepted and respected by the local community. Already they have achieved a great deal.

Liz Meadley, RN, RM
Health Education Officer—HIV/AIDS
Lower North Coast District Health Service

Getting the group started

How the group is established and the atmosphere that is created when it first meets will help determine whether people go to future meetings. It is therefore important to start the group in a way that breaks the ice and enables people to feel comfortable in their surroundings and with each other. If you are organising a group meeting for community development or action work, this may be done fairly informally through introductions and discussion of the particular issues involved. However, for an educational or support group, it might be done more formally.

Icebreakers

A number of things can be done at the beginning of a group's life, and to a lesser extent at the beginning of each group meeting, to break the ice and help relax people into their surroundings. They provide an opportunity for people to introduce themselves to one another and discuss their reasons for being involved with the group or what they want to accomplish. As a result, many of these activities can also serve as goal-setting activities.

Some common icebreaker activities

- A group member interviews another group member and then introduces him or her to the rest of the group. The type of questions asked varies according to the type of group. For example, people attending an asthma education group may discuss their own experiences of asthma and why they have come to the group. One problem with this activity, however, is that people tend to mix up the name of the person who was introduced with the name of the person who did the introducing. For this reason I would be reluctant to use this activity with people who are particularly likely to have difficulty in remembering names.

- Each person introduces himself/herself to the group, answering a series of questions of relevance to it. This overcomes the problem of mixing up names.

- Each person introduces himself/herself and then repeats the names of all the people who have already introduced themselves.

- Each person introduces himself/herself and then throws a ball to someone else, saying the name of that person. You cannot return the ball to the person who threw it.

Introducing the group

Once the ice is broken and people are settled in you can introduce the group and its goals. If you have asked people during the icebreaker to tell you what they want to achieve from the group, you can now all use this information to plan together the group goals. You may find at this time that your own goals for the group go out the window to some extent, and the group together plans its goals.

By the time you have finished the introduction, members should have an understanding of the group and what it will achieve, and should have had an opportunity to change the group plan so that it more accurately meets their needs.

Experiential activity

Having met one another and found out what issues will be covered during the group's life, group members should leave the first meeting also having had a taste of what the group will be doing. You might therefore involve the group in an activity that begins its formal life or demonstrates just what you will achieve. For example, a stress management group might discuss the particular stressors of its members and do a relaxation exercise. In this way, members are able to leave the first meeting with some sense of whether the group is likely to be beneficial for them, and whether they plan to return.

Facilitating discussion

So very often people plan to have a discussion in a group, but they do not plan how it will actually happen. They assume that if they say, 'Let's discuss . . . ' a discussion will just begin. Unfortunately, the times when that will happen are more the exception than the rule. Most times, it is necessary to structure activities that will enable a discussion to develop. You may not need them, but more often than not you will. It will be necessary to have an idea of group members' attitudes to the topic before launching into discussion, so that you have a sense of what approach you can take to it. Can you be provocative in order to encourage a vigorous debate, or do you need to begin gently and lead the group into the controversial areas? You will need to bear this in mind when planning discussion. The following activities may be used to encourage discussion.

Using trigger materials

Show a film or play a game that touches on the issues you hope to cover. If it is slightly controversial, it will motivate people to discuss the issues. Then ask specific questions to draw out the pertinent issues. Make sure that you plan a set of questions before the event, and that these are open-ended so that you do not simply receive yes or no answers.

Debate

Break the group into two, provide both sides with information if necessary, give them time to prepare and then have them debate the issue. Of course, if you want to encourage participation you may be better to keep the debate informal. Having group members argue the position they disagree with is one way of enabling them to clarify their views and hear the views of their 'opponents'.

Brainstorming

Brainstorming is a good way to pool everyone's ideas and come up with innovative ones, especially if you are trying to find solutions to a problem. It could be used, for example, to come up with ways to change the attitudes of local government councillors towards child care facilities, convince businesses to become environmentally responsible, devise effective overeating avoidance tactics or plan stress release activities into a normal working day.

   The typical strategy for brainstorming is the following one. Put the problem or issue to the group. Ask participants to think up as many ideas as possible, without judging their own or other people's ideas. All suggestions are accepted and written down. Keep going until all ideas are exhausted and people cannot think of anything else.

What you do next depends on the reason for the brainstorming. If the group was trying to find the most appropriate solution to a problem, the next step would be to prioritise the suggestions made. This may require group members simply to vote, or there may be lengthy discussion, depending on the issue and the philosophy of the group. If the brainstorming was designed to answer a question, you may want simply to group the answers into similar categories.

Rounds

Rounds are good because they ensure that everyone has an equal opportunity to participate. They can therefore be used both to encourage shy group members to speak and to prevent dominant group members from monopolising conversation.

Ewles and Simnett (1985: 125) suggest three rules that are necessary if rounds are to be successful. They are:

- no interruptions until each person has finished his statement;

- no comments on anybody's contribution until the full round is complete (i.e. no discussion, praise, interpretation, criticism or I-think-that-too type of remark);

- anyone can choose not to participate. Give permission, clearly and emphatically, that anyone who does not want to make a statement can just say 'pass'. This is very important for reinforcing the principle of voluntary participation.

Rounds can be valuable for beginning and ending sessions and getting feedback, or as a measurement of the entire group's opinion.

Conclusion

Awareness of group process is an extremely useful component of working effectively with groups, whether they are work teams, social action groups, participants in a health education group or members of a family. Working with groups in a supportive, enabling way, rather than a limiting or controlling way, is an important part of work to promote health from a Primary Health Care perspective.

REFERENCES AND FURTHER READINGS

Biklen, D. P. 1983. *Community organizing: theory and practice*, Prentice Hall, Englewood Cliffs, New Jersey.

Brown, A. 1986. *Groupwork*, Gower, Aldershot, UK.

Bundey, C., Cullen, J., Denshire, L., Grant, J., Norfor, J. and Nove, T. 1989. *Group leadership: a manual about group leadership and a resource for group leaders*, Western Sydney Area Health Promotion Unit, Westmead.

Community Development in Health Project. 1988. *Community development in health: a resource collection*, Community Development in Health Project, District Health Council, Preston/Northcote.

Douglas, T. 1983. *Groups: understanding people gathered together*, Tavistock, London.

Ewles, L. and Simnett, I. 1985. *Promoting health: a practical guide to health education*, John Wiley and Sons, Chichester, UK.

Green, L. W. and Kreuter, M. W. 1991. *Health promotion planning: an educational and environmental approach*, Mayfield, Mountain View, California.

Hart, L. B. 1981. *Learning from conflict: a handbook for trainers and group leaders*, Addison-Wesley, Reading, Massachusetts.

Hunt, S. 1990. Building alliances: professional and political issues in community participation: examples from a health and community development project, *Health Promotion International*, 5(3), 179–85.

Johnson, D. W. and Johnson, F. P. 1987. *Joining together: group theory and group skills*, Prentice Hall, Englewood Cliffs, New Jersey.

Kearney, J. 1991. The role of self help groups: challenging the system and complementing professionals, *Health Issues*, 28, 29–31.

Lawson, J. and Callaghan, A. 1991. Recreating the village: groups for new mothers, *Australian Journal of Public Health*, (15)1, 64–6.

Markos, S. 1991. *Self help groups and the role they play in the health care system*, Health Issues Centre, Melbourne.

McDonald, M. 1992. *Put your whole self in*, Penguin, Ringwood, Victoria.

Nelson-Jones, R. 1991. *Leading training groups: A manual of practical skills for trainers*, Harcourt Brace Jovanovich, Sydney.

Pfeiffer, J. W. (ed). 1983. *The encyclopedia of icebreakers: structured activities that warm-up, motivate, challenge, acquaint, and energize*, Pfeiffer and Company, San Diego, California.

Pfeiffer, J. W. (ed). 1989. *The encyclopedia of group activities: 150 practical designs for successful facilitating*. University Associates, San Diego, California.

Pfeiffer, J. W. (ed). 1991. *The encyclopedia of team-development activities*, Pfeiffer and Company, San Diego, California.

Pfeiffer, J. W. (ed). 1991. *The encyclopedia of team-building activities*, Pfeiffer and Company, San Diego, California.

Pfeiffer, J. W. and Jones, J. E. (1974–1985). *A handbook of structured experiences for human relations training*, Volumes 1–10, University Associates, San Diego, California.

Richards, C. and Walsh, F. 1990. *Negotiating*, Australian Government Publishing Service, Canberra.

Sampson, E. E. and Marthas, M. 1990. *Group process for the health professions*, Delmar, New York.

Scott, D. 1981. *Don't mourn for me — organise*, Allen and Unwin, Sydney.

Scott, S. 1988. *Positive peer groups*, Human Resource Development Press, Amherst, Massachusetts.

Tyson, T. 1989. *Working with groups*, Macmillan, Melbourne.

Women and Addiction Support Group. 1991. Self help is expert help, *Health Issues*, 28, 22–4.

CHAPTER **9**

Education for health

Education plays a central role in health promotion. Not only is education itself a common health promotion strategy; it is also involved to some extent in just about every other health promotion strategy which is used. Working for public policy change, community development, using the mass media, and working with individuals and groups all involve education in some form or another — whether it be education of policy makers, health workers or community members. Education is therefore inextricably linked with all other forms of health promotion. In this chapter we review some of the principles of health education, or education for health, and consider the particular approaches to education which sit most comfortably with the Primary Health Care approach.

Values in health education

In chapter 2 we reviewed a number of key values in health promotion, and many of these have particular relevance to health education. In particular, the attitudes of health workers towards community members, the presence or absence of victim blaming or labelling, and the role which health workers see education as having, all have a major impact on both the way in which education occurs and the likely outcome of that education.

Health workers using a Primary Health Care approach work in partnership with community members, recognising the expertise which these members bring to the learning process. They are also careful to avoid victim blaming, working with people to help change the environment as well as individual behaviours when people determine they need assistance to change these. Health workers using the Primary Health Care approach also recognise education as an enabling strategy rather than one to encourage compliance with others' wishes. For this to occur the focus is on participation in which community members have decision-making power, not merely token involvement. Because of the central role of these values in health education, you are encouraged to review chapter 2 if you are not familiar with these issues.

187

The changing focus of health education

Until relatively recently, education of individuals to change their behaviours, out of the context of changes to the environment, was regarded as the only goal of health education. With the development of the new public health movement, however, this focus on health education went out of favour as health workers recognised that imploring individuals to change their behaviour would not address problems created by an unhealthy environment or the actions of other people. With this recognition has emerged a focus on health promotion in its broadest sense, and a shift of emphasis away from health education.

However, it would be a mistake to believe that health education is no longer important. Rather, health education remains central to health promotion, both because health education is the basis from which the current approach to health promotion has developed, and because health education plays a vital role in attempts to promote health using other strategies (Green and Kreuter 1991: 14). Moreover, education which focuses on helping individuals aquire new skills and knowledge still has an important place if we are to help people further develop their skills for dealing with the variety of situations which they encounter.

Nonetheless, the change in philosophy that is marked by the new public health movement has resulted in a shift in emphasis within health education. Education has been recognised as having an important role to play in work for social change (Freudenberg 1984: 40), and emphasis has moved away from education of individuals solely to change their behaviour towards recognition of the power of education to help create a healthy environment. Tones et al. (1990: 5) describe the two key ways in which education is used to help create and support a healthy environment as *agenda setting* and *conscientisation*.

Agenda setting is the use of education at the community level to explain and convince people why public policy changes are important. Recent Australian examples of the use of agenda setting include the education campaigns which preceded the reduction of legal blood alcohol levels from 0.08 to 0.05 mg/L; education about the benefits of car seat belt wearing before legislation making car seat belts compulsory; and education about the importance of cycling helmets before legislation making them compulsory. In agenda setting, education can occur through formal education campaigns, and through public discussion and debate within the mass media.

Conscientisation, or critical consciousness raising, may be regarded as the more radical approach to education for social change (Tones et al. 1990: 5). Critical consciousness raising is discussed in further detail below, because of its central importance in Primary Health Care.

Defining health education

A typical definition of health education is: 'any combination of learning experiences designed to facilitate voluntary actions conducive to health' (Green and Kreuter 1991: 17). This definition is important for its recognition that any changes must be made on the voluntary decisions of the person or people concerned, and that health education often involves a variety of strategies or a number of interactions. It also includes scope for a variety of health promoting actions, rather than limiting health education to individual behaviour change, though this point is perhaps less obvious. Freudenberg (1984: 40) has attempted to make this final point more explicit and account for the broader range of activities which form part of education for social change by defining health education as 'those efforts that educate and mobilise people to create more healthful environments, institutions and policies (as well as lifestyles)'. The scope of health education is therefore quite broad, as is reflected in Ewles and Simnett's seven dimensions of health education (1985: 28):

1. Health, and therefore health education, is concerned with the whole person, and encompasses physical, mental, social, emotional, spiritual and societal aspects.

2. Health education is a life-long process from birth to death, helping people to change and adapt at all stages.

3. Health education is concerned with people at all points of health and illness, from the completely healthy to the chronically sick and handicapped, to maximize each person's potential for healthy living.

4. Health education is directed towards individuals, families, groups and whole communities.

5. Health education is concerned with helping people to help themselves and with helping people to work towards creating healthier conditions for everybody, 'making healthy choices easier choices'.

6. Health education involves formal and informal teaching and learning using a range of methods.

7. Health education is concerned with a range of goals, including giving information, attitude change, behaviour change and social change.

Within a Primary Health Care approach, then, health education is used across a broad spectrum of activities, from patient education, through individual education for healthy choices, to education for social change. However, the philosophical positions from which these kinds of education have traditionally occurred is quite different (Tones et al. 1990: 6). Both patient education and health education for individual behaviour change had their roots in the medical model, and much education of this nature remains within the medical model. However, this does not mean that all education of this kind occurs from a medical model perspective. Nor does it mean that all education which can be described as education for social change is necessarily built on a social model of health. The difference between agenda setting and conscientisation provides a clear demonstration of this. Remaining focussed on the principles of Primary Health Care and applying these principles to the conduct of education, no matter what the setting or the impetus for education, is therefore a major challenge for the health worker.

Education for critical consciousness

The concept of education for critical consciousness, critical consciousness-raising, or conscientisation was developed in its original form by Paolo Freire, though similar ways of working have also been developed by others. For example, the consciousness-raising techniques of the women's movement have much in common with Freire's education process. These approaches to education offer a great deal to Primary Health Care because of the way in which they work with people, and because they provide a framework for action to deal with the root causes of problems as recognised by people themselves.

Freire (1973: 13) criticised traditional notions of education and agricultural extension (closely related to community development) for amounting to cultural invasion, since representatives of powerful groups impose their view of the 'facts' on less powerful members of society. He argued that education is never neutral, since it in some way either confirms or challenges the status quo. On the basis of this premise, he argues for education which challenges the status quo, and thus enables the empowerment of oppressed members of society and the development

---

The Murri Mums' Birthing Classes

In 1991, a group of older Aboriginal women living in Moree, New South Wales, approached me as the Coordinator of Community Health with their concern about the lack of pre-natal classes for Aboriginal women in the area. Only a very small number of Aboriginal women were using the pre-natal classes provided, though these classes were well attended by non-Aboriginal women.

The Aboriginal women who approached me were concerned about the quality of life and health of the young Aboriginal mothers and babies, who they recognised were not taking advantage of the service available. As mothers themselves, though, they felt they understood why Aboriginal women were staying away, and wanted to improve the situation. At the same time, the Moree Plains Health Service had identified the need for culturally appropriate health services if they were to have an impact on the poor health status of the local population, one third of whom are Aboriginal.

From the outset, it was recognised that the Aboriginal women themselves needed to be involved in the planning process in order to ensure that any action taken would be relevant to their needs and be owned by the women. Phone calls were made to a number of Aboriginal women working in service agencies around the town and to a local Aboriginal woman who were known to be particularly interested in the classes. We met to discuss the issues. As reasons why they felt Aboriginal women did not attend the available classes, the women cited the lack of specific Aboriginal teaching materials, the fact that Aboriginal women felt uncomfortable being the minority, and their embarrassment at the presence of non-Aboriginal supporting males in what was to them 'women's business'.

The women present agreed to be involved in the process of finding out whether Aboriginal women in the town would support Aboriginal birthing classes. A questionnaire was devised and given to the women. As they worked in areas where they came into contact with young Aboriginal women, they arranged to assist these women to complete the questionnaires.

Analysis of the questionnaires indicated support for the idea of the classes and gave us some useful information about their existing knowledge, and areas where they felt that they needed to know more. A final meeting was held with the Aboriginal service providers at which their commitment to the idea, a plan of proposed sessions (day, time and venue for the classes), the key people who should be involved in the classes, and the questionnaire results were discussed. There was unanimous support for the classes, which they decided to call the 'Murri Mums' Birthing Classes'. A midwife with whom the women felt comfortable and who was already a successful childbirth educator was approached and agreed to lead the classes.

The first six-week program began in February 1992 and was well attended, the plan was to break for two weeks and recommence classes. However, the second program was not attended and it was clear that there was a problem. Discussions with the key Aboriginal women indicated that class-free weeks led to confusion about when the classes were on, so it was decided to offer the classes continually. It also became apparent that transport to the classes was difficult, so a number of Aboriginal workers undertook to provide transport to the classes.

Evaluation of the classes by the Aboriginal women has been very positive. Nonetheless, it would be a mistake to think that we have 'arrived' and that the classes will roll smoothly on. We need to continually listen to the women who attend the classes and adapt what we do according to their needs. This process is as central to the Murri Mums' Birthing Classes as the actual skills and knowledge which we aim to help the women develop.

Jennifer Brett
Coordinator
Community Health
Moree Plains Health Service

---

of a more just social system. Education for critical consciousness focuses on changing the environment rather than the individual alone, by working with people to examine the underlying issues behind their problems and to change the structures around them.

Freire (1968, cited by Minkler and Cox 1980: 312) argues that social change can be achieved only by the active participation of the people as a whole — it cannot be achieved by strong leaders alone. Therefore, action for change must be built on critical reflection and action by everyone concerned. This process of critical reflection and action is described by Freire as 'dialogue', a two-way process occurring between 'teachers' and 'learners', in which they are both teacher–learners.

Education for critical consciousness is a process of problem posing that leads people through analysis of their personal situation and then of the underlying social issues to making a plan for action to address the issues they have discovered. The four steps involved in the process are:

- reflecting upon aspects of their reality (for example, problems of poor health, housing);
- looking behind these immediate problems to their root causes;
- examining the implications and consequences of these issues;

- developing a plan of action to deal with the problems collectively identified

(Minkler and Cox 1980: 312).

However, before such a process can occur, facilitators need to listen carefully to the needs articulated by community members and take the time to understand their problems as they see them (Wallerstein and Bernstein 1980: 382). They also need to observe the dynamics of the groups and individuals concerned to determine what sense of belonging or community exists. Some sense of community or group belonging seems to be important for the conscientisation process to work effectively (Minkler and Cox 1980: 320). It is for this reason that education for critical consciousness often goes hand in hand with community development.

Education for critical consciousness as described by Freire may not fit every learning situation that arises. However, the principles of problem posing, two-way communication and sensitivity to people can be used in any learning situation, so that it becomes an enabling process for the people involved. The following general guidelines for more traditional health education give some indication of how this can occur.

Healthwise

The conscientisation process as described above has been incorporated into the Healthwise programs recently developed in a number of Australian states. Healthwise is a group discussion program which aims to increase awareness of health issues and increase participation in local health issues (Carr et al. 1991: 9). By using the principles of education for critical consciousness, the Healthwise programs provide an opportunity for people to analyse their own experiences with the health system and use this knowledge to consider their own solutions to local health problems in the light of their own analysis. In so doing, the Healthwise programs encourage people to move beyond popularly held health beliefs to a more complex examination of health problems and solutions.

Using the conscientisation process provides a vivid demonstration of the importance of skills in facilitating group process in health education. The health worker's ability to facilitate discussion and enable group members to contribute to the discussion and planning process will be a large determinant in the success of the process. Health workers who attempt to impose their views or be too directive are unlikely to effectively implement the process.

The teaching–learning process

Leddy and Pepper describe three key assumptions which should underpin effective teaching–learning (1989: 317–33):

1. Teaching–learning is a process, not a product — that is, new information

and skills are not the only goals. How that learning occurs is equally important and may contribute greatly to the learning process.

2. The teaching–learning process occurs between people who all bring their own expertise to the situation, whether it be the expertise of personal and collective experiences or the more theoretical expertise carried by health workers.

3. The teaching–learning process needs to be built on effective communication and mutual respect.

What these principles demonstrate is the importance of a partnership approach to working with community members. Both the community member (or members), and the health worker contribute to the discovery of potential solutions in a supportive atmosphere where learners are allowed the dignity of risk, and assume responsibility for decisions they make (Ewles and Simnett 1985: 88). In such an approach, education is a guided problem solving process, in which both 'teacher' and 'learner' are open to learning from each other.

Facilitating the teaching–learning process

A number of principles guide effective teaching–learning, and build on the philosophical base of the teaching–learning process described above. They provide some general guidelines that can be applied to any teaching–learning situation. They are:

- allow people to direct the learning process;
- get to know people's perspective;
- be aware of the context of people's lives;
- build on what people already know;
- be realistic in what you set out to achieve;
- take account of all levels of learning;
- present information in logical steps.

Allow people to direct the learning process

The active participation of community members in the education process is paramount to successful education. Client controlled education is much more likely to address the issues of concern to people when they are ready, and in the order that will help them to learn most effectively.

Participation to the point of control over the education process fits comfortably with the Primary Health Care approach. It is also supported by the principles of adult learning, which recognise the need for learners to direct the learning process and for learning to address the problems that learners themselves want to address. This principle was originally thought to apply only to adult learners, but there is growing recognition that it is just as relevant to child learners (Kalnins et al. 1992).

Client controlled learning is most likely to occur if people themselves set the goals of learning. We discussed in chapter 8 how this can be incorporated into group work, and the same approach can be taken with individuals. Helping people clarify just what it is they want to learn is therefore an important part of the education process.

Active participation can also be encouraged by maximising interactive teaching techniques and activities, rather than taking an 'empty vessel' approach and 'filling' passive recipients with information. People need to be able to have their say, use their initiative, experiment and find out what works for them. Structuring education so that these things are possible is therefore another priority for health workers who are eager to facilitate learning. Which interactive techniques and activities are appropriate will vary depending on the situation and the people involved, and on whether you are involved in education for individual change or education for social change. Commonly used interactive activities include debating contentious issues, using structured group activities, planning action to address a problem, and practising the action required (whether that be drafting a letter to a local councillor, role-playing the negotiation between work colleagues about smoking in the workplace, or preparing a low-fat meal).

It is important to point out, though, that interactive techniques do not by themselves ensure interactive learning, nor is interactive learning precluded by the use of what are traditionally regarded as non-interactive techniques, such as lectures. Rather, it is *how* teaching techniques are used which ultimately determines the extent and success of interactive learning. Once again, emphasis should focus on how the health worker and learners use the teaching techniques, rather than solely on which techniques are used.

Get to know the people's perspective

Teaching–learning is effectively a communication process, and as such is built on an understanding of the background and ideas of the other person or people. This is often a long, slow process, and not necessarily one which can be completed before the teaching–learning begins. Rather, you need to be open to learning about the other person's perspective throughout the teaching–learning process, and to adapt your approach accordingly. A person's attitudes towards relevant issues, their cultural background, their life experience and topics currently of priority for them may all influence their approach to learning and their ability to act. To ensure that communication is effective, pay particular attention to the needs of people who have impaired sight or hearing, low literacy skills, or any other communication problem.

Be aware of the context of people's lives

The active participation of people in directing the learning process will help to ensure that education does not occur out of the context of their lives. This will again enable learning to be directed to the specific needs of the learners, taking account of such things as the particular barriers to action which they need to address and any other issues which may be more important to them than those identified by health workers.

Being aware of the whole situation with which people are dealing will also help to identify what other strategies may be needed to address the issue at hand. Using conscientisation, this would then mean that these other strategies would become part of the education process. For example, letters may be written to members of parliament regarding the re-routing of a main road, while road safety education may be conducted to deal with the problem in the short term.

Build on what people already know

The active participation of community members in the learning process will help to ensure that you start from the point where it is easiest for people to begin to learn. This will enable you to build on what people already know, providing new material in a format and at a pace that is appropriate to the learner or learners. Finding out what people know in a way which does not leave then feeling vulnerable is an important skill here. For example, 'can you tell me what you have heard about osteoporosis?' provides people with more scope to express ideas they are unsure of than asking people what they 'know' about the topic.

Be realistic in what you set out to achieve

Education is much more likely to be effective if you set realistic, achievable goals rather than expecting to achieve too much all at once. It will be useful, therefore, to spend some time with the people you are working with, finding out what they want to achieve and assisting them to adapt their plans if they seem unrealistically high or low. Helping people to plan what they want to achieve so that it is divided into a number of manageable pieces can also help them to keep track of their progress.

Take account of all levels of learning

Learning has traditionally been regarded as occurring on three levels — those of knowledge, attitudes and behaviour. While this schema has been criticised in recent years, it provides a useful guide. Consideration of whether knowledge development, attitudes and values clarification, or behaviour change and skill development are needed will help determine on what level or levels learning needs to occur.

A number of health education books describe teaching strategies and the level or levels of learning to which they are suited. However, these descriptions are, on the whole, of limited use, because it is the way in which strategies are used, rather than the actual strategies, that determines on which levels learning occurs. Also, in reality it is often impossible to separate knowledge, attitudes and behaviour, so attempting to separate them during the learning process is probably unrealistic. Teaching strategies, then, need not be limited to one or two levels of learning, but are limited mainly by the imaginations of the people using them.

Present information in logical steps

If people are to learn effectively, new ideas need to be provided in a logical sequence, in which more complex ideas are built on simpler ones. Some planning is therefore needed to structure ideas so that they are presented in an ordered fashion. Of course these plans may be let go, to some extent, as learners direct the process through their questions and other activities, but the plan remains a useful framework.

The notion of learning having to start with simple ideas before moving on to more complex ones has been questioned in recent years. As with the notion of starting with achievable issues in community development, there is growing recognition that people may be quite able to deal with complex ideas when they relate to their own experiences or the problem to be solved, without needing to discuss the more simple ideas first. In these instances, people are likely to be motivated to learn about the complex issues, since they relate to the problem at hand.

Teaching–learning strategies

By now it is probably quite apparent to you that all the health promotion strategies described in this book so far are useful health education strategies. Mass media campaigns, community development, lobbying and advocacy, and group work often result in education of more than one group of people, and often at a number of stages in the process.

In addition, we discussed conscientisation above, and there are a number of other common health education strategies discussed below. Which strategies are most appropriate depends on the issue at hand, the needs of the people with whom you are working, the context in which the learning is taking place and the particular skills that you and the people you are working with have. In addition, strategies can be adapted and new ones developed to better suit each situation. The following brief descriptions provide an introduction to some common education strategies.

Talks and lectures

Talks and lectures tend to be regarded as a relatively efficient way to pass on a lot of information to a group of people. However, their effectiveness can be limited in a number of ways. Firstly, people may attempt to provide too much information in a talk, swamping the audience in a way which tends to inhibit rather than foster learning. Secondly, unless combined with other strategies, talks tend to be one-way communication in which little interaction (and therefore little participative learning), occurs. When combined with other interactive strategies, though, and using a variety of approaches to get the message across, talks can be a useful teaching tool.

Discussions and debates

Discussions and debates provide an opportunity for people to examine an issue by comparing a variety of views. They are a much more participative approach to learning than talks and lectures, though care still needs to be taken to ensure that they are effective. Firstly, discussion may need to be guided (perhaps through a series of questions) or provoked (such as through a challenging video or opinion). Secondly, if group discussion is to be a participative process for everyone, it may need to be facilitated so that everyone has a chance to participate.

Demonstration and practice of skills

Observing and then practising behaviour can be a valuable way to learn, and may be vital when people are attempting to learn a new skill. If demonstration is to be effective, planning the demonstration as a series of logical steps, and keeping explanation to the necessary key points, will help simplify the process for learners.

Role-play

Role-playing often provides a useful opportunity for people to practise new or unfamiliar behaviour with others. It can also be used to provide an opportunity to explore values and feelings within a group. A word of warning about role-plays, though: they should be used to explore emotional or challenging issues only by health workers with the knowledge and skills to assist participants to come out of the role at the end of the process. Otherwise, role-playing may do more harm than good.

Games

There is a whole variety of educational games or activities which are available to trigger learning. One example of these is the series of structured activities for group learning (Pfeiffer and Jones 1974–1985). However, if games and activities are to be effective learning tools, they need to be relevant to the issue at hand, and to be well facilitated. Like other teaching–learning strategies, games and activities are not ends in themselves, and if used unthinkingly may do little to promote learning.

Self-contracting

Self-contracting provides a mechanism whereby people can contract with themselves to change their behaviour in some way, and then support the behaviour change through rewarding the behaviour they wish to encourage. Despite the discomfort which some people feel with its behaviour modification origins, self-contracting has often been found a useful tool to help people change their behaviour. Very important in this process is the fact that people themselves determine what they should change and how they should support their new behaviour.

Action

Enabling people to act on an issue of concern to them can provide an excellent opportunity for them to learn and make a difference. Writing a letter about an issue of concern, planning and conducting a health survey or media campaign, or developing educational materials for use with their peers, are just some examples of action for change which in itself may teach the protagonists a great deal. In these situations, educators may play an important role as resource people, but otherwise allow people to act independently.

Community level education

Education at the level of the community or population is a more complex process than education at the individual or group level — even more planning and teamwork is needed if it is to be successful. Nonetheless, the same general principles apply. The World Health Organization (1988: 175) suggest three points to keep in mind if you need to develop successful education at the community level:

1. You should get the support of influential people in the community — those who are called 'opinion leaders' or 'key people'.

2. You should be sure that all the people of the community are informed about the problem and are kept up to date on plans and progress. All available channels of communication should be used for this purpose.

3. You should get the maximum number of people involved so that the community will really strengthen its capacity to do things for its health. This can be done through community health committees, advisory or planning boards, etc.

Community-level education draws particularly on mass media and community development strategies. If it is to be effective, it needs to be built on the recognition of the nature of communities as composed of a variety of groups, often with competing interests. This is likely to mean that a variety of different approaches are needed to work effectively with each of these different groups.

The Learn to Drive and Self Esteem Program for isolated rural women

The Learn to Drive and Self Esteem Program for isolated rural women was developed by a Clinical Nurse Consultant in Women's Health, Lorna Neal, and the Coordinator of the Bucketts Way Neighbourhood Centre, Liza Savage. The need for the program was identified as a result of consultation with women living in isolated rural communities, community health centre personnel, staff of the Community Youth Support Scheme, the area Transport Association, and the Manning District Emergency Accommodation Incorporated.

The aim of the program was to extend the independence of rural women who didn't hold a driver's licence. The self esteem component of the program was developed by the group facilitators in response to recognition by the group participants that lack of self confidence had hampered their previous attempts to acquire a driver's licence.

The topography of the Lower North Coast District in New South Wales is largely rugged and inaccessible, consisting of many isolated communities. These factors contribute to personal and family isolation as well as stress in women of all age groups. Single parents in these areas are often disapproved of and domestic violence is tolerated as a way of life (Office of the Status of Women, 1989: 21).

The original target group of the program consisted of women with young children living in small villages, who were unable to drive and therefore unable to access medical services, employment opportunities and further education, and who had to negotiate with partners, friends or relatives for shopping opportunities. Retired women were later identified as another target group. They had come to the area with an ageing partner from cities with adequate public transport, to idyllic beach resorts with no transport or support services and very limited and expensive food outlets.

The pilot programs were financed with a grant from the North Coast Department of Adult Education. The program was developed from modules originally used for Skill Share programs involved with adult literacy. The four modules of the Roads and Traffic Authority handbook have been continually revised by Neal and Savage, and today have very little in common with the original modules. However, they remain easy to understand and are accessible for people with low literacy skills. Women's health education is blended through the program, depending on the needs of each group of women. The program is conducted over six sessions, each of four hours, with up to 12 participants, using two group leaders skilled in assertiveness training and conversant with the Road Traffic Handbook. The support of group members for each other is essential, so the facilitators need a well rounded knowledge of group leadership and group dynamics. The participants are encouraged to apply for their learner's permit at any time during the program and the driving instructor and assessors are introduced to the group.

The course participants and group leaders meet three months after the completion of the course to assess their progress. The comments of the participants allow the group leaders to evaluate the program's outcome. Also at this time, suggestions for future programs are encouraged from the women.

The program outcome has been very exciting, with the women not only gaining their driver's licences, but also making positive lifestyle changes. Many have gained employment, accessed services and undertaken further education. Some women have subsequently left abusive relationships. A few women have decided not to gain their driver's licences, for various reasons. Some of these women have been refused access to the family car and have been coerced by their partner to discontinue. Indeed, the program has challenged a number of relationships, and this is evident in some of the comments made by the women's partners. These comments included that the car wouldn't be available for him when he needed it, 'you can imagine what women get up to if you let them drive', 'she gets smart enough now', and 'I'll take her when she needs to go somewhere'.

One woman recruited for the program cancelled her place because her husband informed her that 'he would give her a good beating if she continued'. This woman has since left the relationship and has gained her driver's licence.

Some of the reasons which women have given for not acquiring a driver's licence before the driving course have been:

- they might hurt someone;

- they would fail both the computer and practical tests;

- they didn't have the skills, ability or temperament to drive;

- they believed they were too old to drive;

- they were told they were too stupid to drive.

Up until the end of 1991, sixty women have participated in the program. These women have ranged in age from 18 years to 70 years old. From the five courses conducted and evaluated, 97 per cent of women have gained their drivers' licences, 12 per cent have left abusive relationships, 50 per cent have attended further education (including Skillshare programs, literacy courses, personal development programs and the Higher School Certificate), and 20 per cent have gained employment since attending the course. However, these figures indicate only some of the impact that the program has had on women's lives. Some comments that indicate this impact include:

- 'It's wonderful — my children are so proud of me since I've gained my licence. I'm able to buy groceries as I need them for the first time in my life';

- 'I take a friend to church every Sunday. I feel marvellous,' a woman who is over seventy years of age stated;

- 'My daughter couldn't have taken the job if I hadn't got my licence,' said a woman living on a farm who was able to transport her sixteen year old daughter to a Saturday job;

- 'I'm going to enter my name on the electoral roll now. I've never felt I was important enough before,' a forty year old woman said at the completion of a course;

- 'Slowly I have come to learn that I am important person';

- 'I now face problems realising my opinion is important';

- 'I think I have a clearer view of how to achieve more independence for myself'.

When asked to name one or more components of the course that were valuable, some of the responses were:

- 'companionship';

- 'accepting the reason why I was not reaching my goals';

- 'learning not to be negative';

- 'I am the same person but facing a problem openly';

- 'I have a quiet time for me';

- 'losing weight';

- 'eating a healthier diet';

- 'I am able to make choices I didn't have before'.

The Learn to Drive and Self Esteem Program provides rural women without a driver's licence with the opportunity to access the basic services most of us take for granted, in an environment which is supportive and positive. As a result, this program has greatly increased the choices available to the women who have participated, and has gone quite some way in promoting the health of these women within the context of their lives.

Lorna Neal
Clinical Nurse Consultant (Women's Health)
Lower North Coast District Health Service

Conclusion

This chapter has briefly reviewed the role of health education in health promotion, and discussed some of the key principles to be considered in education for health from a Primary Health Care perspective. On the whole, health workers already have much scope within their traditional roles to incorporate health education readily into their work, to do so in a way which enables people to take greater control over their lives, and to use education as a springboard to other health promotion strategies when these are of value.

REFERENCES AND FURTHER READINGS

Brookfield, S. 1983. *Adult learners, adult education and the community*, Open University Press, Milton Keynes, UK.

Carr, M., Kuo, H., Fong, A., Jones, L. and Taylor, P. 1991. *Healthwise Tasmania: a handbook for facilitators*, Tasmanian Department of Health, Hobart, Tasmania.

Colquhoun, D. 1992. Dominant discourses in health education, in *Health education: politics and practice*, Deakin University, Geelong, Victoria.

Coutts, L. and Hardy, L. 1985. *Teaching for health: the nurse as health educator*, Churchill Livingstone, Edinburgh, UK.

Cox, K.R. and Ewan, C.E. (eds). 1988. *The medical teacher*, 2nd edn, Churchill Livingstone, Edinburgh, UK.

Draper, P., Griffiths, J., Dennis, J. and Popay, J. 1980. Three types of health education, *British Medical Journal*, 16 August 493–5.

Ewles, L. and Simnett, I. 1985. *Promoting health: a practical guide to health education*, John Wiley and Sons, Chichester, UK.

Freire, P. 1973. *Education for critical consciousness*, Sheed and Ward, London.

Freudenberg, N. 1984. Training health educators for social change, *International Quarterly of Community Health Education*, 5(1), 37–52.

Glanz, K., Lewis, F. M. and Rimer, B. K. (eds). 1991. *Health behavior and health education: theory, research and practice*, Jossey-Bass, San Francisco.

Green, L. W. and Kreuter, M. W. 1991. *Health promotion planning: an educational and environmental approach*, Mayfield, Mountain View, California.

Hill, P. S. and Murphy, G. J. 1992. Cultural identification in Aboriginal and Torres Strait Islander AIDS education, *Australian Journal of Public Health*, 16(2), 150–7.

Johnson, S. (1992). Aboriginal health through primary health care, in Gray, G. and Pratt, R. (eds). *Issues in Australian Nursing 3*, Churchill Livingstone, Melbourne, Victoria.

Kalnins, I., McQueen, D. V., Backett, K. C., Curtice, L. and Currie, C. E. 1992. Children, empowerment and health promotion: some new directions in research and practice, *Health Promotion International*, 7(1), 53–9.

Laura, R. and Heaney, S. 1990. *Philosophical foundations of health education*, Routledge, London.

Leddy, S. and Pepper, J.M. 1989. *Conceptual bases of professional nursing*, J. B. Lippincott, Philadelphia.

Lorig, K. 1991. *Common sense patient education*, Fraser Publications, Ivanhoe, Victoria.

Mather, P. L. 1988. Educating preschoolers about health care, *Childhood Education*, Winter, 94–100.

Minkler, M. and Cox, K. 1980. Creating critical consciousness in health: application of Freire's philosophy and methods to the health care setting, *International Journal of Health Services*, 10(2), 311–22.

Minkler, M. 1989. Health education, health promotion and the open society: an historical perspective, *Health Education Quarterly*, 16(1), 17–30.

Office of the Status of Women. 1989. *National Agenda for Women Implementation Report*, Australian Government Publishing Service, Canberra.

Redman, B. 1988. *The process of patient education*, C. V. Mosby, St Louis, Missouri.

Reid, J. and Trompf, P. (eds).1990. *The health of immigrant Australia*, Harcourt Brace Jovanovich, Sydney.

Tones, K., Tilford, S. and Robinson, Y. 1990. *Health education: effectiveness and efficiency*, Chapman and Hall, London.

Tones, K. 1992. Health promotion, self-empowerment and the concept of control, in *Health education: politics and practice*, Deakin University, Geelong, Victoria.

Wallerstein, N. and Bernstein, E. 1988. Empowerment education: Freire's ideas adapted to health education, *Health Education Quarterly*, 15(4), 379–94.

Werner, D. and Bower, B. 1982. *Helping health workers learn*, The Hesperian Foundation, Palo Alto, California.

World Health Organization. 1988. *Education for health: a manual on health education in primary health care*, World Health Organization, Geneva.

CHAPTER 10

Putting it all together

It is now time to consider how you can put all the approaches and strategies discussed in this book into practice. There are two ways in which to 'put it all together'. Firstly, the principles and skills of health promotion and Primary Health Care can be incorporated into the way in which health workers approach their everyday work. Secondly, the principles and skills of health promotion can be put together to create specific health promotion programs which health workers may implement as individuals or as part of a team.

Applying Primary Health Care principles

No matter where health workers are placed, opportunities exist to apply further the principles of Primary Health Care and make work with community members, clients or patients more health-promoting. Community health centres, workplaces, hospitals and residential institutions such as group homes, hostels and nursing homes all require work on both the structural level and the individual level in order to make action and interaction more health-promoting. Within them, then, you can both be guided by the principles of Primary Health Care in your daily work with community members, clients or patients and work for change at an organisational level so that the organisation is more responsive to the needs of the people it is meant to serve.

On a structural level, services which operate from a Primary Health Care approach respond to the needs of the population they are meant to serve, are operated with an openness to community members, are structured in a way which enables community members to make informed choices, are developed in a way which maintains or increases people's control over their own health, and place emphasis on promoting health. These services make maximum use of appropriate low technology and are guided by an agency philosophy of promoting the health of the community or population whose needs they are designed to address.

Individual interactions should be built on recognition of the expertise which community members have with regard to their own lives and their experiences of living with the issues which have brought them to you. They need to be driven by the right and ability of community members to make informed decisions about their own lives, and so provide what is necessary to enable them to do this.

It is important to reiterate here the importance of the principles of Primary Health Care guiding any work to promote health. This is because while the skills of use in health promotion are valuable, they do not by themselves ensure the implementation of Primary Health Care principles. Any health promotion strategy can be used in a way which is more controlling than enabling. It is the implementation of Primary Health Care principles which ensures that the strategies are used in a way which is supportive of people and therefore enables them to take greater control over their lives.

Focusing in this way on the principles of Primary Health Care rather than on which particular strategy to use is valuable, because you are then able to respond to the situation and the particular needs of people with whom you are working in the way that is most appropriate. From this perspective, a whole range of variations and combinations of strategies may become apparent and be appropriate for the particular situation with which you are working. Focusing on the known strategies alone, rather than on the principles of Primary Health Care, may limit your possible responses and result in your action being driven more by the strategies themselves than the needs of the people and the situation.

As health workers become more experienced in implementing the principles of Primary Health Care, this is exactly what we are seeing occur. Responses to problems and situations are becoming more individualised and more sophisticated, because of the focus on the individual needs of the situation. Effective Primary Health Care practice requires health workers to draw on, rather than rely on, skills and strategies. You are encouraged to examine *Cases for change: CHASP in practice* (Ryan 1992), *The changing face of health: a primary health care casebook* (Phillips-Rees et al. 1992) and the proceedings of recent Australian Community Health Association conferences (Clarke and MacDougall 1993; Australian Community Health Association 1990) for some excellent examples of how health promotion skills and strategies have been tailored to fit local need.

Midwifery care for pregnant teenagers— Primary Health Care in action

At 'The Warehouse', an outreach centre of the Family Planning Association in Penrith, New South Wales, a service is being run to meet the antenatal care needs of pregnant teenagers. The clinic is staffed by midwifery and obstetric staff from the Nepean hospital and staff from the 'The Warehouse'.

'The Warehouse' clinic aims to provide effective, high-quality midwifery and Primary Health Care that meets the needs of its clients. The midwives believe that it is essential to foster a therapeutic relationship so that there can be effective antenatal care (that is, care that has a positive effect on the teenage woman herself, as well as on her pregnancy and parenting). By providing a more appropriate service the clinic is attempting to address the major issue of pregnant adolescents not relating to (and therefore not using) the traditional medical model of care and services. Clark (1984: 16) outlines the common problems described by adolescents attending public hospital clinics as:

seeing a different health worker each time . . . losing confidence in the quality of the service . . . inadequate transport and access . . . perceived moralising attitudes of staff . . . [feeling] that their control and responsibility [are] threatened.

'The Warehouse' clinic attempts to address those issues, and demonstrates a Primary Health Care model in a number of ways:

1. It is socially acceptable and accessible to the clients, being community-based in a Youth Health Centre, easily accessible and located in a central shopping district within easy reach of public transport.

2. The focus of care is on illness prevention and health promotion. Each prenatal clinic session is preceded by an education/discussion group. Topics are broad and include lifestyle review and suggestions for change. In addition, prenatal visits are a time for assessment and reassurance regarding foetal well-being, and provide an opportunity to give positive feedback to the woman about her achievements and progress. There is extensive discussion regarding nutrition, exercise, smoking, lifestyle changes and emotional health. In the optimum situation the midwife is able to provide education and information that are well received and acted upon. As a group, teenagers tend to have poor nutritional habits and in pregnancy this may result in low haemoglobin levels. There is consensus amongst the teenagers themselves that calcium and protein intakes are often inadequate. Added to this are the high levels of psychosocial stressors, including smoking, that may further contribute to a less than optimum foetal environment. In addition, pregnancy for the teenager may contribute to increased feelings of powerlessness, low self-esteem and/or psychological and social difficulties.

3. Assistance with finance, housing and education is available through the Youth Centre staff and hospital social worker. This intersectoral collaboration ensures that all available resources are utilised to provide an optimal service. The collaboration of all disciplines and service groups is essential to facilitate an effective service. There is a strong, vital belief in a social view of health, recognising that for many young women and their partners, the psychosocial stressors and disadvantages of being young parents will far outweigh the physical and practical demands. For this reason, the service aims for a well coordinated holistic approach, with efforts made to minimise the number of health workers with whom each client has to come in contact.

4. The approach to antenatal care is one of shared health assessment, with midwife and client engaging in a relationship that aims to be empowering for the client, maximising her involvement, and endeavouring to promote an atmosphere of mutual trust and respect. The essence of providing effective care to the young pregnant woman is to first examine one's own beliefs and attitudes to teenagers and teenage pregnancy. It is crucial that the midwife likes teenagers and is willing to be their strongest advocate. She or he must be free from the historical beliefs and myths regarding teenage pregnancy and avoid becoming involved in patronising or stigmatising dialogue. Such dialogue serves only to alienate the woman, and once this occurs, it will be virtually impossible to retrace one's steps in order to develop a relationship of mutual trust and respect.

Individualised care provides an excellent opportunity to build effective relationships based on open communication. An atmosphere of mutual trust and respect should be the goal, so that care is effective, productive and rewarding. Once the teenage woman has a strong sense of this occurring, she is perhaps more likely to listen to advice, change some aspects of her lifestyle or make serious attempts to do so. Gillian

Checkley (1990: 26) makes a valuable point when she states: 'Teenagers respond well to sincerity, they don't expect you to be always right but they do expect honesty'.

At 'The Warehouse', antenatal care is provided predominantly by two midwives. This allows for greater continuity of care and is crucial if we are to succeed in building a therapeutic trusting relationship that promotes the teenagers' personal growth, self-esteem and knowledge.

5. Minimal appropriate technology is available on site; routine ultrasound, for example, is not provided. Clients are referred to a visiting obstetrician for any assessment or intervention if it is required. The first antenatal visit takes place, together with the maternity booking-in procedure, at Nepean Hospital with the primary midwife involved in the 'The Warehouse' program and a medical officer.

6. One midwife has a full-time commitment for psychosocial support of the women throughout their pregnancies and the early months of parenting. By making early and regular contact as problems arise, admission rates and length of stay for this previously high-risk group are kept to a minimum.

Midwives in 'The Warehouse' program are aware that they must provide care that meets each person's individual needs, including support, information, encouragement, advocacy and empowerment, through working in partnership with each woman. Through this approach to midwifery services for pregnant teenagers, the health of the women and their babies is promoted.

For further information, contact:
'The Warehouse'
20 Belmore Street
PENRITH NSW 2750
Tel: (047) 21 8330

Pat Brodie
Midwife

Planning health promotion

Planning health promotion will require you to draw on all the information in this book as well as many other skills you have developed as a health worker. That is, planning health promotion requires that you clarify your values, assess the needs of the people for whom the program is being developed and work collaboratively with them to determine the best way to respond to their needs. And because of the involvement of these people themselves and the fact that needs are dynamic, you will have to remain flexible and responsive to changing needs and circumstances.

Health promotion activity is planned on a range of different levels and at different levels of formality and informality. Planning for one activity may take just a few minutes and may be simply thought through by a health worker or community member, while planning for another activity may take considerable time and the involvement of many people. This planning may simply occur and the plan be implemented, or time may be spent documenting the whole planning process. Whichever description best fits the planning you do will depend very much on the situation. Whichever of these approaches is used, the points raised here will be relevant.

The way in which you plan and implement a health promotion program may differ, depending on the particular ways in which things are organised in your state, region and agency. For example, some states and regions allow a more developmental or 'bottom up' approach to health promotion activity in which action is developed with local people, while others expect a more 'top down' approach to health promotion in which action is planned separately from the community and implemented as an intervention. While both approaches may have important roles to play in promoting health, the imposition of centrally planned health promotion at the expense of local response to local need can present real problems for health workers attempting to work from a Primary Health Care approach. Similarly, the particular approach taken by your local administrator will influence the ways in which you can work for health promotion. You will need to work with the realities of your own particular working environment, although you may also be working to change that reality if it does not sit comfortably with a Primary Health Care approach or the needs of your community.

The term 'health promotion program' is used to describe a combination of health promotion activities designed to address a particular need. You may decide that the need you are addressing can be dealt with appropriately by one local health promotion activity or a program consisting of a series of local activities, or that it will require a major national or international campaign. Alternatively, you may plan to design a local program to tie in with a national or state campaign if it is relevant to your area.

When you are planning health promotion, there are a number of key issues you will need to address. These will be useful for you and your partners in the process in enabling you to effectively prepare and implement your ideas. In addition, your own administrators or funding bodies may want to have much of this information in order to judge the merits of your activity or decide whether they will support your plans.

Some of the detail of what will need to be planned will vary depending on the issue you are addressing and the strategy which you decide will be most appropriate. For example, if you decide that health education is the most appropriate response, there will be some issues specific to health education that may need consideration. However, this section will consider the issues common to any health promotion action. Also, the specific details required by the organisation to whom you are accountable may vary, but the sets of issues below should be generally applicable.

In order to plan health promotion effectively, you will need to do the following.

- Assess the needs of the population or community to whom you are responsible.

- Prioritise the needs or issues which you find.

- Examine in some detail the particular issue you are going to act on.

- Clarify who is your critical reference group.

- Set aims and objectives.

- Decide the most appropriate response to the problem.

- Calculate what resources you will need in order to act effectively.

- Plan how you will evaluate your activity.

Of course, planning is not a simple linear process, and the order in which the above steps occur will vary according to the particular situation. Moreover, it is worthwhile to note once again the fine line between all stages of assessment, planning, implementation and evaluation. Indeed, the steps described above may themselves be part of the action of health promotion in some situations, and are not limited to the planning process.

Examine in detail the issue you are planning to act on

In chapter 3 we examined needs assessment and discussed the need to set priorities on the issues you find in order to determine which issue or issues you will address first. Once priorities have been set, you will need to examine in more detail each issue you are going to address. This will require you to draw together as much relevant information as possible. It will also require critical discussion of the issue by the people involved (that is, community members, other health workers and anyone else who has concerns about the issue) so that you can review the issue and determine just what the problem is. This is necessary in order to ensure that the strategies which you then choose for addressing the problem are the most appropriate. This examining of a problem in order to move beyond immediate perceptions to a more complete analysis was also discussed in chapter 3.

Conducting a literature review may enable you to find out more about the problem or issues you are dealing with. It may also enable you to find out how other people have dealt with similar issues if others have already developed a program to meet a similar need. You can then learn from their experiences and mistakes so as to build on their program, or adapt it to meet your needs. Of particular value here is the Health Education and Promotion System (HEAPS), a database containing details of previously developed health promotion programs from around Australia.

Determine your critical reference, host or target group

In order to ensure that you are addressing an issue in the most appropriate way, you will need to clarify just whose needs the particular program is designed to address. For example, an approach which is relevant to a group of teenagers is unlikely to be relevant to a group of older people living in a nursing home. Even if you are addressing a health need that is relevant to an entire community, you may need to take a slightly different approach in order to work appropriately with different groups within the community. Most commonly, the group that a particular health promotion program is meant to be designed for is known as the target group.

Unfortunately, however, the term 'target group' gives the impression that people are passive and waiting to be 'hit' by the program being implemented. As Yoland Wadsworth (1990: 52) has described, this approach regards people as 'sitting ducks'. Such an approach to people does not sit comfortably with Primary Health Care, and I am sure it does not sit all that comfortably with the ducks themselves! For this reason, and to encapsulate the importance of the collaboration of people themselves in the planning and implementation of health promotion activity, the term 'critical reference group' has been coined to refer to the group of people for whom a project is designed (Wadsworth 1991: 10).

Another term, 'host community', has been coined to refer to the community with whom you are working in community development. This term reflects the fact that you are involved with the community at their request — the community is 'hosting' you. This is one more attempt to break free of the disempowering connotations of the term 'target group'. Unfortunately, the term 'host community' is not relevant to all situations and the term 'critical reference group' is somewhat cumbersome and perhaps more directly relevant to evaluation alone, for which it was originally coined. Nonetheless, these two suggested terms constitute important attempts to replace the term 'target group' and the approach it represents.

Clarifying for whom your project or activity is being developed needs to go hand in hand with determining what the problem is. Indeed, these two steps are inextricably linked, since the people for whom the project is developing need to be involved in its development. How this actually occurs, however, will depend very much on the situation. You will need to determine how it can most appropriately occur in each particular instance.

It is important to note that there will be times when the individual or group for whom the action is designed may not be the individual or group with whom you need to work, although they will in these circumstances remain the people for whom you will work. For example, educating local councillors about the dangers of certain environmental toxins used in local industries may be of benefit to members of the community living near those industries if changes occur as a result. In this case, the critical reference group is the community members, not the local councillors. This distinction between who will benefit from the action and whom the action will affect is an important one.

Decide how you will respond

Once you feel you have a good understanding of the problem, you will be able to decide on the most appropriate way to respond. Doing this is not a simple task, and there are no tricks of the trade to make it easy. As Egger et al. (1990: 120) have stated, 'it all depends'. This is the point at which you will have to rely on your assessment skills and judgment, and those of the people with whom you are working. However, the more thoroughly you have examined the issue itself, the more likely you are to be able to respond appropriately. This does not mean that the assessment process must go on interminably, but rather that you must aim to be comprehensive.

As a general rule, addressing an issue on a number of different levels will increase the likelihood that you will be successful. In deciding on what level or levels you need to work, the Ottawa Charter for Health Promotion can be a useful guide. Can you act to work for healthy public policy to address the need? Is there some other way in which you can work for more supportive environments? Will you need to encourage and support community action? Can you help people further develop their own skills in dealing with the issue? Do you need to work for a reorientation of the system so that more emphasis is put on the prevention of this problem?

Take some time to consider (perhaps through brainstorming with the community members involved or some of your colleagues) what strategies you could implement to address the problem on each of these levels. This is a good way of ensuring you do not assume that the most appropriate strategy is education alone, an assumption that health workers often make.

Set aims and objectives

You can make clear for yourself and any funding or management bodies what you want to achieve from the program or activity by setting aims and objectives. This may occur relatively informally, with community members taking the time to decide exactly what it is they want to achieve and how they want to achieve it. It may also occur more formally, with health workers documenting aims and objectives against which the program may be evaluated.

This is one area where a great deal of apparently contradictory information has appeared in recent years. Many books on health promotion and guidelines for the development of health promotion programs outline varying combinations of goals, aims, targets and objectives, often defined differently. The following use of 'aims' and 'objectives' has been chosen for its simplicity, though it is not meant to be definitive. The key element here, which is likely to be found in any good combination of categories used, is that one is a broad statement of what you wish to achieve and the other is a more detailed explanation of the steps required to achieve it. In larger programs, other categories may need to be used in order to break the program activities down into manageable pieces.

An aim is a clear statement of what you wish to achieve through your program or activity. There is some disagreement amongst authors as to whether an aim should be a very general statement of intent or a specific measurable goal against which the program is evaluated. However that may be, it is probably valuable to establish both a general statement of intent, towards which your activity will contribute, and a more specific aim against which your action can be evaluated.

Objectives describe the steps that you will need to take in order to achieve your aim. As much as realistically possible, they are written in a manner which enables them to be evaluated: that is, they are specific and measurable. Objectives may describe what action will occur (for example, an environmental action group may set objectives of writing letters to their local member of parliament, the minister for the environment and the chief executive officers of a number of companies in their local areas to express concern at pollution levels) or they may describe what changes will occur as a result of the action (for example, the same group may set objectives of putting environmental health issues firmly on the local and state government agendas). Generally, evaluating against objectives which describe the changes that will occur will more readily enable you to determine whether your program or activity has been effective than evaluating against objectives which simply describe the action of the protagonists. While the action which occurs may be very valuable, you may want to know whether it has actually made the difference you hoped it would. Change-oriented objectives are extremely valuable because they enable you to do that.

Within health education, these two types of objectives are described as learner-centred and teacher-centred objectives. Teacher-centred objectives describe what the teacher will have accomplished as a result of his or her activity (for example, the teacher will have explained the principles of effective writing), while learner-centred objectives describe the change which you hope will result (for example, the learner will be able to write a letter for publication in the local paper on an issue about which he or she is concerned). Once again you can see how the implementation of the teacher-centred objective may be important, but its value may be reduced if it does not result in the changes described by the learner-centred objective.

You may decide that it is appropriate for you to set both action-oriented and change-oriented objectives in order to make clear just what you want to achieve and how you are going to achieve it. Indeed, working with community members, you may find it useful to set four groups of objectives — what you as a health worker want to do, what you as a health worker wish to accomplish, what community members wish to do and what community members wish to accomplish.

Objectives, then, make clear statements about what you want to achieve and how you want to achieve it. It is worth noting that the more clearly you have defined the need you are addressing, the easier it will be to set objectives for the program. This is one example of how each of the steps in planning a health promotion program or activity described here is inextricably linked to the others.

Calculate what resources you will need

You will also have to calculate just what resources you will need in order to implement your ideas and what resources you already have. A key component of this is examination of what skills are needed and whether staff members or community members have these skills or whether others will need to be involved in order to pass them on or to participate directly in the program.

It is important that you make maximum use of the skills of people who are available to work with you. Doing that makes good sense, since it means effective use of resources. It may also be a positive process for community members themselves, because recognition of and respect for their abilities is something which most people appreciate. Also, working with community members so that they develop the skills to continue the activity will enable them to keep working for their health and will result in increasing the resources of the community.

Other health workers can also be regarded as valuable resources. For instance, workplace health promotion programs implemented from outside the organisation need to actively involve any occupational health and safety workers in the organisation, since these people also have a health promotion responsibility and work in the organisation on a daily basis. Similarly, involvement of teachers in school health promotion programs, Aboriginal health workers in Aboriginal health promotion programs and local midwives or women's health nurses in women's health promotion programs will increase the chances that local people will have access to local resources and that the program will continue in the community in one form or another. Indeed, you will need to seriously consider whether these people should be leaders in health promotion activity in these areas, with other health workers acting as resources.

You will have to estimate how much time, in terms of preparation, implementation and evaluation, the program will take, so that you can make an informed decision about what it will cost the agency and decide whether it is worth the effort that will go into it. You will then be in a better position to decide whether the agency can run the program using existing resources, or whether you will need to apply for additional funds. Alternatively, if the program appears too costly, it may be able to be adapted in order to reduce its cost. Maintaining the spirit of the program then becomes an important issue.

You will also need to consider just what physical resources you will need. This will depend very much on the particular strategy you will be using. For example, if you are planning a social action campaign, you may need access to typing and photocopying facilities, telephones and stationery. You may also need a hall for large meetings and smaller rooms for committee meetings, easily accessible to members of the community. Or, if you are planning a formal health education program, you may need teaching aids, an appropriate venue, and perhaps child care facilities.

Once you have assessed what resources you require, you may need to find out what resources are available elsewhere. For example, if you decide that your plans cannot be implemented without outside assistance, you will need to find out what outside resources are available. Once again, people are probably the most valuable resources. Health promotion specialists, perhaps working in other areas of the health department, may be able to contribute a great deal of expertise. People from volunteer or self-help groups may also contribute much about the issues which they face.

Another form of outside resources is money! External funding sources may be available to fund some of the activity which you want to carry out. Most funding of this kind is available only at certain times of the year rather than on a continual basis, but it is well worth checking whether any funds are available at the time you need them. Keep an eye on the major papers in your area for details.

Plan how you will evaluate your action

Planning an evaluation is vital to the development of any health promotion program, and will be an integral part of it. Evaluating what you are doing will enable you to improve what you are doing as you are doing it, thus maximising the chances that your activity will be successful. It will also enable you to report any successes and lessons learned to other people working for health promotion and to the community, funding bodies and administrators to whom you are accountable.

You will need to plan how you are going to evaluate so that you can ask the appropriate questions throughout the implementation of your activity. It will not be possible to evaluate effectively if you leave consideration of evaluation until after your activity has finished. We examined evaluation in some depth in chapter 4, to which you are referred for more detail.

Implement your plans

When the time comes to put your plans into action, you should have a fairly strong sense of what you are doing and how you are doing it. You will need to remain flexible, however, being sensitive to the possibility that needs, circumstances and available resources may change and your responses may thus need to change. Continued communication and critique will therefore be an important component of your action.

Conclusion

In this book we have reviewed the importance of health workers promoting health, the values which should drive health promotion practice and some of the key strategies which are of use in working with members of the community to promote their health. In drawing those elements together to help create effective health promotion action, this chapter has provided an overview of a number of important issues. The challenge for each health worker lies in drawing the same elements together for the purpose of effective action based on the principles of social justice and on the right of ordinary people to make effective decisions about their lives.

REFERENCES AND FURTHER READINGS

Australian Community Health Association. 1990. *Healthy environments in the 90's: the community health approach, papers from the 3rd National Conference of the Australian Community Health Association*, Australian Community Health Association, Sydney.

Checkley, G. 1990. Talking to teenagers, *Healthright*, 9(4), 25–8.

Clark, M. A. 1984. *Facts, myths and stigma: a report on teenage pregnancy and parenting*, NSW Department of Health, Sydney.

Clarke, B. and MacDougall, C. (eds). 1993. *The 1993 Community Health Conference, vol. 1, papers and workshops: proceedings of the Fourth National Australian Community Health Association Conference*, Australian Community Health Association, Sydney.

Egger, G., Spark, R. and Lawson, J. 1990. *Health promotion strategies and methods*, McGraw-Hill, Sydney.

Ewles, L. and Simnett, I. 1985. *Promoting health: A practical guide to health education*, John Wiley and Sons, Chichester, UK.

Johnson, S. 1992. Aboriginal health through primary health care, in Gray, G. and Pratt, R. (eds), *Issues in Australian nursing 3*, Churchill Livingstone, Melbourne.

Lorig, K. 1991. *Common sense patient education*, Fraser Publications, Ivanhoe, Victoria.

McKenzie, J. F. and Jurs, J. L. 1993. *Planning, implementing, and evaluating health promotion programs: a primer*, Macmillan, New York.

Northrop, M. 1991. Screening in medicine: a right or a risk, *Health Issues*, 29, 35–9.

Phillips-Rees, S., Sanderson, C., Herriot, M. and May, A. 1992. *The changing face of health: a primary health care casebook*, South Australian Health Commission and South Australian Community Health Association, Adelaide.

Ryan, P. 1992. *Cases for change: CHASP in practice*, Australian Community Health Association, Sydney.

Shaw, L. and Tilden, J. 1990. *Creating health for women: a community health promotion handbook*, Women's Health Development Program, Brisbane Women's Community Health Centre, Brisbane.

Stoker, L. 1988. *Healthy women: an introduction to health for women from non-English-speaking backgrounds*, New South Wales Department of Health, Sydney.

Wadsworth, Y. 1990. The consumer contribution to public health research and its funding administration, in Matrice, D. and Brown, V. (eds), *Widening the research focus: consumer roles in public health research*, Consumers' Health Forum, Curtin, ACT.

Wadsworth, Y. 1991. *Everyday evaluation on the run*, Action Research Issues Association (Incorporated), Melbourne.

CONCLUSION

Where to from here?

Having read through this book and used the information in it to further develop your skills, where do you go from here? As will have become progressively clearer throughout the preceding 10 chapters, this book can only provide an introduction to the particular skills you can use in promoting health and the approaches you can take. It is now up to you to build on this information. There are a number of things you can do from this point on to keep developing your skills and expertise in the area of health promotion.

1. *Use the information in this book to develop your skills.* Put the ideas into practice and see which ones work for you and your community.

2. *Keep reading about the areas we have covered in this book.* Each of them has a substantial theoretical basis, and as you develop your background in them, you will be more effective in developing your own theory and practice.

3. *Talk with your colleagues.* Discuss your ideas, your successes and your failures with anyone who is interested to learn with you.

4. *Ask questions.* Get help when you need it, and don't be afraid to ask for help. Successful people use their expertise, and the expertise of others, to its best advantage. And don't forget to include those people you are employed to serve amongst the people you ask questions of. The partnership with community members needs to include learning from each other as you develop.

5. *Share your learning professionally by attending conferences and presenting papers on your work.* So many people who do great work fail to realise that many people would like to hear about their work and learn from it. Don't judge your work too harshly.

6. *Work together, supporting and encouraging each other and promoting the health of the team.* A great many of the strategies described in this book cannot be implemented fully if health workers themselves have not experienced them. This is particularly so with the empowerment strategies. Traditionally, the health care system has encouraged compliance and discouraged lateral

thinking and creativity. It has worked to stifle, rather than empower, people working within it. Health workers who do not feel able to impact on the world around them will find it very difficult to help develop these skills in others. If you are one of those people, or you are working in a team with people who feel that way, then a vital step towards working to promote the health of your community is to use empowerment strategies within the team, so as to enable the development of the team and the self-efficacy of everyone in it. Too often health workers write each other off, ignoring the strong socialisation processes that have impacted on them. It is not possible to ignore health promotion issues within your own team and yet achieve your potential in promoting the health of the community. The ripples of this work will be felt far beyond the confines of the staffroom, and you will be able to establish a team environment that will achieve so much more than individuals alone can achieve.

7. *Continue working to keep the development of a Primary Health Care system on the agenda, and to ensure that the system develops towards a greater emphasis on the promotion of health.* There is some important work to be done in lobbying to break up the current trend towards medicalisation of community health, which is threatening the establishment of a comprehensive Primary Health Care approach. An important component of this will be working for the continuing reorientation — towards a Primary Health Care approach — of undergraduate and postgraduate education of health workers and others whose actions impact on health.

Only through a concerted effort by health workers and community members will the health care system be effectively reoriented to a focus on the promotion of health and the needs of the community. Don't underestimate the importance of your role in this process. You *can* make a difference, and I wish you all the best in your health promotion work!

APPENDIX 1

The Declaration of Alma-Ata

On 12 September 1978, at Alma-Ata in Soviet Kazakhstan, representatives of 134 nations agreed to the terms of a solemn Declaration pledging urgent action by all governments, all health and development workers, and the world community to protect and promote the health of all the people of the world. The climax of a major International Conference on Primary Health Care, jointly sponsored by WHO and UNICEF, this Declaration stated:

1. The conference strongly reaffirms that health, which is a state of complete physical, mental and social well-being, and not merely the absence of disease or infirmity, is a fundamental human right and that the attainment of the highest possible level of health is a most important world-wide social goal whose realisation requires the action of many other social and economic sectors in addition to the health sector.

2. The existing gross inequality in the health status of the people, particularly between developed and developing countries as well as within countries, is politically, socially and economically unacceptable and is, therefore, of common concern to all countries.

3. Economic and social development, based on a New International Economic Order, is of basic importance to the fullest attainment of health for all and to the reduction of the gap between the health status of the developing and developed countries. The promotion and protection of the health of the people is essential to sustained economic and social development and contributes to a better quality of life and to world peace.

4. The people have the right and duty to participate individually and collectively in the planning and implementation of their health care.

5. Governments have a responsibility for the health of their people which can be fulfilled only by the provision of adequate health and social measures. A main social target of governments, international organizations and the whole world community in the coming decades should be the attainment by all peoples of the world by the year 2000 of a level of health that will permit them to lead a socially and economically productive life.

Primary health care is the key to attaining this target as part of development in the spirit of social justice.

6. Primary health care is essential health care based on practical, scientifically sound and socially acceptable methods and technology made universally accessible to individuals and families in the community through their full participation and at a cost that the community and country can afford to maintain at every stage of their development in the spirit of self-reliance and self-determination. It forms an integral part both of the country's health system, of which it is the central function and main focus, and of the overall social and economic development of the community. It is the first level of contact of individuals, the family and community with the national health system, bringing health care as close as possible to where people live and work, and constitutes the first element of a continuing health care process.

7. Primary health care:

i. reflects and evolves from the economic conditions and socio-cultural and political characteristics of the country and its communities, and is based on the application of the relevant results of social, biomedical and health services research and public health experience;

ii. addresses the main health problems in the community, providing promotive, preventive, curative, and rehabilitative services accordingly;

iii. includes at least: education concerning prevailing health problems and the methods of preventing and controlling them; promotion of food supply and proper nutrition; an adequate supply of safe water and basic sanitation; maternal and child health care, including family planning; immunization against the major infectious diseases; prevention and control of locally endemic diseases; appropriate treatment of common diseases and injuries; and provision of essential drugs;

iv. involves, in addition to the health sector, all related sectors and aspects of national and community development, in particular agriculture, animal husbandry, food, industry, education, housing, public works, communication and other sectors; and demands the coordinated efforts of all those sectors;

v. requires and promotes maximum community and individual self-reliance and participation in the planning, organization, operation and control of primary health care, making fullest use of local, national and other available resources, and to this end develops through appropriate education the ability of communities to participate;

vi. should be sustained by integrated, functional and mutually-supportive referral systems, leading to the progressive improvement of comprehensive health care for all, and giving priority to those most in need;

vii. relies, at local and referral levels, on health workers, including physicians, nurses, midwives, auxiliaries and community workers as applicable, as well as traditional practitioners as needed, suitably trained socially and technically to work as a health team and to respond to the expressed health needs of the community.

8. All governments should formulate national policies, strategies and plans of action to launch and sustain primary health care as part of a comprehensive national health system and in coordination with other sectors. To this end, it will be necessary to exercise political will, to mobilise the country's resources and to use available external resources rationally.

9. All countries should cooperate in a spirit of partnership and service to ensure primary health care for all people since the attainment of health by people in any one country directly concerns and benefits every other country. In this context the joint WHO/UNICEF report on primary health care constitutes a solid basis for the further development and operation of primary health care throughout the world.

10. An acceptable level of health for all the people of the world by the year 2000 can be attained through a fuller and better use of the world's resources, a considerable part of which is now spent on armaments and military conflicts. A genuine policy of independence, peace, détente and disarmament could and should release additional resources that could well be devoted to peaceful aims and in particular to the acceleration of social and economic development of which primary health care, as an essential part, should be allotted its proper share.

The International Conference on Primary Health Care calls for urgent and effective national and international action to develop and implement primary health care throughout the world and particularly in developing countries in a spirit of technical cooperation and in keeping with a New International Economic Order. It urges governments, WHO and UNICEF, and other international organizations, as well as multilateral and bilateral agencies, non-governmental organizations, funding agencies, all health workers and the whole world community to support national and international commitment to primary health care and to channel increased technical and financial support to it, particularly in developing countries. The Conference calls on all the aforementioned to collaborate in introducing, developing and maintaining primary health care in accordance with the spirit and content of this Declaration.

World Health, August/September 1988, 16–17.

APPENDIX 2

The Ottawa Charter
for Health Promotion

The first International Conference on Health Promotion, meeting in Ottawa this 21st day of November 1986, hereby presents this CHARTER for action to achieve Health for All by the year 2000 and beyond.

This conference was primarily a response to growing expectations for a new public health movement around the world. Discussions focused on the needs in industrialized countries, but took into account similar concerns in all other regions. It built on the progress made through the Declaration on Primary Health Care at Alma Ata, the World Health Organization's Targets for Health for All document, and the recent debate at the World Health Assembly on intersectoral action for health.

Health promotion

Health promotion is the process of enabling people to increase control over, and to improve, their health. To reach a state of complete physical, mental and social wellbeing, an individual or group must be able to identify and to realize aspirations, to satisfy needs, and to change or cope with the environment. Health is, therefore, seen as a resource for everyday life, not the objective of living. Health is a positive concept emphasizing social and personal resources, as well as physical capacities. Therefore, health promotion is not just the responsibility of the health sector, but goes beyond healthy lifestyles to well-being.

Prerequisites for health

The fundamental conditions and resources for health are peace, shelter, education, food, income, a stable ecosystem, sustainable resources, social justice and equity. Improvement in health requires a secure foundation in these basic prerequisites.

Advocate

Good health is a major resource for social, economic and personal development and an important dimension of quality of life. Political, economic, social, cultural, environmental, behavioural and biological factors can all favour health or be harmful to it. Health promotion action aims at making these conditions favourable through *advocacy* for health.

Enable

Health promotion focuses on achieving equity in health. Health promotion action aims at reducing differences in current health status and ensuring equal opportunities and resources to *enable* all people to achieve their fullest health potential. This includes a secure foundation in a supportive environment, access to information, life skills and opportunities for making healthy choices. People cannot achieve their fullest health potential unless they are able to take control of those things which determine their health. This must apply equally to women and men.

Mediate

The prerequisites and prospects for health cannot be ensured by the health sector alone. More importantly, health promotion demands coordinated action by all concerned: by governments, by health and other social and economic sectors, by non-governmental and voluntary organizations, by local authorities, by industry and by the media. People in all walks of life are involved as individuals, families and communities. Professional and social groups and health personnel have a major responsibility to *mediate* between differing interests in society for the pursuit of health.

Health promotion strategies and programmes should be adapted to the local needs and possibilities of individual countries and regions to take into account differing social, cultural and economic systems.

Health promotion action means:

Build healthy public policy

Health promotion goes beyond health care. It puts health on the agenda of policy makers in all sectors and at all levels, directing them to be aware of the health consequences of their decisions and to accept their responsibilities for health.

Health promotion policy combines diverse but complementary approaches including legislation, fiscal measures, taxation and organizational change. It is coordinated action that leads to health, income and social policies that foster greater equity. Joint action contributes to ensuring safer and healthier goods and services, healthier public services, and cleaner, more enjoyable environments.

Health promotion policy requires the identification of obstacles to the adoption of healthy public policies in non-health sectors, and ways of removing them. The aim must be to make the healthier choice the easier choice for policy makers as well.

Create supportive environments

Our societies are complex and interrelated. Health cannot be separated from other goals. The inextricable links between people and their environment constitutes the basis for a socio-ecological approach to health. The overall guiding principle for the world, nations, regions and communities alike, is the need to encourage reciprocal maintenance — to take care of each other, our communities and our natural environment. The conservation of natural resources throughout the world should be emphasized as a global responsibility.

Changing patterns of life, work and leisure have a significant impact on health. Work and leisure should be a source of health for people. The way society organizes work should help create a healthy society. Health promotion generates living and working conditions that are safe, stimulating, satisfying and enjoyable.

Systematic assessment of the health impact of a rapidly changing environment — particularly in areas of technology, work, energy production and urbanization — is essential and must be followed by action to ensure positive benefit to the health of the public. The protection of the natural and built environments and the conservation of natural resources must be addressed in any health promotion strategy.

Strengthen community action

Health promotion works through concrete and effective community action in setting priorities, making decisions, planning strategies and implementing them to achieve better health. At the heart of this process is the empowerment of communities, their ownership and control of their own endeavours and destinies.

Community development draws on existing human and material resources in the community to enhance selfhelp and social support, and to develop flexible systems for strengthening public participation and direction of health matters. This requires full and continuous access to information, learning opportunities for health, as well as funding support.

Develop personal skills

Health promotion supports personal and social development through providing information, education for health and enhancing life skills. By so doing, it increases the options available to people to exercise more control over their own health and over their environments, and to make choices conducive to health.

Enabling people to learn throughout life, to prepare themselves for all of its stages and to cope with chronic illness and injuries is essential. This has to be facilitated in school, home, work and community settings. Action is required through educational, professional, commercial and voluntary bodies, and within the institutions themselves.

Reorient health services

The responsibility for health promotion in health services is shared among individuals, community groups, health professionals, health service institutions and governments. They must work together towards a health care system which contributes to the pursuit of health.

The role of the health sector must move increasingly in a health promotion direction, beyond its responsibility for providing clinical and curative services. Health services need to embrace an expanded mandate which is sensitive and respects cultural needs. This mandate should support the needs of individuals and communities for a healthier life, and open channels between the health sector and broader social, political, economic and physical environmental components.

Reorienting health services also requires stronger attention to health research as well as changes in professional education and training. This must lead to a change of attitude and organization of health services, which refocuses on the total needs of the individual as a whole person.

Moving into the future

Health is created and lived by people within the settings of their everyday life; where they learn, work, play and love. Health is created by caring for oneself and others, by being able to take decisions and have control over one's life circumstances, and by ensuring that the society one lives in creates conditions that allow the attainment of health by all its members.

Caring, holism and ecology are essential issues in developing strategies for health promotion. Therefore, those involved should take as a guiding principle that, in each phase of planning, implementation and evaluation of health promotion activities, women and men should become equal partners.

Commitment to health promotion

The participants in this conference pledge:

- to move into the arena of healthy public policy, and to advocate a clear political commitment to health and equity in all sectors;

- to counteract the pressures towards harmful products, resource depletion, unhealthy living conditions and environments, and bad nutrition; and to focus attention on public health issues such as pollution, occupational hazards, housing and settlements;

- to respond to the health gap within and between societies, and to tackle the inequities in health produced by the rules and practices of these societies;

- to acknowledge people as the main health resource; to support and enable them to keep themselves, their families and friends healthy through financial and other means, and to accept the community as the essential voice in matters of its health, living conditions and well-being;

- to reorient health services and their resources towards the promotion of health; and to share power with other sectors, other disciplines and most importantly with people themselves;

- to recognize health and its maintenance as a major social investment and challenge; and to address the overall ecological issue of our ways of living.

The conference urges all concerned to join them in their commitment to a strong public health alliance.

Call for international action

The Conference calls on the World Health Organization and other international organizations to advocate the promotion of health in all appropriate forums and to support countries in setting up strategies and programmes for health promotion.

The Conference is firmly convinced that if people in all walks of life, nongovernmental and voluntary organizations, governments, the World Health Organization and all other bodies concerned join forces in introducing strategies for health promotion, in line with the moral and social values that form the basis of this CHARTER, Health For All by the year 2000 will become a reality.

This CHARTER for action was developed and adopted by an international conference, jointly organized by the World Health Organization, Health and Welfare Canada and the Canadian Public Health Association. Two hundred and twelve participants from 38 countries met from November 17 to 21,1986, in Ottawa, Canada to exchange experiences and share knowledge of health promotion.

The Conference stimulated an open dialogue among lay, health and other professional workers, among representatives of governmental, voluntary and community organizations, and among politicians, administrators, academics and practitioners. Participants coordinated their efforts and came to a clearer definition of the major challenges ahead. They strengthened their individual and collective commitment to the common goal of Health for All by the Year 2000.

This CHARTER for action reflects the spirit of earlier public charters through which the needs of people were recognized and acted upon. The CHARTER presents fundamental strategies and approaches for health promotion which the participants considered vital for major progress. The Conference report develops the issues raised, gives concrete examples and practical suggestions regarding how real advances can be achieved, and outlines the action required of countries and relevant groups.

The move towards a new public health is now evident worldwide. This was reaffirmed not only by the experiences but by the pledges of Conference participants who were invited as individuals on the basis of their expertise. The following countries were represented: Antigua, Australia, Austria, Belgium, Bulgaria, Canada, Czechoslovakia, Denmark, Eire, England, Finland, France, German Democratic Republic, Federal Republic of Germany, Ghana, Hungary, Iceland, Israel, Italy, Japan, Malta, Netherlands, New Zealand, Northern Ireland, Norway, Poland, Portugal, Romania, St. Kitts-Nevis, Scotland, Spain, Sudan, Sweden, Switzerland, Union of Soviet Socialist Republic, United States of America, Wales and Yugoslavia.

INDEX

This index was compiled by Jonathan Jermey.

5 6 7 8 9 0 1 2
C D E F G H I